CREATIVE IDEAS FOR CHRISTMAS 1987

COMPILED AND EDITED BY NANCY JANICE FITZPATRICK

Oxmoor House®

Library of Congress Catalog Number: 84-63033
ISBN: 0-8487-0708-7
ISSN: 0883-9085
Manufactured in the United States of America
First Printing

Executive Editor: Candace N. Conard
Production Manager: Jerry Higdon
Associate Production Manager: Rick Litton
Art Director: Bob Nance

Creative Ideas for Christmas 1987

Senior Editor: Nancy Janice Fitzpatrick
Editor: Kathleen English
Assistant Editor: Alison Nichols
Recipe Development: Elizabeth Taliaferro, Foods
    Assistant, *Creative Ideas for Living*® magazine
Editorial Assistant: Josie E. Lee
Production Assistant: Theresa L. Beste
Copy Chief: Mary Jean Haddin
Artists: Barbara Ball, David Morrison
Designer: Cindy Cooper

CONTENTS

Continued

INTRODUCTION

Love shows in a handmade gift, a gathering of friends, a welcoming door decoration. Christmas 1987 awaits your loving touch. Choose from the multitude of new and exciting ideas on the following pages to show loved ones your affection.

HOME FOR THE HOLIDAYS

In this chapter, we visit with people in eight states whose Christmases at home are remarkable for their individual styles. Each of these festive examples is unique, and yet all share a bond. Our hosts used their talents to make the holidays very personal and meaningful. Enjoy their colorful, creative celebrations and let them inspire the Christmas spirit in you.

MEET ONE OF
SANTA'S HELPERS

If Santa knew Madeline Smith, he would make her an honorary elf. This Cincinnati woman spends days arranging and rearranging a collection of some 3,000 ornaments and a dozen Christmas trees, as well as swags of greenery, groups of candles, and miniature Christmas villages, before she considers her home decorated. After all this preparation, Madeline likes to open her house to visitors, who can number as many as 200 during the month of December. "It's

Above: Here Madeline samples some of the home-made sausage she makes for gifts. The Santa bread figures at left are baked in molds. Madeline bakes them at a very low temperature for about ten hours to remove all moisture from the dough, and then seals the figures with a satin varnish.

fun to share what you have," she explains. "That's what Christmas is all about."

Collecting decorations (some of which date back to the late 1800s) began as a hobby for Madeline, and then developed into a rewarding business. But as all collectors understand, no collection is ever really complete, and Madeline continues to attend flea markets, auctions, and estate sales in search of decorations. "Things just keep mushrooming, and one thing leads to another," Madeline says. To date, her antique acquisitions include feather trees, German glass ornaments, toys, vintage children's clothing, and German Belsnickle Santas (figurines representing Santa's helpers). But just as special to Madeline are the sentimental ornaments, such as the dime store ring her son gave her years ago and the baby shoes of

Left: The bountiful variety of antique German glass ornaments is the product of many trips to estate auctions and flea markets. Close scrutiny reveals that the lights are wired to the tree. Only the bulbs are replaced as needed.

her daughter, that embellish her family tree.

Although Madeline's home looks as if she decorates with no thought to cost, she does have a secret: "I tell people never to throw anything away!" And Madeline practices what she preaches. When the decorations come down, every popcorn garland is stored in a metal box and used again—some for up to seven years.

As if decorating to the hilt weren't enough, Madeline and her husband, Herbert, make homemade sausage to give to friends. After ten years of sausage making and experimenting, the Smiths believe the recipe is just

Above: Why decorate with one tree when two look so nice? In the breakfast room, Madeline displays two of the 40 feather trees she has collected. Classic Christmas books and stuffed animals are scattered about the base of the large tree. And some of the dolls on display wear clothes Madeline made for her children.

about perfect. Madeline admits that now Herbert can make the sausage and "he's not even a cook." The Smiths' smoked sausage can be frozen for up to six months and will keep in the refrigerator for up to four months. To enjoy the Smiths' sausage, follow the recipe on page 7.

Left: Santas reign in this bedroom. Almost every Santa on this tree is an antique German ornament. Although she prizes the entire collection, Madeline does have her favorites, such as the Santa that is "so ugly I just love him!"

Right: Four feather trees, crocheted ornaments, and vintage children's clothing form this Victorian Christmas vignette. Popular in the late 1800s, feather trees have a wooden base and wire branches to which chicken feathers (bleached white or dyed green) are attached. Several of the ornaments were cut from old linens or doilies and starched. The cone-shaped icicles are made entirely of cotton, and tiny glass beads strung on wire form a delicate garland. Feather trees such as Madeline's can be costly and hard to find. But to make your own, see page 62.

SMOKED BEEF SAUSAGE

5 pounds ground chuck
¼ cup firmly packed brown sugar
¼ cup Burgundy or other dry red wine
8 large cloves garlic, minced
3 tablespoons plus 1½ teaspoons pickling salt
2 tablespoons liquid smoke
1 tablespoon dried whole basil, crushed
1 tablespoon rubbed sage
1 tablespoon ground savory
2½ teaspoons whole mustard seeds
2½ teaspoons cracked black pepper
1 teaspoon ground thyme
½ teaspoon ascorbic acid
¼ teaspoon ground ginger

Combine all ingredients, stirring well. Shape mixture into a large ball. Store in an airtight container in refrigerator 4 to 5 days. Knead mixture 5 to 10 minutes each day. Shape mixture into 5 (9-inch-long) rolls.

Prepare charcoal fire in smoker. When coals become gray-white, sprinkle with wet hickory chips. Place water pan in smoker, and fill with water. Arrange sausage rolls on upper food rack. Cover smoker with lid. Smoke sausage rolls 7 to 8 hours, turning rolls after 3½ hours. Refill water pan with water, and add additional charcoal as necessary. Remove sausage from smoker. Slice and serve immediately or refrigerate for later use. Yield: 5 (1-pound) sausage rolls.

Above: Beeswax candles, cranberry garlands, and cookie cutters decorate one of the feather trees in Madeline Smith's breakfast room. At the base of the tree are very small feather trees and a variety of Santa collectibles. The figurines holding twigs are German Belsnickle Santas, which are really Santa's helpers. Each is outfitted with a twig, symbolizing the old custom of giving a switch to a naughty child.

A DOLLMAKER'S WORKSHOP

For seven years, Judie Tasch has been making primitive cloth dolls. But she has loved dolls forever. And this can be seen throughout her home. Dolls decorate mantels and tables, dolls are propped in corners, and a cribful of dolls sleep next to the fireplace. "I collect antique dolls, and I'm inspired by them," says Judie.

After perfecting the cotton layering process for making her cloth dolls, Judie added Father Christmas dolls to her repertoire. An interpretation of the classical European figure, Father Christmas is more of a decorative piece than her other dolls. His face is cloth,

---

Left: Judie always uses her dolls in decorations at Christmas. She makes seven variations of Father Christmas and is considering an eighth one this coming year. "I have always loved Santas," says Judie. "That was my inspiration." The Father Christmas dolls are the favorites of Judie's husband and two sons.

Below: Dressed in suede robes and wearing long white beards, this trio of Father Christmases is ready for Christmas Eve rounds. All the pinecones, berries, and greenery that embellish the dolls have been preserved naturally. "There is absolutely nothing store-bought on these," says Judie.

but his body is wooden and secured to a stand. Judie has always been crazy about Santas, which is obvious from her earlier work. ("My mother still decorates with one I made in the tenth grade.") The seven variations of Father Christmas all sport mohair and wool beards and robes of suede cloth trimmed in rabbit fur. A very special Victorian Father Christmas, made in a limited edition, is elaborately detailed, down to the mink trim of his robe. And because these figures are often used as holiday centerpieces, to make every angle appealing, Judie has trinkets spilling from the sack that Father Christmas carries on his back.

Though Judie's first dolls were reproductions of traditional porcelain dolls, she soon realized her interest was in a different area.

"I enjoy collecting primitive antiques so much that making the primitive cloth dolls just seemed to fit into my style," explains Judie. Working from her home in Austin, Texas, Judie has created a community of 24 varieties of dolls. All are made from a cotton layering process, and then painted and varnished. This gives the dolls a durable composition and a timeworn appearance. "Some people think the dolls are made of leather," Judie says. But most people just think they are wonderful.

9

TRADITIONS WROUGHT FROM TIN

In the warmth of his kitchen, Carl Thorne gently held Lynlee's small hand on the paper and traced around each finger. Sitting in her father's lap, she watched her uncle Carl with interest for a while, but holding still is a big job for a six-year-old. If her hand had been much larger, she might not have made it.

The job finished, Carl withdrew to his workshop. Lynlee showed her Aunt Lee the nutcracker she took to school that day, and in what seemed like minutes, Carl returned with a tin cookie cutter the shape of Lynlee's hand.

Not many people can draw on their professions for Christmas decorations. In fact, very few craftsmen have the wealth of material that Carl Thorne has. But cookie cutters, candle molds, miniature chandeliers,

Above: Fletcher, a new mouser-to-be, turns a Christmas wreath into an obstacle course—the obstacle being how to get down. He must have been disappointed to find that the red clusters were peppers.

Above: In the rolling hills east of Winston-Salem, the Thornes have breathed new life into this old house and the adjoining buildings.

Right: Carl traded one of his tin pieces for an old gate, which now hangs above an antique meal bin in the Thornes' living room. On the meal bin sit a wooden box and lantern that Carl made.

10

Above: Lee Thorne holds a candle tree made by her husband, Carl, as he lights the tiny candles. Carl learned to make these trees during his apprenticeship and has continued to make them through the years. Hanging over the kitchen table is a chandelier Carl made, combining his woodworking and tinsmithing talents. The design in the metal is achieved with artfully applied solder. Decorating the table are two of his candle molds adorned with greenery and ribbon.

Left: Bolstered by her dad and her nutcracker, Lynlee holds as still as she can while her Uncle Carl traces the outline of her hand. Carl and Tom, Lynlee's father, both comment on how much her hand has grown since the last time it was traced for a cookie cutter.

11

and small candle trees—all wrought from tin—make touching and personal Christmas decorations.

For six years Carl was a master tinsmith at Old Salem, North Carolina. Then in 1986 he went out on his own. He has since added woodworking to his skills, often combining wood and metal in one-of-a-kind creations.

"I was a surgical assistant, but I grew dissatisfied with it," Carl said. "I wanted something tangible to show. I wanted to feel good about what I did.

"I was at someone's house and saw all kinds of utilitarian pieces made of tin. I grew curious," he explained. "I'd always worked with my hands." Carl heard that the person who'd made the tin pieces was looking for an apprentice, and almost before he had time to realize what was happening, he had apprenticed, mastering the craft quickly. He had no trouble in obtaining the position at Old Salem.

In Kernersville, a short drive east of Winston-Salem, Carl and his wife, Lee, live in a house that was built for her great-grandmother in 1932. It sits on almost three acres of land, along with a building Carl converted into his workshop, a corncrib, and a barn patrolled by a cat named Mousy. Carl and Lee have completely upgraded and remodeled the old house.

"Lee and I both enjoy collecting antiques, and we're using the house as a place to combine our antiques with some of the more contemporary art and accessories we are beginning to collect," Carl said.

Those pieces mix well with Carl's creations, and the combination of antiques and

modern furnishings lends itself to an understated, distinctive holiday treatment. Lee makes candles using Carl's candle molds. Their Christmas tree is sprinkled with candle balls, old-fashioned counter-weighted candle holders, and cookie cutters. Items Carl obtained by bartering his tinware—an old gate piece mounted on their living room wall and a pine hutch in the kitchen—wear bits of greenery and ribbon.

The singular pieces, simply treated, reflect the man who has chosen a separate path. "Years ago the craftsman's work was the epitome. Today there's so much exactness. I like things that aren't perfect," he said, "that are unique."

Below: "The candle ball is my original design and is used primarily at Christmas, although I do know a few folks who use it year-round," Carl says. "I've seen it hung on a Christmas tree, which was its original purpose, and hung in the doorway as a mistletoe ornament—nice to have such wonderful vibrations occurring under my work!"

Above: Lee singes the tiny beeswax candles, which are too small to actually burn, in a chandelier ornament Carl made. The Thornes' Christmas tree is filled with Carl's handiwork combined with treasured ornaments Lee has collected.

A CREATIVE WOMAN'S DESIGNS ON CHRISTMAS

St. Simon's Island, off the coast of Georgia, offers the expected resort attractions of sand, sea, and sky. But it is the island's woods and marshes, still on the wild side, that haunt the imagination. It was here that Teri Bonds began creating her handmade natural decorations, inspired by the resources at hand. It was a simple beginning. As Teri explains, "I was working for a shop on the island, and I made moss baskets for sale there. A friend took one of my baskets to the Atlanta Gift Show, where a catalog representative saw it and expressed interest."

When Teri agreed to make over 200 baskets for the catalog company, her friend told her she was crazy, and predicted, "It's going to take many hands to do it." It did. Teri got help to fulfill the order, and her company was born, aptly named Many Hands.

Teri's designs are now available in some 4,000 retail shops, department stores, and catalogs. In many homes, people are enjoying her handsome decorative accessories at Christmas and year-round. The moss baskets were just the beginning of a continually expanding line, created from a natural harvest that includes dried flowers such as yarrow, tansy, goldenrod, heather, and statice; grapevine; corn husks; green and Spanish mosses; herbs and spices including cinnamon, rose

Above: Teri's husband, Mose, steals a smooch under a kissing ball, one of her creations. Grapevine rings trace the ball and a cheery gingerbread man acts as cupid. Berries, eucalyptus, fir, and ribbons accent the orb, top and bottom.

Left: Teri welcomes friends through the back gate with a basket overflowing with fir, magnolia, and holly. Of loosely woven grapevine, this basket is flat on the back for hanging.

Left: When Teri's girls requested something pretty to put in their long hair, Teri began experimenting with barrettes and bands topped with ribbons, tiny dried flowers, greenery, and cones. Many Hands now makes the pretty wearable ornaments, and the packaging reads "to Kelly and Memory." Here, Teri places a delicate flowery barrette in daughter Kelly's hair. Teri is wearing one of the tiny floral bouquets as a pin.

Below: The simple charm of Teri's spice crèche takes one's breath away. Five cinnamon stick logs, laced together with raffia, form the stable. Bits of cinnamon stick, a tiny cone, and cloves form the figures. A star of anise hangs above.

Left: For this napkin ornament, Teri shaped the heart of a palmetto palm frond with scissors. Bits of cedar, pepper berries, and a ribbon bow were glued to the top of the scalloped leaf. Ribbon, glued to the back of the leaf, is tied around the napkin.

hips, anise star, mint, dock, and tarragon; eucalyptus; and more. Many of the materials are still plucked from the wild woods and marshes of St. Simon's Island. (A few of Teri's Christmas specialties are shown on these pages, including her kissing ball, spice crèche ornament, and flowery hair and clothing accessories.)

Teri carefully considers each addition to her line. For instance, she contemplated developing a Della Robbia wreath for some time. She reasoned, "People love the Williamsburg look. And when they buy high-end products (expensive, quality items), they want to be able to use them again and again." Using artificial fruit in the wreath made good sense, especially with the realistic fruit reproductions that were available. But Teri was hesitant since her business was built on natural products. A trip to Williamsburg last year convinced her. As she discovered, "Even Williamsburg is using artificial fruit. If they can, we can." So this past Christmas, Teri introduced the Della Robbia wreath, and it proved to be very popular.

Left: This quaint structure reminds Teri of St. Simon's Island. It is also similar in character to a gingerbread house, only of less perishable materials. The house is plastered cardboard, and the roof is covered with moss. Burlap cutouts outlined with moss are windows and the door. A tiny grapevine wreath adorns the door. Teri is designing a smaller version to offer to her customers.

Opposite: A breath of spring is refreshing at the Christmas table. This centerpiece is based on a straw wreath covered with sheet moss. Here and there, live flowering plants (the small potted ones that you can buy in the grocery store) and resurrection ferns are pressed into the moss. Teri pulled the ferns, which spring to life with watering, from the bark of live oaks. The rich pink berries are pepper berries, which hold peppercorns, and the green ones are ligustrum berries. Scattered through the foliage are kumquats, lady apples, and mushrooms.

Teri lives in Atlanta, Georgia, now, with her husband, Mose, and her almost-grown daughters, Kelly and Memory, but she still maintains a home on the island for her frequent visits to oversee Many Hands work. Teri's designs are based on tradition and fine materials, qualities which, she feels, make them timeless as home decorations. And that may be why her business continues to grow. In many homes at Christmas time, people all across the country display and give her decorations. That must give Teri a nice, warm feeling of fulfillment.

Right: Teri surrounds a soulful hand-carved Santa, accompanied by a deer, with a woodsy harvest of dried leaves and grapes (still clinging to the vine), and airplane plantlets. Teri knows how to let natural materials work their simple charm.

A BIG FAMILY CHRISTMAS IN UTAH

Big families make for big Christmases. And the Liljenquists (Gorman, Katherine, and their seven children) know about that kind of holiday. One daughter recalls, "It seemed to me as a child that—with all the decorations, presents, food, and everyone at home—our house was full to the ceiling!"

Home for the Liljenquists is Ogden, Utah, about 30 miles from Salt Lake City, and flanked to the east by the often-snowy Wasatch Mountains. Gorman and Katherine's kids are married now, with children of their own (except for the youngest, John, who is a student at Brigham Young University). The five girls attended colleges in Utah, married Ogden men, and, all but one, live in their hometown. The eldest in the family is Joe, who, like his father, is a veterinarian. Joe lives in the nearby town of Bountiful with his wife and their five children.

When the Liljenquists were growing up, Christmases in this household were starred by Katherine's festive spirit, an enthusiasm that infused the whole family. They always had two fresh green trees, and Katherine cut backyard greenery to deck the halls. Evergreen pungency mingled with sweet aromas wafting from a crowded kitchen, where Katherine and the girls cooked (and, no doubt, the boys tasted) batches of goodies.

According to Katherine, "We've always made candies—pecan rolls, chocolate-dipped sweets, and the family favorite, buttermints—

Top right: Two small balsam firs grace the hearth and a large one stands in the center of the room. Their strong, straight branches grow at right angles to the trunk and provide perches for Ann's doll collection. Dolls, handmade and collectible, have been given to Ann and Emily over the years, and now, Ann's baby daughter, Ellen, will be getting some of her own.

Right: Emily plays the piano, while Charlie, Daniel, Nathan, and Ann (holding an enraptured Ellen) sing carols. Emily and her dad, Bruce, perform sacred music for their church. The yellow stars on the piano's music stand are Trice's design.

18

for friends, neighbors, and ourselves.'' She also makes the buttermints, as well as wreaths, for church and school benefits. Her handsome wreaths are the result of careful attention to materials and good craftsmanship. (Wreaths, instructions, and the melt-in-your-mouth buttermint recipe are on the following pages.)

The photos on these two pages were taken at the home of the eldest daughter, Ann Gladwell, homemaker and mother of five. Every Christmas, Ann plants a holiday forest in her living room. Ann and Emily, Ann's eldest daughter, decorate three trees in that area with their collection of dainty dolls. That's not a job for the younger children, but Ann understands the joys of tree trimming for

Above: Gathered at the home of Ann Gladwell are the talented Liljenquist ladies. From left to right—Ann, Katherine (mom), Katie, (and standing) Barbara and Trice. (Liz, a busy school teacher and administrator, was not available for the photo.)

Ann found the unusual set of reverse appliqué stockings at a crafts fair. The intricate handwork, called flower cloth, is by the Hmong people. Several families from this Laotian tribe have settled in the area.

Ann's coffee table is a nice, safe way to put pretty things close to the floor so that children can enjoy them, too. It's an old display case with sliding glass doors to protect the contents.

any age. As she explains, ''I get a fourth tree for the playroom, so that they can have free rein with their very own tree.''

The second eldest Liljenquist daughter is

19

Liz Mueller. She applies her teaching skills to a Christmas party for her two little ones and the other children in the family. Before the party, she gathers the makings for a cake-decorating session: small individual cakes, colorful icings, and assorted decorations. When the children arrive, she serves them raisins, apples, and cheese—a healthy snack to help discourage candy eating later. They play games, sing Christmas songs, and for the party finale, frost their cakes and trim them with sugar beads and candies. Liz provides wire baskets, which the children weave with pretty ribbons, to carry the cakes home.

Trice Boerens, middle child and mother of two, is a designer and art director for the Vanessa-Ann Collection, a company that produces designs for needlecraft and other mediums. Early on, Trice's art took precedence over candy making. Katherine remembers, "One Christmas when Trice was about 10, we were all involved in the candy making, and there was Trice in the middle of the floor with her watercolors." Trice shares her designs for several painted wooden cutouts on these pages. She sometimes asks a carpenter to cut out the shapes, and then Trice, her mother, and her sisters decorate the pieces. (See photo captions for pattern pages.)

The youngest daughters, Barbara Curtis and Katie Smith, are working mothers (each with a baby boy), but they still find time for handcrafts. Barbara's family lives in Richmond, Virginia. When they come home for the holidays, she may bring gifts of stained glass, quilting, and cross-stitch. Barbara once gave her mom a cross-stitched calendar of family birthdates. According to Katherine, it now needs some more work. "I need to get it caught up again," a challenge with this fast-growing family.

This year Katie made painted wooden decorations, but she is also an exceptional seamstress. She made her own wedding dress, and now makes bridal gowns for friends.

Fond memories of big family Christmases, and now, the added incentive of grandchildren, inspire the creative and personal ideas that Katherine and her daughters share with us here.

Opposite below: Trice designed the wooden trees in the foreground. These trees, painted and stenciled in soft pastels, can be used on the mantel, as a centerpiece, in a window, all around the house. The patterns for the trees and stencils can be found on pages 146 and 147. Trice's elder son, Andrew, hangs ornaments (shown at right, patterns on page 148) on the top half of the tree only, safely out of reach of baby brother, Cole. These bear and ball ornaments are richly colored with wood stains and diluted paints.

Right: Cole and Andrew roll a pony plaything (featured on page 90), a classic pull toy updated with Trice's graphic design and distinctive color sense. This toy style never went out of favor with the little ones, and now enjoys even greater popularity as a decorative folk accessory.

Above: Katherine collected the delicate petals (bougainvillea bracts) adorning this wreath on a visit to California. You might substitute similar flowers native to your area. Wreath instructions are on these pages. The small wooden tree, stenciled with a single star, is Trice's design, and the pattern is on page 153.

Flower Blossom Wreath

Tie a string hanger around a 12" straw or Spanish moss wreath form to hold the wreath while attaching the fragile blossoms. (Katherine gathered the dried blossoms shown from beneath a bougainvillea plant. They are actually bracts, as are the showy "petals" of a poinsettia. If these plants are not available to you, try similar materials found in your area.) Attach blossoms to the wreath with craft glue, covering the sides first and the top last. Attach a wire hanger to the back of the wreath and remove the string.

Eucalyptus, Garlic, and Raffia Wreath

Wire overlapping eucalyptus branches to a straw wreath form, or buy a eucalyptus wreath. At three intervals on the wreath, wrap 6 to 8 raffia pieces (long enough to knot and leave 2" excess when trimmed). Tie

raffia, securing a cluster of artificial berries into the knot, and trim the raffia. Between the raffia ties, attach clusters of 3 garlic heads to the wreath with raffia. Attach a wire hanger.

Hoya Wreath

Reshape a wire coat hanger into a circle (hook is top of wreath). Wrap 15" to 18" lengths of hoya plant (or other evergreen shrub) around the wire, securing with florists' tape. Add ribbon trim as desired.

Red Pepper Wreath

You'll need 3 to 4 dozen fresh red peppers. Sort the peppers by size and shape and tie a 20" length of raffia to each stem. Use them to cover a 12" straw or Spanish moss wreath form, one side at a time. Use bigger, curved peppers at the bottom of the wreath and

Above: Katherine trimmed the eucalyptus wreath (left) with garlic bulbs, raffia, and berries. The center wreath, nestled in the straw, is woven from branches of a hoya plant, and fresh red peppers spice up the wreath on the right. Wreath instructions are below. The small wooden ducks are Trice's pattern, which appears on page 153.

smaller peppers on the sides and top. Tie the peppers to the wreath, winding the excess raffia around the wreath. (As you add more peppers, use the raffia to secure the first layers.) Attach a sprig of greenery to the top of the wreath and a wire hanger to the back.

Buttermint Recipe
3 cups sugar
1 cup hot water
½ cup butter
1 teaspoon vanilla extract

Combine sugar, water, and butter in a large saucepan; bring to a boil, stirring constantly. Cover and cook, without stirring, over high heat 3 minutes, to wash down sugar crystals from sides of pan.

Uncover and continue cooking, without stirring, until mixture reaches hard ball stage (260°). During the first five minutes, wash down sugar crystals that have formed on sides of pan as needed, using a pastry brush dipped in hot water. Remove from heat, and immediately pour syrup onto a buttered marble slab.

Sprinkle vanilla over surface of hot syrup; let rest 2 minutes or until edges begin to set. Work syrup into a mound. Divide mound of candy in half. With buttered hands, pull, fold, and twist each portion until candy is opaque and begins to stiffen. This takes 5 to 10 minutes, depending on the weather and your skill.

Shape mint mixture into 2 (½"-thick) twisted ropes. Using kitchen shears, cut ropes into 1" segments. Place mints on waxed paper to cool. Let mints sit overnight or until they become creamy. Store in an airtight container. Yield: about 150 mints.

ROMANCING THE SEASON

From first light to lights out, Christmas decorations frame Susan and Bruce Jaeger's December days. The Jaegers' bedroom was born of heritage and romance; holiday decorations merely extend the mood.

Susan grew up in Port Tobacco, Maryland, near the mouth of the Chesapeake Bay. When she married and moved to Crofton, just west of Annapolis, she took along family antiques and treasures from her childhood home.

In the recent remodeling of their house, Susan and Bruce enlarged the bedroom to three times its original size. For Christmas, Susan drew upon her legacy from the past to decorate the new space. "I decided I wanted to do as many things typical of Maryland and the (Chesapeake) Bay as I could," she said.

She dangled oyster shells from the tree with ribbon. Norway spruce, boxwood, and seashells sprang from crab shells placed on a salesmen's sample chest.

Since Maryland is one of the natural flyways for geese, Susan arranged a brass goose in an antique cast-iron sleigh. And she showcased two wooden swans given to her by her son, Bart, and daughter, Julie.

When Susan's children were young, she often took them to a nearby pond to watch the resident swans. "They've always been one of my favorite waterfowl," she said.

"They're so graceful, so elegant." The hand-carved swans celebrated completion of the remodeled bedroom.

Nostalgia provided material where homage to Maryland left off. On the tree, Susan hung Julie's and Bart's silver baby rattles and spoons, as well as lace doilies crocheted by her grandmother. On a fireside table, she arranged her collection of crystal trees, many of which Bruce had brought her from his travels to Bethlehem and countries including Germany, the Netherlands, Switzerland, and the Bahamas.

In this medley of lace and legacy, cast in shades of peach and ecru, the standard seasonal red isn't needed. Hunter green is the link, and sentiment is the shading.

Above: Wallpaper placed over gold foil is pleated into a fan shape and caught with a decorative metal knob. Below it, a hand-carved swan dons festive ribbon and floats in a pond of greenery.

Below: Susan Jaeger selects articles for decorating that reflect her heritage. The tree displays baby rattles and spoons, doilies made by her grandmother, and oyster shells, plentiful in Susan's native Maryland. Arranged with teddies, quilts, and sprays of greenery, this corner entertains the eye at every turn.

Above: In this scene, an angel watches over the Nativity in a frosted thicket of trees, the crystal figurines rising delicately from a deep green "hillside."

Opposite: Susan and Bruce's bedroom epitomizes the romance of the season. Beside a blazing fire rises their graceful tree. Echoing it by the bed is a boxwood tree ornamented with baby's breath and swans, and over the mantel hangs a straw wreath form that has been cut and reshaped to become a swag embellished with flowers, lace, and ribbon.

BORN CHRISTMAS PEOPLE

When Nancy Stanton redecorated her living room in peach and beige tones, she wasn't thinking ahead to Christmas and the tree that would stand in that room. But her daughter Laura Kluvo knows how much her mom loves Christmas. For instance, how many people who live in south Florida have fireplaces for Nancy's reason? As she explains, "We have a mantel, added most particularly so that our heirloom stockings have a proper hanging place. Our children are adults now, but those handmade needlepoint stockings had better be hanging from the hooks."

Laura knew that her mom would want everything to be just right for the holiday, and the ornaments and decorations made and collected over the years by the family would seem out of place in the pastel setting. So she designed all new ornaments in the Victorian style. Laura and her sister, Leah, made a treeful of baubles in colors to suit the new decor.

The exquisite ornaments—angels, fans, nosegays, hearts, and cornucopias—are of peach, ivory, gold, and aqua fabrics with moiré ribbon and lace trims. (The old ornaments are, of course, still treasured and displayed on a tree in the family room where the colors fit right in.) Laura also made a puffed wreath of layered ivory lace and taffeta to hang over the mantel.

Although the new collection of ornaments amazed Nancy, it didn't surprise her at all that Laura would try such an undertaking. She has been making ornaments for relatives since she was six years old. One aunt covers her tree with decorations that she calls "early Laura."

That childhood interest in handcrafts never waned and, a few years ago, Laura founded the Southern Handcraft Society. Nancy and Laura's grandmother, Ruth Moe, are also members, and they all contribute to the society's Country Christmas craft show described on page 38. As Nancy puts it, "We are truly immersed in this holiday. I think there are those of us who are just born Christmas people. But it is important to guard against turning Christmas into a hectic, pressured time. It all comes down to attitude, planning, and cooperation."

Nancy shares one of her secrets for making time for Christmas crafts: "I am known as the catalog queen, but I accept that title because it is a good system for me. I shop leisurely at home through catalogs all year-round."

After the early-December Country Christmas show is behind them, Nancy, Laura, and Ruth concentrate on their family holiday. Five generations of Stantons gather at Nancy's home. (They have been known to splash in her pool on Christmas Day.) They all bring their specialties for a buffet. There are the traditional holiday dishes—turkey, ham, vegetables, and sweets—but, thanks to

---

Below: Laura's Victorian cornucopia, made in moiré fabric, overflows with baby's breath, star flowers, and ribbon roses. Instructions are on page 28.

the tropical location, there are also recipes containing fresh citrus and seafood.

Lots of people and food can mean chaos in the kitchen, but Nancy's husband comes to the rescue. As Nancy proudly explains, "Peter is a human trash compactor/dishwasher. He has an amazing talent for making mincemeat out of any mess. This is definitely my favorite tradition."

As Nancy describes their family day, "Our Christmas is a wonderful, magical, warm holiday because we love each other, we care, we support, and we think every new child is an amazing miracle—to be cherished and enjoyed." And you know that when Nancy says "warm," she's talking about much more than the weather on a sunny Christmas day in Florida.

Above: When Nancy Stanton (seated) redecorated her living room, daughter Laura Kluvo designed all new ornaments to color-coordinate with the new look. (Laura tells us how to make one of her ornaments on the following page.) Laura's son finds a spot on the floor close to the presents as Laura, holding her baby daughter, and Laura's grandmother, Ruth Moe, stand. The French hand-sewn stocking on the chair to the left is one of a pair that Ruth made last year for two new baby girls in the family (Ruth's granddaughter and great-granddaughter). The christening gown hung on the wall, an unusual display idea, is also Ruth's work.

Above: Laura made this ivory cloud of a wreath with layered fabrics—taffeta and lace. The fabric is gathered, lightly stuffed, and attached to a commercial wreath form. She shares directions for her puffy wreath on this page.

LAURA'S VICTORIAN DECORATIONS

Laura used soft pastel shades to coordinate with her mom's furnishings. Choose fabric colors that will enhance your decor.

Cornucopia Ornament

From the patterns on page 149, construct cones from poster board and fabric. Slip the poster board cone into the fabric cone, aligning seams. Fold excess fabric to the inside of the cone, and glue to secure.

Glue gold cord around the cone in a spiral. Glue a decorative lace ruffle or other trim around the cone opening. Cut a length of ⅛"-wide ribbon for a hanger. Glue ends of ribbon to the sides of the cone. From more ribbon, tie ribbon bows with streamers and glue over the hanger ends. Embellish the center of the bows with ribbon roses or other trim as desired.

Fill the cone with Spanish moss. Touch stems of baby's breath with glue and insert into the moss. Add dried starflowers and ribbon roses on wire stems, or other dried flowers, as desired.

Puffy Wreath

You'll need a 14" Handicraft wreath form. (These forms, available at most craft stores, are wire circles with wire clips at right angles to the circles and at regular intervals.)

Fold a 4½-yard length of 45"-wide taffeta in half (at 2¼ yards) and mark fold line. Measure 11" on either side of the line and draw a second and third line across the fabric. Continue measuring and marking 11" intervals for a total of 15 lines, with some fabric left over on each end.

Pin a 4½-yard length of 45"-wide lace fabric on top of the taffeta. (You should be able to see the lines through the lace.) With a long stitch, baste through both layers of fabric along each line. Gather fabric and knot thread to secure.

Open clips on the wreath form. Place fabric at the first gathered line in the clip and close the clip to secure. Repeat for remaining gathers, forming a puff of fabric between clips. Last gather will overlap fabric in the first clip. Trim excess fabric from the ends. Insert a handful of stuffing (you'll need about ½ pound) from the back into each fabric puff.

Pull the wires and caps out of 7 glass balls, 3½" in diameter. Squeeze craft glue into the caps, replace the caps, and let glue dry before proceeding. With fine-gauge wire, attach a ball to the front of every other clip.

WREATHS THAT REVEAL
THE UNEXPECTED

A wreath is a wreath, of course, of course, unless it's designed to delight a horse. Carrots and sweets, tethered to a muzzle-level ring of cedar, fetch appreciative snorts from one of Jo Harris's equine friends, shown *at right*.

Each year Jo makes wreaths for the horses at her farm in Pell City, Alabama. She and her husband, Paul, celebrate Christmas in the country with decorations suiting their lifestyle. An antique dealer as well as a riding instructor, Jo enjoys country and folk art objects. The wreath *below* shows how she makes creative use of her finds—a group of antique tools becomes the center of a spray.

Jo Harris understands the impact of simple greenery that contains the unexpected. For totally different reasons, so do her horses.

WELCOME THE SEASON

"The stockings were hung by the chimney with care." The homespun stockings shown here were *made* with care. Fabrics were chosen and patterns cut out; hearts and flowers were fashioned and seams stitched closed. From the festive collection on the following pages, you can make your own decorations to deck halls, doors, trees, and mantels.

HOMESPUN STOCKING THREESOME

Embroidered with flowers and stenciled with hearts, these homespun stockings will warm up a country interior and give Santa the chance to prove that the best presents do come in small packages. Though not the usual stocking size (they're only 6½" tall), this trio packs quite a decorating punch. The heels and toes are highlighted with a contrasting fabric, and the sturdy lining will accommodate a variety of stocking stuffers.

Consider using them separately as an alternative to the usual gift wrapping; just line a stocking with a complementary color of tissue paper and tie a gift card to the hanger.

Materials (for 3 stockings):
patterns on page 133
¾ yard (45"-wide) lightweight woven fabric (homespun or muslin)
¾ yard (45"-wide) cotton print fabric (for lining)
contrasting scraps of fabric for inserts, heels, and toes
thread to match
acetate (for stencil)
craft knife
hole punch that makes ⅛"-wide holes
masking tape
2 small stencil brushes
acrylic paints (red, green)
crewel needle
perle cotton embroidery floss (red, green)
lightweight rope

STENCILED STOCKING

Transfer patterns to fabrics and cut out. There are 3 pieces to the front of the stenciled stockings: a bottom, a top, and a middle insert. Stocking back is one whole piece. Transfer toe and heel appliqué placement markings to fabric.

Transfer heart and circle stencil designs to acetate. Cut out hearts with craft knife, and use hole punch to make the circles.

Place stencil on top of fabric piece in line with placement marks and secure with masking tape. Dip brush in red paint and dab it on paper towel to remove excess. Stencil hearts, using an up-and-down motion. Paint green circles in same way. Let dry. With right sides together, stitch top section of stocking to insert piece. Press seam open. With right sides together, sew insert to bottom section of stocking. Press seam open.

Pin heel and toe to stocking front as indicated on pattern. Tuck raw edges under slightly and hand-sew to stocking front. With one strand of embroidery floss and a running stitch, embroider as marked on pattern.

With right sides facing, stitch stocking front and back. Clip and turn. With right sides facing, stitch lining front and back. Clip; do not turn. Place lining in stocking, pushing it down into toe and heel area of stocking. Roll top edge of lining over top of stocking so that ¾" of lining shows. Fold raw edge of lining under ¼" and attach to stocking with blind stitch. Loop rope in half, and stitch ends together. Stitch loop to back left side of stocking.

EMBROIDERED STOCKING

Cut out 2 whole stocking pieces for front and back. (No insert piece.) Transfer all embroidery markings to stocking front. Use a running stitch and 1 strand of green floss to embroider all horizontal and vertical lines. Use a lazy daisy stitch and 1 strand of red floss to embroider flowers. Appliqué heel and toe same as for other stockings. Assemble stocking and lining same as for other stockings.

32

COLORS CAST TO THE WIND

Fluttering ribbons in brilliant Christmas colors tease the wind and flash on the landscape. This wind sock is perfect for a bit of holiday daydreaming.

Easy enough for a child to make, it's designed to touch the child in all of us. Simply secure woven weatherproof ribbon to a plastic ring, stitching the ribbon in place either by hand or with a machine; then hang your holiday wind sock from a tree in the yard, a hook on your porch, or anywhere you can enjoy its movement and life.

Materials:
12¼ yards (1⅜"-wide) green grosgrain weatherproof ribbon
12¼ yards (1⅜"-wide) red moiré weatherproof ribbon
8"-diameter plastic macramé ring
red, green thread
1 yard (1/16"-wide) green satin ribbon
½" plastic curtain ring
7 yards (1⅜"-wide) white moiré weatherproof ribbon
white thread

Cut wide red and green ribbon into 49" lengths, 9 of each color. Fold 1" of each length over macramé ring, alternating colors, and stitch in place with matching thread.

To make hanger, cut three 1-foot lengths of narrow green ribbon. Tie one end of each length to the macramé ring between every sixth ribbon. Gather loose ends and knot around curtain ring.

Hang the sock at arm level to weave. Cut nine 28" lengths of white ribbon. Weave a ribbon around the sock, over and under vertical ribbons, keeping white ribbon next to the ring. Pin in place. Continue weaving, alternating over-and-under pattern as shown in photo. Begin and end each strip at the same spot on the sock, overlapping ends, to form a back seam, and pin in place as you work.

When all strips are woven, pin bottom strip to each ribbon it passes. Remove other pins except those securing back seam. Sew bottom white strip to colored strips all around. Sew overlapped white ribbons to form back seam. Trim trailing wide ribbon ends on the diagonal.

33

NOT A CREATURE
WAS STIRRING

This little mouse has donned his nightcap, ready to settle down for a long winter's nap. Stitched with red, green, and white print fabrics, mouse and his bed illustrate the famous image from Clement C. Moore's *A Visit from St. Nicholas.*

Little ones will especially enjoy tucking in their tiny friend as they hear about Santa's unexpected arrival that snowy night. And quilters will appreciate the clever design of this stuffed creature and his fluffy pillow and mini-quilt.

Materials:
patterns on page 137
9" square of fabric (for mouse body)
thread to match
stuffing
white quilting thread
2 (⅛"-diameter) black buttons for eyes
6" x 8" piece of fabric for nightcap
thread to match
Fray Check
5" x 15" piece of white print fabric
3" x 11" piece of green print fabric
4" square piece of red print fabric
5" x 6" piece of bleached muslin
5" x 6" piece of batting
green embroidery floss

MOUSE: Transfer patterns for mouse to fabric, and cut out. Right sides facing, sew nose gusset to head on mouse front as indicated on pattern. Sew center seam of mouse front from nose down. Clip at neck.

Sew ears, leaving open where marked, trim seam, clip, and turn. Blind-stitch the rest of side closed, leaving bottom open. Baste ears to front of head, centering on each gusset seam, raw edges aligned. Pin mouse back in place, with ears to inside, and sew back to front, leaving open where marked. Clip seam at neck.

Cut a 1" x 7¾" piece of fabric for tail, fold in half lengthwise, sew long side, leaving ends open, and turn. To finish, tie the tail in a knot ½" from one raw end. Baste the other end to back of mouse. Stuff mouse firmly, carefully working stuffing into small places. Blind-stitch body closed, catching raw edges of tail in closure. Tack tail in position under mouse so that it lies to the back.

Sew arms and legs, leaving open where marked. Clip and trim where necessary; turn. Stuff firmly; blind-stitch openings closed. With quilting thread and a long needle, sew from the inside of one arm to the outside and back; then sew through the mouse where indicated on pattern, through the other arm, and back. Continue until the arms are securely attached. Repeat for legs.

With quilting thread, sew on eyes, where marked, sewing through head from one eye to the other and pulling thread tightly to contour face. Sew four 6" strands of white quilting thread through the tip of the nose. Tie strands together in a knot on each side of the nose. Trim whiskers to about 2".

CAP: Transfer pattern to fabric and cut out. Cut ear holes where marked, and coat with Fray Check.

When thoroughly dry, sew center front seam and press open. Press under ¼" of cap, and sew the hem. With right sides together, sew center back seam. Turn right side out.

To form tassel, sew seven 8" pieces of matching thread through point of cap. Braid threads and tie loose ends with matching thread. Trim ends evenly. Fold top of cap over so that tip is ½" from bottom of back and tack top of braid to back seam.

PILLOW: Cut a 3" x 4½" white print fabric rectangle for pillow and a 4½" x 1" green print fabric rectangle for border. All seams are ¼". With right sides facing and 4½" raw edges aligned, sew green border strip to pillow. Press seam toward green. Press border edge opposite seam ¼" to wrong side, and then in half. Fold pillow in half, right sides facing and short ends together. Sew bottom and side seams. Turn.

Quilt any pattern you wish in green border, traveling from one design area to another by pushing the needle between the layers. Fill pillow with stuffing.

QUILT: Transferring pattern to fabric, cut 12 red print triangles and 12 white print triangles. Sew together, referring to photo for placement. Cut 2 (1" x 4½") and 2 (1" x 5½") border strips from green print fabric. Sew 4½" strips to short ends of quilt, right sides facing, stopping and starting ¼" from edges of quilt. Repeat with 5½" strips on each side. Fold pieces together at corners to miter as shown in photo. Sew together, and trim excess.

Layer bleached muslin, batting, and quilt top, and baste together. With three strands of green embroidery floss, make French knots (with three wraps) in the middle of each triangle on both the front and back of the quilt. Travel from one triangle to next between the layers.

With white quilting thread, quilt the green border in any pattern you wish. This quilt has hearts and scallops along the border. Cut a 1" x 15" strip of white print fabric for bias binding. Sew to quilt top, right sides facing. Press raw edge of binding ¼" to wrong side, and fold around edge of quilt. Blind-stitch in place on underside of quilt.

PARTY WITH A SNOWMAN

Set the tone for a fun-for-all kids' Christmas celebration with this snappy snowman set. It's a festive table decoration and party favor all rolled up in one. The snowman, disguised as a napkin holder, is really a take-home ornament. Because the set is so quick and easy to assemble, you can make up a dozen or so for a party that kids will remember.

To make the snowman, follow patterns on page 138 to cut 2 body pieces from light-weight white felt. Match body pieces and stitch edges, leaving opening to turn. Turn, stuff lightly, and sew opening closed. Sew on small black beads or button eyes. For nose, glue on a tiny pink felt circle. Use red embroidery thread to stitch stars on each cheek and black thread to stitch, or glue on, mouth and arms (see photo).

Cut 2 snowman hat patterns from red felt, cutting a slash in one of them as shown on pattern. Match hat pieces and blanket-stitch outer edge of hat with red embroidery floss.

Slip hat over snowman's head through the slash. Secure hat with red thread and tiny stitches. To trim hat, glue on strips of rickrack and a ⅛" red pom-pom (see photo). For an ornament hanger, tack a doubled length of ribbon or thread to the back of the snowman.

Buy purchased mats and napkins in Christmas colors, or make your own. For a mat, cut an 11" x 16"-piece of pre-quilted green fabric. Cut to round corners. Finish mat with red bias tape, matching raw edges with right sides together, and stitch. Fold tape to back of mat, encasing edge, and zigzag-stitch in place. Cut a 20" strip of ½" red dotted bias tape. Stitch midpoint of tape at center left of place mat, 3½" from outer edge. If desired, sew red star buttons randomly at top of mat to finish. For napkin, cut a 12½" x 12½"-piece of Christmas print fabric. Fold edges under ¼", repeat, and hem.

Place folded napkin over dotted tape on mat, place snowman on top of napkin, and tie tape at snowman's neck.

DON'T FORGET THE DOORKNOBS

Merry doorknob wreaths spread season's greetings even before guests ring your bell. The wreaths are so easy to make, you'll want to post welcoming festivity at every portal.

Tie one into an overall room scheme by using scraps of fabric left over from decorating. Make enough for your home, and then make some more for a bazaar or for gifts. You'll enjoy these decorations for years to come.

Materials:
patterns on page 136
10" x 10" piece of green fabric
9" x 7" piece of red fabric
9" x 18" piece of single-sided fusible web fabric
9" x 18" piece of backing fabric
9" x 18" piece of fleece
red thread
fabric glue
2" x 7" piece of double-sided fusible web fabric, prebacked if available
backing sheet, if web isn't prebacked

Transfer wreath pattern to green fabric and bow and heart patterns to red fabric. Do not cut out; marked outlines are stitching lines. Cut away fabric section with hearts, and set aside. Iron to fuse wreath and bow to single-sided fusible web fabric, following manufacturer's directions. Layer backing fabric, fleece, and marked fabric with web, right sides of fabric to outside. Pin together.

With red thread, machine-zigzag a close satin stitch around wreath and bow. Top tension may be slightly lessened so that stitch draws to the underside.

For bow, begin stitching at left section of ribbon. Stitching one section at a time, move clockwise, stitching center circle last.

For wreath, begin stitching where indicated on pattern. Stop at each point with needle in fabric, lift presser foot, and turn design as you work.

Being careful not to cut satin stitches, cut

out wreath and bow with sharp scissors. Glue bow to wreath with fabric glue.

Following manufacturer's directions, iron to fuse heart strip to double-sided fusible web, using backing sheet if web isn't prebacked. Cut out hearts. Remove backing, and position hearts on wreath. Iron to fuse in place.

THE KEY TO A SUCCESSFUL BAZAAR

A well-planned Christmas bazaar can be a joy to all who attend, providing shoppers a chance to buy unique handcrafts for holiday decorating and gift giving. Such an event can also be a great fund-raiser for the sponsoring group. But planning is a key word. Where there's a crowd and money changing hands, confusion can occur. Adequate preparation will minimize these problems.

The Southern Handcraft Society (SHS) of Boca Raton, Florida, produces a holiday crafts sale, called Country Christmas, the weekend after Thanksgiving. It has grown bigger and better in each of its four years. Laura Kluvo (featured on page 26 with her family) was the 1986 president of the society. She is also the founder of the group, which now numbers 120 members. Laura explains, "Country Christmas provides the funds to further our goals of preserving, enriching, and sharing the creative arts."

By sharing the details behind their show's success, the Southern Handcraft Society may help you and your group stage an enjoyable and profitable sale of your own.

The Quality Distinction
The Country Christmas sale is known for its fine-quality items. To maintain that reputation, SHS asks artists to submit slides of their work for consideration. Since 50 artists (including some SHS members) from all over the South are chosen to be featured in the show, Country Christmas customers have the opportunity to buy works that might not be shown in the area otherwise. And out-of-town artists don't have to sit and sell their work all weekend—members inventory shipments, set up displays, sell the items, return unsold items, and mail checks.

Good Business
Members assume responsibility for show expenses and have a separate bank account for Country Christmas. They collect and pay sales tax. They accept checks, but not credit cards. The participating artists (SHS members

as well) contribute 20 percent of their proceeds to the society. In addition, members make items (including 100 "special limited edition" ornaments) to sell at the show, and 100 percent of the proceeds of these sales goes into the treasury.

At the sale, each cashier has an adding machine, cash box, and logbook. She logs each sale in the book by inventory code number, artist's initials, and price. Baggers double-check receipts. The club treasurer collects money hourly and makes deposits several times a day. Professional security guards are hired for the show.

A Good Location Helps Things Flow Smoothly
Since Country Christmas is held inside the recreation center at Patch Reef Park in Boca

Raton, inclement weather doesn't mean cancellation, and the facilities can accommodate a crowd. There's plenty of parking, as well as a kitchen, rest rooms, and a janitorial staff. Signs clearly mark the entrance and exit. The City of Boca Raton's Parks and Recreation Department and the Greater Boca Raton Beach Tax District co-sponsor the show, providing the location and assisting with publicity.

If No One Knows, No One Shows
Publicity is crucial to a big turnout, and SHS members do an excellent job of spreading the word about Country Christmas. They send press releases on individual artists, the society itself, and the club's annual recipe and crafts book, *Country Christmas Year-Round*, to local and national publications to

Above: Southern Handcraft Society members excel at display. Shelves are filled with folk art, miniatures, florals, stuffed animals, dolls, and more. Pillows fill seats. Quilts are hung on the walls or draped over screens, chair backs, and cabinet doors. Tables are set with place mats and pottery. Prints and original watercolors are hung on the walls or propped in open drawers. Baskets overflow with goodies or live poinsettias, and holiday music fills the air. The room is scented with pine, cinnamon, and potpourri, including the society's specially formulated potpourri named Country Christmas, which is for sale.

provide advance coverage.

All materials carry the SHS registered logo in distinctive, coordinating colors. Members post some 2,000 flyers in local shops and distribute them at other events, and mail or hand out 6,000 postcards. (A gentle request on cards and posters, "Moms and Dads only, please," heads off a potential problem.)

The society places ads in local newspapers and invites the press to preview the show on Friday before it opens to the public, so that articles may appear in the paper on opening day. SHS members follow up with thank-you notes to reporters who cover the event and personally invite them to subsequent events staged by the society.

Business members of SHS and local craft and decorating shops receive free program ads in return for help in publicizing the event.

Display

The Country Christmas show has a warm, homey atmosphere. Arrangements are made with dealers of country pine and bent twig furniture to bring in armoires, cabinets, chests, tables, chairs, and screens as a backdrop for the crafts. The furniture is also for sale.

Five live trees are set up and decorated with handcrafted ornaments. (Over 1,000 ornaments were sold this year.) Each tree has a theme: Victorian, traditional, children's, cross-stitch, and hearts. Live garland is swagged around the ceiling perimeter of the room. Huge grapevine wreaths decorate the outside of the building. For the preview party, the walk is lined with luminarias.

Crowd Control

SHS members arrive well in advance of the customers and wear distinctive navy blue aprons with cross-stitched bibs. A hostess greets shoppers with programs that describe the history and highlights of the show, and asks them to sign a guest register for a head count and future mailing list.

During the peak hours of the sale, there are eight cashiers and eight baggers with an abundant supply of tissue, bags, and boxes in several sizes. Floating cashiers write up sales receipts for waiting customers to speed things along at the cashier's table.

The room has a 250-person capacity. At the entrance, every shopper receives a large brown bag (one of 250). When all the bags are handed out, members ask shoppers to wait for a few minutes before entering. At the checkout, baggers empty the brown bags and resack purchases in white bags sealed with an SHS sticker. A runner recycles brown bags to incoming guests.

DOILY CHRISTMAS TREE WALL HANGING
Materials:
pattern on page 145 (for border)
20 doilies (2½" to 5" in diameter)
1 yard dark green fabric
¼ yard black cotton fabric
½ yard dark red cotton print fabric
¾ yard print fabric for backing
¾ yard thin batting or fleece
red and green quilting thread
ecru sewing thread
dowel or rod for hanging

Cut a 20" x 30" piece of dark green fabric. Arrange doilies on fabric in the shape of a tree. Pin and baste doilies to fabric. Blind-stitch doilies in place.

For first border, cut 2 (1½" x 30") strips and 2 (1½" x 22½") strips from black fabric. With right sides together, sew side strips to green fabric; then sew top and bottom strips. For second border, cut 2 (3½" x 31½") strips and 2 (3½" x 28½") strips from dark red fabric. With right sides together, sew side strips to black strips; then sew top and bottom strips.

Mark quilting lines radiating from top center of the green panel and the border pattern (shown on page 145). From backing fabric and batting, cut 30" x 40" pieces. Layer backing (right side down), batting, and quilt top (right side up) on a flat surface. Pin and baste all 3 layers together.

First, quilt around each doily; then quilt

along the radiating lines on green panel; and finally, quilt along the borders.

For binding, cut 2 (1" x 29") strips and 2 (1" x 39") strips from dark green fabric. With right sides together, sew strips to edges of green panel, turn, and blind-stitch to back, mitering corners.

To form a hanging sleeve, cut a strip 4½" x 24" from backing fabric. Hem short ends. Turn under ¼" on long sides, place right side up on back of hanging, and whipstitch in place. Insert dowel or rod.

Above: One of the many skilled craftspeople who contribute to the success of Country Christmas is Marilyn Dorwart. Her appliquéd and quilted pieces bring return customers. (Marilyn was the Florida state winner in the 1986 Great American Quilt contest.) The small wall hanging displayed on a screen behind Marilyn has a Christmas tree made up of tiny doily circles that are family heirlooms. Doilies also embellish her remarkable dress.

41

ANGELS IN CROSS-STITCH

This heavenly ensemble is made of pinwale corduroy in that divine grayed hue known as Williamsburg blue. Angels in cross-stitch float on creamy backgrounds. Singly or in trios, they adorn an ornament, a small personalized stocking, a tree skirt, and a pillow stitched with the theme—"Hark! The Herald Angels Sing." Angelic details—flaxen hair, rosy robes, shimmery wings, and occasional pink hearts—complement the dominant blues.

Because this design has a strong graphic quality, other colored fabrics and flosses can be easily substituted to match your decor. The design also translates effectively to a larger scale, as on the tree skirt, which is simply stitched on fabric with a bigger mesh.

TREE SKIRT
Materials:
chart and color key on page 134
1⅞ yards (60"-wide) blue pinwale corduroy
27" square (6-count) ecru Herta cloth
⅔ yard unbleached muslin
#32 gold braid
embroidery floss (see color key)
#20 tapestry needle
1 yard (¹⁄₁₆"-wide) blue satin ribbon
1 yard (¹⁄₁₆"-wide) light blue satin ribbon
5¼ yards (1½"-wide) gathered ecru eyelet lace

From corduroy, cut a 60" circle. Fold circle in half, right sides together, and mark fold (diameter) on wrong side. Fold in half again, straight edges together, and mark fold. Repeat folding and marking process once more. Cut out ⅛ of the circle along fold lines. Use this cutout as a pattern to cut 1 matching piece from Herta cloth and 1 from muslin. Zigzag-stitch the raw edges of the Herta cloth panel to keep it from raveling.

Following the chart and color key, center design 2" above bottom edge of Herta cloth. Use 1 strand of gold braid to stitch wings and 4 strands of floss for rest of design. Complete cross-stitching; then with 2 strands of brown floss, backstitch along dark lines on chart. Make French knot eyes with 2 strands of blue floss. Cut ribbon into 12" pieces. Under each angel's chin, thread a ribbon of each color, tie bows, and trim ends to 2½".

With wrong sides together and a ½" seam allowance, machine-baste stitchery panel to muslin panel. With right sides together and a ⅝" seam allowance, stitch panel to corduroy to complete circle. Press seams open.

On wrong side of fabric, mark a circle with a radius of 5" from center. Cut out. Opposite from stitchery panel, cut a straight line from edge to center opening along a previously marked fold.

Stitch around center opening ⅝" from edge. Clip close to stitching, and press under along seam. Topstitch ½" from pressed edge. With right sides and raw edges together,

stitch eyelet along outer circumference of tree skirt. Press seam towards skirt. To keep ruffle flat, zigzag-stitch bottom edge of skirt on right side. Press under ½" twice along both remaining straight edges. Topstitch ¼" from pressed edge.

ORNAMENT
Materials:
chart and color key on page 134
5" x 6" (28-count) piece of ivory linen
gold metallic thread
embroidery floss (see color key)
#24 tapestry needle
2⅝" x 3⅝" pre-stick padded oval
3" x 4" piece of ivory felt
glue syringe
craft glue
⅓ yard (¼"-wide) gathered ivory lace
6" (¹⁄₁₆"-wide) blue satin ribbon
⅝ yard (⅛"-wide) light blue satin ribbon
scissors

Following chart and color key, cross-stitch 1 angel without hearts on linen. (Stitch over 2 threads per stitch.) Use 3 strands of gold metallic thread for wings and 1 strand of embroidery floss for rest of design. Complete cross-stitching; then backstitch with 1 strand of brown floss along dark lines on pattern. Make French knot eyes with 1 strand of blue floss.

Trace padded oval shape onto felt and cut out felt. Mount stitchery on oval according to manufacturer's directions. Trim stitchery ½" beyond edge of oval. Using a glue syringe, apply a thin line of glue around the back edge of the oval. Fold stitchery fabric to back over glue. Let dry. Reapply glue over fabric on oval back. Starting at the bottom of the oval, place lace (finished edge extending outward) on glue. Overlap ends slightly and trim excess. Let dry.

For a hanger, cut 9" of ⅛"-wide ribbon, fold in half, and glue ends to back of oval, 1" below top center edge. Glue felt oval to ornament back. Apply a thin line of glue around outer edge of ornament on stitchery cloth. Starting at bottom, attach remaining

⅛"-wide ribbon over glue. Overlap ends slightly and trim. Tie a bow from ¹⁄₁₆"-wide ribbon and glue under angel's chin.

PILLOW
Materials:
chart and color key on page 134
11" x 13" (14-count) ecru Aida or pre-printed fabric as shown in photo
gold metallic thread
embroidery floss (see color key)
#24 tapestry needle
½ yard (¹⁄₁₆"-wide) blue satin ribbon
1¼ yards (¾"-wide) gathered ecru lace
9" x 11" and 5" x 72" pieces of blue pin-wale corduroy
stuffing

Finished pillow size: 12" x 14". Following chart and color key, stitch 3 angels and words centered on fabric, using 3 strands of gold metallic thread for wings and 1 strand of embroidery floss for rest of angel. Use 1 strand of brown floss to backstitch dark lines indicated on chart. Backstitch words with 1 strand of blue floss.

Cut ribbon into 3 (6") lengths and tack midpoint of ribbons under angels' chins. Tie into bows and trim ends.

Trim stitchery to 9" x 11". Starting at center bottom edge, machine-baste lace to fabric with a ¼" seam allowance, right sides and raw edges together. Tuck under top end and overlap ends slightly.

With right sides together and a ¼" seam allowance, sew 5" edges of corduroy strip together to form a large circular piece. Press seam open. Fold piece in half lengthwise, wrong sides together, and press. Gather ¼" from raw edge, and pull to fit around edges of pillow top.

With raw edges together and a ¼" seam allowance, baste ruffle to pillow top. Pin 9" x 11" piece of corduroy to pillow top, right sides together and ruffle inside. With a ½" seam allowance, stitch around pillow, leaving opening at bottom edge for turning. Clip corners. Turn right side out. Stuff pillow and hand-sew opening closed.

STOCKING
Materials:

pattern on page 139
chart and color key on page 134
5" x 6" (14-count) piece of ecru Aida cloth
gold metallic thread
embroidery floss (see color key)
#24 tapestry needle
6" (1/16"-wide) blue satin ribbon
8" x 9" and 8" x 12" pieces of blue pinwale
   corduroy
5" (3/4"-wide) gathered ecru lace
5" (7/16"-wide) light blue satin ribbon
2 (4" x 5") pieces of unbleached muslin
   (for lining)

Finished stocking size: 6¾" x 11½". Center desired name, plotted from alphabet chart, under an angel with 1 square between bottom of angel and top of name.

Following chart and color key, stitch middle angel, hearts, and name centered on Aida cloth. Use 3 strands of gold metallic thread for wings and 1 strand of embroidery floss for rest of design. Backstitch with brown floss along dark lines indicated on pattern. Tack 1/16"-wide blue ribbon under chin, tie

into bow, and trim ends. Trim finished stitchery to 4" x 5". From pattern, cut out bottom of stocking front from smaller piece of corduroy. Machine-baste lace to top edge of corduroy stocking with a ¼" seam allowance, right sides up and raw edges together. Trim lace even with corduroy at side edges.

With right sides together and a ¼" seam allowance, stitch bottom of stitchery to top of stocking. Press seam up. With wrong sides together, place stocking over larger piece of corduroy and cut stocking back to match entire front. Pin stocking front to back, right sides together, and stitch sides with a ¼" seam allowance. Clip curves, turn right side out, and press.

Fold 7/16"-wide light blue ribbon in half, wrong sides together. Pin to right side of stocking top at back seam, raw edges together. Machine-baste in place. Cut 2 muslin stocking pieces and stitch pieces together at 4" ends with ¼" seam. Press seams open. Press bottom edge under ¼".

With right sides and raw edges together, stitch muslin facing to top of stocking with ¼" seam allowance. Turn facing to inside of stocking and press.

45

IMPISH SANTA ADDS HEARTHSIDE CHEER

This jolly old elf resides fireside, spreading his impish cheer throughout the house. A cartoonish character, he seems to pop from the scene with all the magic and mirth of that medium. Cut from plywood and painted with acrylics, the figure is supported by a hinged stand, which folds flat for storage.

Materials:
patterns on page 130-131
20" x 26" x ½" piece of plywood (Santa)
7½" x 2" x 1" piece of pine (stand)
jigsaw or band saw
sandpaper: #120, #180, #220
acrylic paint or folk art paint (white, red, black, blue, gold, and green)
paintbrushes: flat bristle—2", ¾", ¼" and round sable—#1, #3
black oil paint marker
mat varnish
4 (½" x 1") hinges
4 screws (shorter than ½")
drill and bit to match screw size
small screwdriver

Cut out Santa and stand pieces. Sand all surfaces (front and back with grain), using coarse- to fine-grain sandpaper.

Set pieces on wood scraps for ease in painting edges. Paint all surfaces with 3 coats of thinned white acrylic paint. Mix red and white paints and coat entire Santa front with pink. (When Santa's suit is painted from the pattern, this pink undercoat will help build a rich red since red acrylic paint tends toward transparency.)

Paint Santa back and stand pieces red. Repeat coats for complete coverage. (Thin paints with water as needed for smooth coats.) Don't let paint build up on edges. Let dry thoroughly. Transfer Santa details to the painted cutout and follow pattern to paint. Let dry overnight. Paint surfaces with mat varnish. Let dry.

Position stand pieces on Santa back as indicated. (For easy storage, make sure stand will fold flat inward before attaching hinges.) Mark screw holes, start holes with drill, and screw hinges in place.

MAKE THEM FROM SCRAPS

Dig into your scrap basket and pull out this whimsical array of ornaments. Transform bits of material and ribbon into a reindeer that flies on cinnamon legs, a soft, white kitten that fits inside her own heart-appliquéd mitten, or a trio of ragpoint ornaments that will give your country Christmas a new twist.

REINDEER ORNAMENT
Materials:
patterns on page 135
¼" yard brown mini-print fabric
scraps of red mini-print fabric
thread to match
stuffing
scrap (¼"-wide) red polka-dot ribbon
navy embroidery thread
1 (¼") red pom-pom
1 small jingle bell
1 (6"-long) soft-sculpture
    sewing needle
brown embroidery thread
4 (3½"-long) cinnamon sticks
4 (8 mm) red or green wooden beads
2 twigs of similar size (for antlers)
small (no. 001) artists' paintbrush
gold metallic paint
craft glue

Fold brown fabric in half, right sides together. Transfer body pattern to wrong side of brown fabric. Do not cut out. With right sides together and leaving an opening for turning, stitch reindeer body on pattern lines. Cut out. Place remaining brown fabric on red fabric with right sides together. Transfer ear and tail pattern to wrong side. Do not cut out. Leaving an opening for turning, stitch along pattern line. Cut out. Clip corners of reindeer body at neck and back as indicated on pattern. Turn pieces. Stuff reindeer body firmly and stitch opening closed.

Hand-stitch ear piece closed and gather along line as indicated. With red fabric down, tack to back of head. Tie a small ribbon bow and glue between ears. Lightly stuff tail, turn opening under ⅛", and stitch closed, pulling thread slightly to give tail a puff. Tack tail to body as indicated. Tie a small ribbon bow and tack in front of tail.

Use 2 strands of navy embroidery floss and satin stitch to make eyes. Glue on red pom-pom for nose. Transfer heart pattern to red fabric and cut out. Glue to reindeer as indicated on pattern. Tack jingle bell to reindeer as shown in photograph, and tie a ribbon bow around the neck.

To attach the back legs, thread the soft-sculpture needle with three 24" strands of brown embroidery floss. Start at left back side and stitch through reindeer to right back side. See photograph. Insert needle through cinnamon stick, add on wooden bead, and stitch back through cinnamon stick. Slip needle back through reindeer body to right front side. Repeat for other three legs. Knot securely. Using 6 strands of brown floss, make a loop hanger, and tack to head in front of ears. Knot end.

Paint antlers with gold paint and let dry. To attach antlers, snip 2 small holes in head, as indicated on pattern. Cut twig ends at an angle, apply a small amount of glue to the ends, and insert in holes.

RAGPOINT ORNAMENTS

TIPS ON RAGPOINT: Blends tend to ravel less than 100% cotton fabrics. Material of broadcloth weight works best. Do not pull stitching too tight, or canvas will stretch out of shape. Too loose stitches, however, will allow canvas to show through. If using different size canvas (more or less than 3.3 stitches per inch) adjust size of canvas to allow for design stitches plus 4 unworked holes on all sides of design.

Materials (for all 3 ornaments):
charts on page 134
½" x 30" cloth, ribbon, or bias strips in
    colors shown in photograph
masking tape
3 (7" x 7") pieces of 3.3-stitch rug canvas
size 16 or 22 blunt tapestry needle
3 (5½" square) pieces of fabric for backing
thread to match
3 (12") pieces of matching-color ribbon or
    braid

Use masking tape to reinforce all edges of canvas. Thread tapestry needle with rag strip and, following stitch graphs, use continental needlepoint stitch to work canvas. Work all stitches in the same direction, turning canvas as necessary. Work until only one border row of blank canvas remains visible on front. Before stitching borders, remove masking tape and turn edges of canvas to back of ornament. Stitch the last border row through the 2 layers created by folding excess canvas to back of ornament. Trim off excess canvas.

Finish ornaments by stitching around outside of ornament with same color as last row of stitching, using 2 to 3 stitches in each corner to completely cover canvas.

Center the 5½" squares of fabric on backs of ornaments. Fold all edges under so that backing pieces fit the ornaments, and pin.

With matching thread, whipstitch backing pieces in place.

Tack ribbon or braid to center top of ornaments and tie bows to make hangers. If ornaments are not rectangular in shape, dampen slightly and block into shape by pinning on ironing board. Steam with light pressure and let dry in place.

CHRISTMAS KITTEN-IN-A-MITTEN ORNAMENT

Materials:
patterns on page 138
8" x 10" piece of white felt
embroidery floss: pink, black, white
stuffing
5" x 10" piece of red pin dot fabric
scraps of green pin dot fabric
craft glue
¾ yard (1½"-wide) red plaid ribbon
tiny jingle bell

Transfer kitten and paw patterns to felt and cut out. On one kitten piece, use black embroidery floss to satin-stitch eyes and straight-stitch eyelashes as indicated on pattern. On same piece, use pink floss to satin-stitch nose. Place kitten pieces wrong sides together with embroidered piece on top, and leaving an opening for stuffing, blanket-stitch together. Stuff lightly and stitch opening closed. Repeat for a pair of paws. Set aside.

Transfer large mitten pattern to red fabric and cut out. Transfer trim patterns to green fabric and cut out. Appliqué the trim pieces to one mitten piece as indicated on pattern. Place mittens right sides together. Using a ¼" seam allowance and leaving straight edge open, stitch together. Turn and press. Stuff thumb and bottom of mitten. Fold top edge of mitten under ⅛" and tack. Insert kitten into mitten. Glue tops of paws to kitten, side by side, as indicated on pattern, so that bottoms of paws hang over mitten.

Fold ribbon into bow, pinch at center, and tack to hold. Attach bow to kitten and mitten as shown in photograph. Sew tiny bell at center of bow. Take several running stitches along thumb line as indicated on pattern.

FROSTY ETCHED ORNAMENTS

Light rays glint off etched and faceted glass ornaments frosted with a string of hearts, two turtledoves, and a pudgy little bear. The glass bevels (available in craft shops) come unadorned, already drilled for hanging. To customize them, you'll need backed adhesive shelf paper and etching cream.

First, cut out pieces of shelf paper large enough to cover one side of each glass bevel and overhang the edges slightly. Remove backing, and affix the paper to the glass. Smooth out any bubbles.

Transfer patterns from page 131 to the shelf paper, and cut out the shapes with a craft knife. Burnish the cut edges with a craft stick so that no etching cream can bleed underneath. With your finger, roll up any adhesive on the glass in cutout areas.

Working in a well-ventilated room and on a protected surface, stir etching cream well, and rapidly paint a thick layer of it over the whole surface of shelf paper. Leave it on only 5 to 10 minutes. (Do not allow cream to dry on glass.) Wash the cream off, being careful to prevent it from contacting unetched glass. Remove shelf paper, and clean the ornaments with glass cleaner.

MINI-QUILTS ALL ON A LINE

Marvelously detailed miniature quilts have captured the imagination of needleworkers and collectors everywhere. Sometimes diminutive versions of the full-sized variety, sometimes a composite of techniques and styles, mini-quilts pack a lot of charm in a small space. They also offer interesting decorating possibilities.

The mini-quilt featured here is five inches square and is based on the traditional Dutch Rose quilt pattern, also known as Carpenter's Wheel or Broken Star. It's stitched with scraps of red and green print fabric and owes its thinness to batting split in half and to the detailed quilting that embellishes the piecework.

This mini-quilt and the ones festooning the fireplace are just a handful of the hundred made by the Cobblestone Quilters Guild in Charleston, South Carolina. Guild member Diane Weed suggested stitching them to garland the Guild's entry in a festival of trees, shown opposite. And the quilters probably wouldn't mind if another group borrowed the idea. In addition to the one given here, another mini-quilt pattern can be found in "Not a Creature Was Stirring" on page 34.

Materials:
patterns on page 132
mylar template material
(*Note:* all fabrics preshrunk 100% cotton)
scraps of red and green print, muslin
6" x 9" piece of light green print
thread to match
6" square of batting, split in half

Diagram—Quilt Assembly

Sew four Unit 2s.

Sew four Unit 3s.

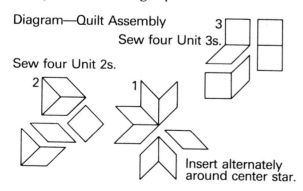

Insert alternately around center star.

Make templates from patterns. Following the cutting chart below, trace templates onto the back of the fabrics. Center fabrics' motifs in shapes, if appropriate. (See light green print squares in photo.)

CUTTING CHART:
Template A:
  16 of red print fabric
  16 of dark green print fabric
Template B:
  8 of light green print
  12 of muslin
Template C:
  8 of muslin

Cut out pieces, and cut a 6" square from light green print for the backing.

Arrange pieces as shown in photo. Pin together and stitch, following the order shown in Diagram. Begin and end with a backstitch (do not sew to edge), and use a small running stitch with a single thread. Iron the seam allowances flat to one side, and trim away any points extending beyond the seam allowances.

Lay the backing square right side down, lay the thin batting on top, and center the completed top right side up on the batting. The top will be slightly smaller than the other layers. Baste from corner to corner so that the layers don't shift during quilting.

Using a single strand of white thread, quilt with a small running stitch, hiding small knots by jerking them through the top layer into the batting. Quilt any pattern you wish, but try not to quilt close to the seam allowances. The more quilting you do, the flatter your quilt will be.

When finished quilting, trim the batting even with the top. To bind quilt, first roll 2 opposite sides of the light green print over twice, and bring to front to cover the raw edges of the quilt top. Check that you do not cover the outer points of the pattern diamonds, and pin in place. Sew these sides down with a small slipstitch. Then roll, pin, and sew the last 2 sides, mitering and sewing the corners.

Above: Here's a mantel treatment that defies the cold. A row of mini-quilts clipped to twine with small clothespins evokes thoughts of quilts airing on a clear spring day, brilliant colors waving in the wind. Make your own swag of quilts by rebinding blocks from tattered old quilts, stenciling and then quilting small patterns, or quilting a piece of cross-stitch.

53

CHUBBY POM-POM SANTA

As full of charm as his pack is of toys, this Santa is ready to hit the reindeer trail and deliver presents to all the good children. Made from knit fabric, Santa can be stuffed to his chubbiest. And with striped boots, pin-dot cap, and mittens, he sports some of the newest fashions this side of the North Pole.

Place him on a table, a mantel, or a door, and Santa will make sure that there is not a pout in the house.

Materials:
patterns on pages 128 and 129
diagrams on page 129
¼ yard flesh-colored knit fabric
stuffing
2 (½") black half-round buttons
soft white yarn
8" x 10" piece red pin-dot fabric (for cap)
scrap of green pin-dot fabric (for mittens)
scrap of red-and-white striped knit fabric
½ yard red knit fabric
½ yard (⅝"-wide) black velvet ribbon
1½ yards (⅛"-wide) green satin ribbon
1 tiny bell (for cap)
6 (½") red pom-poms
7 (½") white pom-poms
2 (2") holly leaves (purchased)
2 (1") green pom-poms
scrap of green knit fabric (for pack)
purchased toys (2"- 4" high) for pack
1"-diameter hanging loop
30" (⅛"-wide) satin ribbon

Note: Use ¼" seam allowance unless otherwise indicated.

Fold 7" x 14" piece of flesh fabric in half, long sides together and right sides facing. Transfer head pattern to fabric, but do not cut out. Leaving open where indicated, stitch around head. Cut out and turn. Stuff fully without stretching, and sew opening closed. Transfer nose pattern to flesh knit fabric and cut out 1. Sew running stitches around the outer edge, and pull thread slightly to gather. Stuff nose to measure 1" in diameter. Pull

thread and knot. Stitch nose to face. For eyes, stitch buttons to face by pushing needle through back of head and knotting tightly so that eyes look deep-set.

To make beard, wrap white yarn around 2 fingers 6 times, pull off, tie a bit of yarn around the center, and stitch loops to face as shown on pattern. Repeat until yarn covers the front and back of head from beard line down to chin as indicated on pattern. Make 2 "one-finger" loops for eyebrows and attach to face where indicated on pattern.

Cut 2 cap pieces from red pin-dot fabric. With right sides facing and leaving straight edge open, stitch pieces together. Clip curves and turn. Fold raw edge under ¼", press, and stitch. Stuff cap slightly and stitch to top of Santa's head. Set aside.

Double flesh fabric with right sides facing, and transfer body pattern to fabric. Leaving arm ends open as indicated, stitch pieces together. Cut out body, turn and stuff fully.

Transfer mitten pattern to green pin dot, and cut out 4 (2 reversed). With right sides facing and leaving an opening for stuffing, stitch each pair together. Turn and stuff. Insert mittens into arm openings, fold in raw edges of arms, and stitch mittens to arms.

Double red and white fabric with right sides facing. Transfer boot pattern to doubled fabric. Leaving open as indicated, stitch around boot and cut out. Repeat for other boot. Turn and stuff boots. Fold raw edges under and sew boots to body.

To make Santa shirt, cut 2 (12½" x 6") pieces of red knit fabric and place right sides facing. With 12½" edges as top and bottom, cut a 2" square out of each lower corner, leaving T-shaped shirt pieces. Leaving bottom and sleeve ends open, use a ½" seam allowance to stitch around piece. See Diagram 1. Turn shirt and place on Santa body. Sew a running stitch ½" from sleeve ends, pull thread tightly inward, and knot so stitching is concealed. Stuff lightly between body and suit front to shape stomach. Set aside.

To make pants, cut 2 (7¼" x 5¼") pieces from red knit and place them with right sides together. From the center of fabric, make a

1¾" line to a 7¼" edge. This is the bottom of pants. Leaving top and bottom open, use a ½" seam allowance to stitch sides and around the center line. See Diagram 2. Clip center line and turn. Pull pants on Santa, and turn top of pants piece down, so that wrong side of leg edges faces up. Sew running stitches around bottom edge of each pant leg. Pull thread tightly for a snug fit, and pull pants up. Stuff pant legs lightly. Fold bottom edge of shirt top under and sew to top of pants.

For belt, use the black ribbon to cover the shirt/pant seam. Overlap ribbon edges in back and stitch together.

Stitch head to body. Cut a 9" length of green ribbon and tie into a bow. Tack bell to center of bow; tack both to peak of cap.

Where front of cap meets face, glue alternating red and white pom-poms to cap to make a brim. See photograph. Glue 2 white pom-poms to suit front for buttons. Tack 2

holly leaves to left corner of cap. Cut remaining green ribbon into 4 equal lengths. Tack centers of 2 ribbon lengths to bottom of each foot. Bring both ribbons to top of foot, and tie in a bow. Tack bows to top of each foot. Glue a green pom-pom to center of each bow.

For Santa's pack, cut a 9" x 14" piece from green knit fabric, and fold in half, short ends together. If desired, trim unfolded 9" edges with pinking shears for top of bag. Leaving top open, stitch sides and bottom of bag, making a U-shape, close to edges of fabric. Turn and stuff to 3" from top. Tack one corner of pack to inside of left mitten. Pull mitten close to body and stitch mitten to body. Stitch bottom of pack to Santa's hip.

Decorate the top of Santa's bag with several lightweight toys tacked to bag. Tack hanger loop to Santa's back at base of head. Thread 30" length of ribbon through loop and knot ends to make hanger.

CUSTOM-TAILORED ENVELOPES FOR HOLIDAY NOTES

What is the well-tailored envelope wearing this year? Custom-designed fabric liners, of course. They add that important element of surprise when your Christmas cards, letters, and gift certificates or checks are opened. Simply combine a bit of pretty fabric and a colorful envelope to convey your greetings before the recipient even discovers the contents of your correspondence.

Spray a scrap of the fabric you've chosen for your liner with spray glue to test it for staining and bleeding. If it checks out, open the flap of the envelope to be lined and trace the outline of the flap and envelope onto fabric. Draw a line inside the outline that will clear the glue on the flap and allow at least ¼" on remaining sides to clear the envelope when the liner is inserted. Cut out.

On the wrong side of the fabric, spray the entire flap lining and about ½" of the fabric that will line the inside of the envelope. Position the liner in the envelope, smoothing the glued fabric and tucking the unglued portion in place. When the glue is dry, carefully crease the fabric on the fold.

A RIPPLING RIBBON STOCKING

New twists and turns for pleating lend movement and surprise to this roomy stocking. Pleats turn one way in the center and do an about-face on the edges. Then ribbon follows along creating the intricate effect seen here.

Made with a small Christmas print, the stocking has a homey, country look. Substitute pastel moiré and lace, and the same technique will look elegantly feminine.

Materials:
pattern on page 139
⅞ yard (45"-wide) fabric for stocking body
¼ yard (45"-wide) fabric for cuff
8 yards (⅛"-wide) satin ribbon
thread to match
fabric glue (optional)

Cut a 13½" x 45" piece from main fabric. Fold short end of fabric over 2", wrong side to inside. Press and stitch ½" from fold. Open fabric, and press pleat toward closest edge. Fold next pleat 1" from stitching line of first pleat. Stitch ½" from fold and press in same direction as first pleat. Continue folding 1" from stitching line and stitching pleats until last one is 1½" from edge of fabric. Press all pleats in the same direction.

Place stocking pattern on front of pleated fabric so that pleats are turned toward bottom, and cut out. Mark a line lengthwise down the center of the pleated stocking front. Cut a piece of ribbon for each pleat so that pieces are the same length as the width of stocking. Place ribbon underneath pleats, pin in place, and stitch down center line.

Starting with the pleat at bottom edge of stocking, reverse direction of the pleat at edge (turning it toward top), and twist ribbon over pleat, slipping it under same pleat (now reversed) at edge. Tack together in seam allowance to hold new direction. Repeat at both sides of stocking for all pleats.

For stocking back and lining, letter-fold remaining fabric in thirds with right side to inside. Folded dimensions will be 15" x 18".

Transfer stocking pattern to flap side of fabric, and cut out through all 3 layers.

With right sides facing, stitch stocking front and back (one of 3 just cut) together. Check to make sure all pleated edges are stitched, clip curves, trim seam, and turn right side out.

With right sides facing, stitch together stocking lining (last 2 pieces). Trim seams, and insert lining in stocking with top edges even.

Cut 5½" x 15" piece of fabric for cuff. Fold fabric in half (5½" x 7½") with wrong side out. Stitch short edges together. Press seam open and fold in half again, with raw edges together and right side out. Slip fold side down over outside top of stocking so that all raw edges are even. Zigzag-stitch together and turn up cuff.

Fold a 4½" piece of ribbon in half to make a hanging loop. Bar-tack between front and back of cuff at back seam of stocking. Make 5 small bows from remaining ribbon. Stitch or glue bows along stitched center line on every fourth pleat of stocking front.

SEA ANGELS

Scallop shells, Nature's pleated fans of near-perfect symmetry, are the shirred robes donned by these darling angels. And bread dough, made from flour, salt, and water, is the substance that shapes and binds everything together.

Rolled into balls, dough makes heads, hands, and feet. Pressed into strips, it becomes arms and wings. And squiggled with a garlic press, it is angel hair. Tiny shells clasped in chubby cherubic hands and gold wire halos are charming details.

Whether hovering with shell baubles, or heralding the season with spiral shell trumpets, the angels (in the sizes and configurations pictured here) can be easily constructed as detailed below.

BREAD DOUGH ANGELS

BREAD DOUGH: Place 1 cup flour and ¼ cup salt in a bowl and stir. (To color dough, add poster paint to desired intensity.) Add 6 tablespoons hot water and stir until dough forms a ball. Knead for 5 minutes, or until salt is worked in and you can roll dough between hands without sticking. Dough will keep in sealed plastic bags in the refrigerator for 5 days.

FINISHING: Follow instructions below to shape angels, moistening dough to join pieces; then bake and paint as follows. Preheat oven to 275 degrees. Bake ornaments for 2 hours or until hard. Let cool. Bend halos forward. Paint cheeks with diluted red acrylic paint, dot eyes with black acrylic paint, and let dry. Varnish with high-gloss polyurethane; let dry. Store ornaments in sealable plastic bags—bread dough is susceptible to humidity.

Hovering Angels (face forward)
Note: These instructions are for an angel made from a medium scallop shell (2½" across). Decrease or increase dough balls in proportion to size of shell used.

Form a 1" uncolored dough ball for wings. Press center of the ball and roll to form a dumbbell shape. Center top edge of shell on dough, and press gently. Roughly shape wing tip by pinching dough; then scallop by cutting a ⅛" slice into dough at 3 intervals with a butter knife. Flatten scalloped edge with finger. Cut a drinking straw in half lengthwise and press into dough to imprint half circles for the feather pattern.

Roll ¼" uncolored dough ball for a head support. Center on wings, above and touching shell. For head, roll a 1" uncolored dough ball. Position head with half on the support piece and half on the shell; press together to attach.

For arms, roll 2 (½") colored balls into oblong shapes; attach at base of head. Shape arms and bend toward center of shell (see photo). Roll a ½" colored dough ball for feet. Place ½ of ball under shell and press gently to attach. Press knife in center of ball to create feet.

Roll 2 (¼") uncolored dough balls for hands and attach. Press a tiny shell or starfish into hands. To make hair, put colored dough into garlic press. Squeeze desired amount through press and style to head with a toothpick.

Bend a 1" length of 20-gauge copper wire in half in a U-shape and insert at back of head for a hanger. For a halo, take a 3" piece of wire and twist ends together. Insert twisted ends into head just in front of hanger. (Do not bend halo forward until the ornament has been baked according to instructions for finishing.) See FINISHING to complete angel.

Trio of Angels
Make an angel, as above, from a medium shell (2½") across. Make 2 angels from smaller shells (2" across) as for medium angel, decreasing size of dough balls proportionately. Add small angels' halos but no hangers. Don't bake or paint angels.

Form 2 (2") uncolored dough strips. Position medium angel so shell sides (about ¼" below wings) overlap strips ½"; press gently. Position small angels' wings over dough strips, bending wings adjacent to medium

angel. Press angels into strips to attach to one another. See FINISHING to complete angels.

Herald Angel (profile)
Note: Instructions are for large angel (scallop shell, 4" across). If using other shells, decrease dough balls proportionately.

For bottom wing, roll a 1" uncolored dough ball into a 1" x 2" strip. Roughly form wing tip by pinching dough; then scallop by cutting a ⅛" slice into dough at 3 intervals with a butter knife. Flatten wing with finger. Cut a drinking straw in half lengthwise and imprint half circles on wing for feather pattern. Lay shell edge on wing with wing front at center of shell edge. Press to attach.

For head and arm supports, roll 2 (½") uncolored balls. Place 1 ball in front of wing and the other just below first and along shell edge. Press to attach. For head, roll a 1" uncolored dough ball. Place head half on top support ball and half on shell.

For arms, roll 2 (1") colored balls into oblong shapes. Attach bottom arm to support ball and touching bottom of head. Shape arm and bend upward (see photo). Roll a ¼" uncolored dough ball for hand and attach. Insert shell trumpet into head where mouth would be and rest shell on top of hand. Attach top arm beneath head. Shape to match bottom arm, and lay hand (¼" ball) over trumpet.

To make hair, put colored dough into garlic press. Squeeze desired amount through press and style hair to head with a toothpick. For feet, lay 2 (¼") colored dough balls side by side; place top half of balls under shell and press to attach.

For top wing, roll a 1" uncolored dough ball into 1" x 1½" shape. Pinch wing front to same width as arm at shoulder. Pinch wing tip. Make scalloped edge and feather design as for bottom wing. Attach wing to arm over hair. For hair bow, roll colored dough into a ⅛" coil; shape into bow and streamers. Bend a 1" length of 20-gauge copper wire in half and insert into bottom wing for a hanger. See FINISHING to complete angel.

RIBBON AND FELT MAKE HANDSOME HEARTS

Let your sentiments be known this Christmas by making one or all of this trio of ornaments. Folk art patterns woven with satin ribbon are centered on layers of pastel felt and bordered by scalloped edges. Create a garland of hearts with several attached to a long ribbon. Whether tied to the tree, to packages, or a wreath, these ornaments are a fond expression of the season.

TIPS ON FELT AND RIBBON WEAVING:

To weave, insert ribbon over and under, over and under, etc., through openings cut in felt. Clip ends, and if necessary, glue to hold. Begin next row and alternate by weaving under and over, under and over, etc. Continue alternating with each row.

Materials (for all three ornaments):
patterns on page 129
12" square of peach felt
12" square of spring green felt
1½ yards (³⁄₁₆"-wide) white satin picot ribbon
3½ yards (³⁄₈"-wide) white satin picot ribbon
craft glue
9" x 12" piece cardboard
pinking shears

On peach felt, mark 2 small heart patterns, 1 large heart, a 4½" x 7½" piece, a 4¼" square, and weaving lines as indicated on pattern. Cut out. On green felt, mark the hand pattern, a 5¼" x 5¾" piece, a 4" square, and weaving lines. Cut out. Cut weaving lines on hearts according to patterns. Using the ³⁄₁₆" ribbon, weave through hearts. Cut from ³⁄₈" ribbon six 20" lengths. (Remaining piece is for hand.) After ornament assembly (instructions below), use pinking shears to trim around ornaments. Loop one length of ³⁄₈" ribbon in half and glue to back of each ornament, allowing ends to extend below ornament. Tie another 20" length into a bow. Glue to base of loop.

SQUARE ORNAMENT

Center small woven heart on green 4" felt square and glue. From cardboard, cut out a 3½" square, and glue to back of green square. Glue ornament to 4¼" peach square. Finish ornament as above.

HEART ORNAMENT

Following inner line, cut out a heart-shaped piece of cardboard, and glue to back of large woven peach heart. Glue ornament to the 5¼" x 5¾" green felt piece. Finish ornament as above.

HEART-IN-HAND ORNAMENT

Use ³⁄₈"-wide ribbon to weave the one row on hand pattern. Center the small woven heart on bottom of hand and glue. Follow inner lines of hand pattern and cut out a piece of cardboard. Glue green felt to cardboard. Glue ornament to the 4½" x 7½" piece of peach felt. Finish ornament as above.

FEATHERY FOLK ART TREE

Harking back to a time of immigrants bearing gifts of their traditions, this small tree is a modern nod to the past. Early German settlers shared their technique of using goose feathers to make beautiful miniature Christmas trees, and by 1910, Sears, Roebuck and Co. offered mail-order feather trees that came fully decorated.

A contemporary fondness for folk art has given new generations the opportunity to enjoy these decorations, though the trees are often quite expensive. A clever alternative is this version, which calls for the simplicity of artificial greenery affixed to a dowel. Embellishing it are *scherenschnitte* (cut paper) ornaments that have been antiqued with tea.

Materials:
wooden base (at least 2" thick)
24" (½" diameter) dowel
drill with ½" and ⅛" bits
craft glue
artificial greenery stems
brown florists' tape
brown paint (optional)
artificial red berries

With ½" bit, drill a hole 1" deep in base, put glue in hole, insert dowel and allow to dry.

Tape ⅛" from end of ⅛" bit to keep holes shallow. Measure 6" from base, mark dowel, and drill 6 holes around stick. Continue to measure, mark, and drill as follows: 5 holes 4" above first set of holes, then 5 holes 4" up, 4 holes 3" up, 4 holes 3" up, and 3 holes 2" up. Finally, drill a hole in top of dowel.

Cut greenery the following lengths: 6 branches 9" long, 5 (7"), 5 (6"), 4 (5"), 4 (4"), 3 (3"), and top branch 3" long. Working from the bottom up, trim some of the greenery away at the ends that attach to dowel, dip in glue, insert in holes, and twist into place. Allow to dry.

Wrap florists' tape around dowel. If wood shows through anywhere, touch up with brown paint. Glue red berries at ends of branches. Add lightweight decorations of your choice.

PAINT FESTIVE PLACE SETTINGS

Delight holiday diners with artfully presented food. Quick tole painting techniques transform plain wooden plates into a colorful frame for Christmas cuisine. Simply top them with sparkling glass dishes, to protect the painted surfaces while letting their vivid hues enhance your holiday table.

Materials:
patterns on pages 150 and 151
sponge brush
acrylic paints (deep red, medium red, deep green, medium green, white)
wooden plates
fine sandpaper
size 6 synthetic flat brush
size 2 synthetic liner

Using sponge brush, paint top of plate deep red. Let dry. Paint plate bottom. When dry, sand lightly and wipe off with lint-free rag. Apply a second coat to both sides and let dry. Transfer holly pattern to top of plate.

Note: When painting with acrylics, rinse brush often.

Using the flat brush, paint holly leaves medium green. Let dry. Apply a second coat if needed. Pick up deep green on corner of brush and shade center veins and areas directly behind overlapping leaves. Wash brush. Pick up white on corner of brush, blend brush down on palette, and shade edges of leaves. Dilute a bit of white with water, and use liner to paint veins.

Using the liner, paint the ribbons medium green. For depth, use the corner of flat brush to apply deep green next to the leaves and areas that appear behind the leaves.

Dip handle end of brush in medium red paint and spin in place for berries. While berries are still wet, mix a bit of medium red and white to make pink. Using the liner, blend pink into red on one side of a few berries. Let dry. Touch a white dot on a few berries to highlight.

WEAVE MINIBASKETS WITH COUNTRY CHARM

Three little baskets, all in a row, add country sweetness to your Christmas tree, and continue to warm your home through the rest of the year. Make these minibaskets in multiples and scatter them over a tabletop tree. Then garland it with raffia and fill it out with baby's breath. You might tuck candy into a single minibasket and leave it on a nightstand as a welcoming present for overnight guests. Or, as shown here, arrange a group of minibaskets on a wall to carry Christmas color and cheer throughout your home.

BASKETRY TIPS

Soak reeds in a small bucket or pan of water. Soaking time will vary with quality and size. Guard against oversoaking. Reed should be pliable without splitting or breaking. Cover soaked reeds with a damp cloth to keep them moist while you work, and resoak reeds and basket frame if they dry out.

Work on a protected surface. Weave with the smooth side of flat reeds to outside. Weave rows close to each other, packing tightly. Trim reeds with old scissors or hand pruners, and use a basketry awl or screwdriver to work ends into tight places. To add in (or splice) a new weaver, back-weave new reed on top of last weaver for a couple of spokes. Use clothespins with springs to secure reeds as you work. For lashing ribbon around rims of elbow and heart baskets, use a large-eyed, blunt needle.

EGG MINIBASKET
Materials:
2 (32"-long) pieces of #3 round reed for handle and rim
glue or beige quilting thread
4 (36"-long) pieces of ¼" flat reed split to ⅛" width for weavers
45" of #4 round reed for spokes
24" (⅛"-wide) red satin ribbon

Using the #3 round reed (or some vines of similar size), form 2 circles, 3" in diameter, by twisting 3 thicknesses of reed together. Position circles as in Diagram 1. Glue, or tie with quilting thread.

With split ¼" reed, follow Diagram 2 to make a God's Eye at the intersections of the rim and handle on each side of basket, going around for 6 rows. Clip excess reed to side with clothespin.

Cut spokes for basket from #4 round reed as follows: 2 (5¼" long), 2 (6"), 2 (5½"), 2 (5"). Cut all ends at an angle. Insert on inside of God's Eyes on each side of basket, in order listed above, with 5¼" pieces next to rim and 5" on each side of bottom spoke. Keep evenly spaced. Clip in place with clothespins.

Diagram 1—Egg Basket

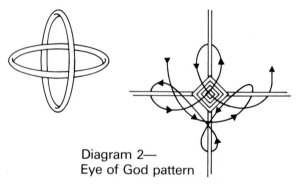

Diagram 2—
Eye of God pattern

Begin over and under weaving pattern with the excess reed from God's Eyes on both sides of basket. Make sure weavers from both sides meet in an alternate pattern, and splice ends.

Leaving a 5" length, wrap ribbon around handle, crisscross back, tie ends in bow, and trim.

ELBOW MINIBASKET
Materials:
8 (12"-long) pieces of ¼" flat reed for spokes
#2 round reed for twining
12 (8"-long) pieces of ¼" flat reed for weaver
2 (8"-long) pieces of ¼" flat reed, dyed red with textile dye, for weaver
2 pieces 24"-long (⅛"-wide) red satin ribbon

Weave together the 8 (12") pieces of flat reed as shown in Diagram 3. Keep reeds aligned and spaced about ¼" apart. With 6" ends at top, follow order on Diagram 3 and bend the first 3 reeds back on themselves, using finger to keep them from breaking. Begin weaving over and under pattern with the fourth reed, bending it under first and over third. Weave fifth under second, then over. Sixth begins over first; seventh, over second; and eighth, under first.

All reeds should be bent back directly on themselves and evenly spaced. Using #2 round reed, twine around 2 top sections of basket, or lobes. To twine, fold reed in half and slip it over the second upright spoke from center V. Twist reed around spokes for 2 rows, and tuck ends into previous rows. See Diagram 4.

Weave 2 rows of natural ¼" flat reed next to twining, 1 row of red, and 1 row of natural. Begin rows at different points of lobes. Splice ends of weavers. Cut spokes 1" from basket top. Wet spokes again if necessary, and bend to inside of lobes. Using awl, tuck in ends. Place 8" pieces of ¼" flat reed around inside of lobes following last rows of weaving, overlapping ends. Place a piece around outside of same row, overlapping ends. Alternate sides of baskets for beginning points, and clip to hold in place.

Leaving a 5" length of ribbon and starting on side, lash each rim with ribbon. Tie ends in bow, and trim.

To make a handle, loop one end of #2 reed at top of lobe between two innermost spokes with end to inside. Draw other end through same point of opposite lobe, arching handle to desired length. Twist reed back on itself, insert through lobe again at starting point, and twist around itself back to other side, looping again. Twist to starting point, trim reed, and tuck end in weaving.

HEART MINIBASKET
Materials:
10 (10"-long) pieces of ¼" flat reed for spokes
#2 round reed for twining
7 (14"-long) pieces of ¼" flat reed for weavers and rim
30" (⅛"-wide) red satin ribbon

Weave 10 spokes together as shown in Diagram 5, smooth side down, unweaving top 2 spokes for heart's top indentation. Spokes should be about ¼" apart. Bend all spokes up in a 90 degree angle, over your finger so as not to break them. Begin twining with #2 round reed at top right-hand side of heart where spokes bend, and twine for 2 rows, bending twining at corners to conform to heart shape.

Next weave 5 rows with ¼" flat reed, splicing ends. Cut spokes 1" from top of basket. Using awl, insert all ends into previous rows of weaving on inside of basket. Place 1 piece of ¼" flat reed along top row of weaving on inside lip of basket. Repeat on outside of basket to form rim. Secure with clothespins.

Thread needle with ribbon. Beginning at bottom point of heart and leaving 5" length of ribbon, tightly lash around rim, tie ends in a bow, and trim. Loop a 6" length of #2 reed through twining for hanger.

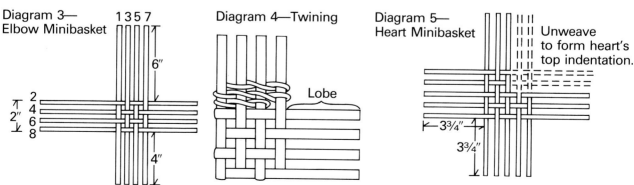

Diagram 3—Elbow Minibasket

Diagram 4—Twining   Lobe

Diagram 5—Heart Minibasket   Unweave to form heart's top indentation.

WINDING IVY
RINGS THIS SKIRT

Delicately winding ivy, green and thriving even in coldest winter, is the inspiration for this stenciled canvas tree skirt. Only two stencils are used, one for the lilting ribbon of leaves around the skirt's edge and the other to randomly branch off vines.

The subtle green works with any color scheme, and the ivy motif allows many ways to tie your decorations together. Drape the skirt across a tabletop and center it with an ivy tree. Try a sprig of ivy as a package topper, wind some around your tree as a garland, and tuck it into flower arrangements. Then use your stencils to personalize wrapping paper. The possibilities are many, and the effect is simple and sophisticated.

Materials:
patterns on page 132
47" square of canvas
10½" x 16½" sheet of plastic
craft knife
green stencil paint
soft-bristle stencil brush
4½ yards (½"-wide) bias tape (same color as canvas)
matching thread

Fold canvas in half twice to form quarters. Working from corner with no raw edges, draw a quarter-circle arc with a 22½" radius. Pin layers together, and cut along arc with sharp scissors. From the same corner, mark a 3" radius, and cut to form an opening for the tree. Remove pins, open the skirt, and cut a straight line from the skirt's outer edge to the center opening.

Transfer ivy patterns to plastic, and cut out each stencil separately. Using stencil A and green paint, stencil ivy swirls around skirt approximately 2" from edge and ¾" apart. Use stencil B, positioning as indicated on pattern, to add ivy clusters every few swirls until you have desired effect. Wrap bias tape around raw edges, mitering corners neatly, and stitch in place.

A HERALD ANGEL

Gliding through the clouds on white wings, flaxen hair flowing behind her, this painted metal angel heralds the coming season with such verve one can almost hear the lyrical tones of her horn. Freehand shading gives depth to her gown, and easy detailing brings a glow to her halo and life to her face. Lightweight sheet metal allows this angel to top a tree or fly high in an arrangement.

Start by transferring the pattern found on page 135 to a piece of sheet metal, either tin or aluminum. Trace the pattern with an awl and use a pair of metal snips to cut out the angel. With a hammer and the awl, punch a hole for a hanger in the top of the metal as marked on the pattern.

Wash the cut metal piece in hot, sudsy water, rinse and let dry. When dry, use a sponge brush to apply metal sealer to both sides. Let sealer dry several hours. Then apply three coats of base coat (light blue was used on the angel shown), and let that dry for several hours.

Using sizes 1, 3, and 5 paintbrushes, and acrylic paints, transfer the painting details to the angel. Consider matching paint colors to a specific color scheme. Or if your little angel is a brunette, or a redhead, surprise her with her own angelic likeness.

Where the pattern indicates shading on the wings and gown, make long sweeping brushstrokes. Let the paint dry for several hours.

Use a sponge brush to apply a metal varnish to both sides of the angel. If you plan to use this decoration out-of-doors, use an oil-base varnish for this final coating. Let the varnish dry, run a ribbon cord through the punched hole, and tie for a hanger.

SIMPLE SILVERY WREATH

This silvery ring of mirrored leaves is a dazzling decoration year-round. With its multi-planed surfaces and delicate tracery of leaf veins, this creation may seem to be a demanding project. But the secret is simplicity; if you can cut out paper dolls, you can make this elegant wreath.

Materials:
pattern on page 147
¼ yard 5-mil mylar (mirrored plastic film, available by the yard at retail display stores and art supply stores)
roll (1"-wide) mirrored plastic tape
10" Styrofoam wreath form
scrap of construction paper
fine-point felt-tip pen
craft knife and blades
small, sharp embroidery scissors (optional)
straight pins

Note: When cutting and scoring leaves, a sharp blade is very important. Replace blades in craft knife as necessary.

Wrap wreath form with mirrored plastic tape. Transfer leaf pattern to construction paper and cut out. With pen, trace leaf outline onto mylar 24 to 30 times. Cut out leaves with craft knife or scissors.

Draw vein lines on leaf. Score lightly along major veins (broken lines) on one side of leaf. Fold and pinch along scored lines to shape. Turn leaf over and score lightly along secondary veins (dotted lines). Pinch along these lines to shape leaf in opposite direction. Use damp, soft cloth or paper towel to clean ink smudges and fingerprints.

Attach a leaf to the wreath form, pinning stem at base of leaf. Use a second pin to anchor leaf, inserting pin at a point which will be covered by next overlapping leaf. Continue attaching leaves around wreath form, overlapping them and alternating the angle of the leaves to the left and right.

A WREATH FOR ALL SEASONS

No longer just simple circles of evergreen placed on a door at Christmas, wreaths are displayed more and more throughout the year. By incorporating a range of colors and techniques, wreaths have become a re-sourceful decoration for doors and walls.

The wreaths shown here are examples of such innovation. A simple weaving tech-nique using wooden reeds produces an intri-cate, seemingly endless wrap encircling the wreath form. The natural color of the wood acts as a neutral canvas on which to create a motif and color scheme appropriate for the room or occasion.

TIPS ON WORKING WITH WOOD WEAVER

The weaver should be soaked in water for 2-3 minutes. Work with 2' to 3' lengths of weaver to prevent fraying. A 1-pound bag of weaver should produce 2-3 wreaths. Any leftover wet weaver should be allowed to dry thoroughly.

Materials:
12" Styrofoam wreath form
1 lb. #6 round reed
scissors
sharp knife
70 wire florists' pole pins
1 lb. ³⁄₁₆" flat reed (for weaver)
pan or bowl of water
screwdriver or awl
glue gun (optional)

From the #6 round reed (do not soak), cut 7 lengths as follows: 2 (29" long), 2 (35"), 2 (38"), and 1 (40"). These are the ribs of the wreath. Place the 40" length at the broadest point of the wreath (most forms have a seam line to follow here), and curve round reed

around the outer edge, fastening it to the form with several pole pins. This is the center rib. (With a sharp knife, taper overlapping ends to lie flat on top of each other and form a complete circle.) Measure ¾" down from the center rib and wrap the 38" length around the wreath form in the same way. Continuing down, place the 35" rib ¾" from the previous rib, and the 29" length last. Repeat for other side. When all ribs are pinned into place, there will be a 2½" distance at the inner circle of the wreath between the last 2 (29" long) ribs.

Soak just a few flat weavers at a time, adding new weavers as needed. Three inches from a rib overlap, with the smooth side of the weaver on the outside, begin weaving over and under the ribs. Overlap the weaver slightly on the inner circle of the wreath to cover the wreath form.

When finished weaving with one piece, tuck the end under one of the ribs. Start new weaver where the previous one ended. Continue weaving around the entire wreath, covering the form. Remove pole pins only as you come to them during the weaving.

Continue to weave around the wreath form until the weaving meets at the inner circle. Tuck weaver end under the nearest rib. If any openings remain in the weaving, choose another length of weaver, and insert the tapered end into the weaving pattern. Work this area, without encircling the entire wreath, until the form is covered. Use a screwdriver or awl to raise the ribs and push under the end of the final weaver.

To make a loop for hanging, wrap a short length of weaver around the top rib twice, allowing the third wrap to extend ½" above wreath. Wrap the weaver 2-3 more times around rib to finish.

Decorate the wreath with silk flowers, greenery, ribbon, or porcelain figures, as desired, and attach with a hot glue gun.

HOLLY-DAY
CARD GARLAND

Bright green holly leaves cut from light-weight felt make a graceful backdrop for your Christmas cards when draped across the mantel or a doorway or pinned to a wall.

Whether holiday greetings come from your neighbor two blocks away or from a former college roommate five states away, Christmas cards are always a delight to receive. It is only fitting that these wishes of joy and peace be given a prominent place in your seasonal decor. And won't friends be pleased to see their cards on display.

You'll need ⅓ yard of green felt and a length of green upholstery trim to fit across your mantel. Transfer the holly leaf pattern on page 140 to the felt and cut out 12 leaves. Turn the ends of the trim back 2" and tack in place. This forms loops for hanging. Using the photograph for placement, pin the leaves to the trim, allowing the edges of the leaves to overlap.

Cut 12 (4") lengths of ¹⁄₁₆"-wide green ribbon, thread through a tapestry needle, and from back of garland, stitch ribbon through the trim and leaves, bringing needle to front. String a paper clip and a bead on needle; then bring needle to back of garland. Tie ribbon securely on back and trim off ends. Repeat until all 12 leaves are secured to trim.

Hang garland by loops and slip cards into paper clips to display.

THE ELEGANCE OF ETCHED GLASSWARE

Break the ice at your holiday parties with a custom-etched punch set sure to spark comment. The pineapple motif echoes your words of welcome, and the tiny holly design elegantly accents simply designed cups.

First, assemble etching cream (available at craft and stained glass shops), backed adhesive shelf paper, and a craft knife. (You might want to practice the technique on an old jelly jar.) Make sure area to be etched is clean. Cushion round pieces on a protected surface that prevents them from rolling.

Cut a piece of shelf paper at least 1" larger than the area you plan to etch, remove the backing, and smooth paper over the glass surface, working out any bubbles. Transfer the pattern on page 141 to shelf paper, and carefully cut it out with a craft knife. Burnish the cut edges to prevent etching cream from bleeding underneath. Use your finger to roll up any adhesive on the glass.

Following directions on the etching cream, stir it well, and rapidly paint a thick, smooth layer over the area to be etched, overlapping onto the shelf paper. Pick out any dry lumps. Leave the cream on only 5 to 10 minutes; do not allow it to dry. Wash cream off under running water, being careful to prevent it from contacting unetched glass. Remove the shelf paper and clean the pieces with glass cleaner.

HANDMADE WITH LOVE

When a gift is handmade, it has a value beyond estimation. It is a token that speaks of time, effort, and thoughtfulness. With the thorough instructions and patterns that follow, you can confidently create keepsake presents for those special people in your life. Start now and look forward to happy smiles of appreciation when your labors of love appear.

APRONS FOR CHRISTMAS COOKERY

For mother, grandmother, aunt, or friend, few memories are as poignant as those of sharing Christmas cookery with a little girl. The precious moments call for fitting attire, and quickly cross-stitched aprons are the icing on the cake!

Materials (for mother's apron):
chart and color key on page 152
12" x 9" piece 11-count white Aida cloth
embroidery floss (see color key)
#24 tapestry needle
23" x 32" piece red cotton duck fabric
red thread
6½ yards (½"-wide) red double-fold bias
  tape
30" (½"-wide) red pin-dot single-fold bias
  tape

Materials (for child's apron):
chart and color key on page 152
8" x 10" piece 11-count white Aida cloth
embroidery floss (see color key)
#24 tapestry needle
16" x 21" piece red cotton duck fabric
red thread
4½ yards (½"-wide) red double-fold bias
  tape
¾ yard (½"-wide) red pin-dot single-fold
  bias tape

Center design on Aida cloth and work according to chart. For adult apron, use 3 strands of floss to cross-stitch and 2 strands to backstitch. For child apron, use 2 strands to cross-stitch and 1 strand to backstitch.

Refer to Diagram 1 to make apron patterns. Place the half pattern on fabric fold, and cut out along pattern line. (Do not add seam allowances.)

Fold apron top under ½" and stitch. Fold apron bottom under 1" and stitch. Bind all raw edges with red double-fold bias tape. Cut remaining bias tape into 2 equal lengths. Match the center of each length of tape to the center of each arm curve and pin in place for binding. Tape extending beyond the curve will become neck and waist ties. (Clip tape seam allowances where tape will bind a curve.) Stitch tape in place.

Stitch the open edges of the bias tape neck and waist ties, tucking the cut ends of the tape under. Cut the stitched Aida for bib as shown in Diagram 2. Center the cross-stitched piece on the apron bib, and pin in place. Place red pin-dot single-fold bias tape over the raw edges of the Aida cloth. Machine-stitch in place, mitering corners.

Diagram 1—Cutting Layout
for Adult and Child Aprons

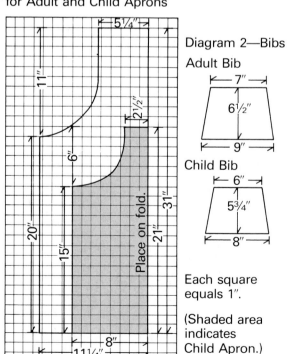

Diagram 2—Bibs

Adult Bib
7"
6½"
9"

Child Bib
6"
5¾"
8"

Each square equals 1".

(Shaded area indicates Child Apron.)

TOP IT OFF WITH HEARTS AND APPLES

A tisket, a tasket, a green and red cover for your basket. Fit any size round basket with a painted, quilted cover to make it all the more special. A basket has so many possibilities, especially at Christmas. After the holidays, pack it with provisions and head out on a picnic.

Materials:
patterns on pages 140 and 141
purchased round basket
newspaper
muslin fabric
pre-quilted fabric
acrylic paints (red, green, yellow, black, white, umber)
single-fold bias tape (for binding)
fabric for inner ruffle
eyelet lace
fabric for lining
ribbon
Velcro

Place newspaper over top of basket; trace around the opening and cut out for pattern. Add ¾" seam allowance to pattern and cut out muslin and pre-quilted fabric. Transfer painting patterns to muslin, and paint according to pattern. Shade apples and heart with umber for a dark shading and yellow for a light shading. Use red or umber to shade leaves. Let dry.

To make the ruffle, you will need a piece of fabric 4"-wide and twice the circumference of the muslin circle. Fold fabric in half lengthwise, wrong sides facing. Beginning ¼" from the raw edge, stitch 2 rows of gathering stitches along entire length of fabric. Pull thread to fit around muslin circle, and fasten off. With right sides facing, align raw edge of ruffle with raw edge of muslin circle, folded edge towards center, and baste. Stitch and press.

Bind edges of quilted circle with bias tape. Place quilted circle on wrong side of muslin circle and attach with blindstitch. Quilt around painted heart, apples, and ribbons. On right side of painted muslin circle, align plain edge of lace to edge of circle, and blindstitch.

To make the lining, place the basket on a piece of paper and trace the bottom. Using this as a pattern, and including a ¼" seam allowance, cut out a circle from lining fabric. Double the circumference of basket and add 8" to the depth of basket. Cut a piece of fabric to this measurement. (For example, for a basket 20" around and 5" deep you would cut a 40" x 13" piece.) Cut piece in half across the width. With ¼" seam allowance and right sides facing, sew pieces together across width, stopping both seams so that lining will fit 1" below handles. Press seam open. Finish off sides of openings for handles. Turn under top edge of lining ¼" and press. Turn under 2½" more, press, and stitch. Stitch another row 1" up from hem to make ribbon casing. Attach safety pin to the end of one length of ribbon and thread through casing. Repeat for other side.

Beginning ¼" from bottom edge, run a gathering stitch around raw edge of fabric. Pull thread to fit fabric circle, and fasten. Align raw edge to edge of circle, right sides facing. Pin and stitch. Place lining in basket with hem hanging over top. Pull ribbon ends to gather. Tie ribbons around basket handles. Attach 2-3 small pieces of Velcro to basket lining and basket lid to hold both in place.

KEEPSAKE CHRISTMAS CONTAINERS

Cross-stitch a lid for a three-quart food keeper that will delight everyone from the half-pints up. Homemade treats are even more appreciated when they're packed in a holiday jar that can be used again and again.

The "Christmas Quilt" jar features a variation of the popular Ohio Star pattern centered with bright red hearts. And ruffled eyelet lace dresses up a jar "For a Special Neighbor" and one "To Warm You."

Materials:
charts on pages 142 and 143
6" square of 14-count white Aida cloth
2 (6½") squares 14-count red Aida cloth
embroidery floss (see color keys)
6" square quilt batting
6" square muslin
2 heart-shaped 3-quart food keepers
round 3-quart food keeper
50" (1½"-wide) eyelet lace
craft glue

Center designs on Aida cloth and work according to chart. For Christmas Quilt design, place batting between Aida cloth and muslin, with Aida right side out. Baste together. Using red floss, follow chart to quilt with backstitch through all 3 layers.

For each jar, remove plastic insert from frame. Center on back of stitchery and trace. Cut along line.

For each lace ruffle, cut a 25" piece of lace, baste along plain edge, and gather to fit outside edge of stitchery. Place on stitchery, right sides facing and raw edges together, and zigzag-stitch together.

Position work in frame. Run glue around outside edge of plastic backing, and insert plastic into back of frame. Hold in place until glue is set.

SALUTATIONS ON DISPLAY

Appliquéd, quilted, and embroidered with salutations, this card holder is a premier spot to stash Christmas cards. The ribbon ties will expand to hold large bundles of holiday cheer. After the holidays, leave it up to hold mail or recipes, and to remind friends that they are always welcome.

Materials:
patterns on page 143
⅓ yard white print fabric
⅓ yard green print fabric
scrap of red print fabric (for apple)
scrap of green print fabric (for holly leaves)
craft glue
water-soluble fabric marker
tear-away backing for appliqué
thread (green, brown, red, white)
⅓ yard (1¾"-wide) eyelet lace
2½ yards (½"-wide) red grosgrain ribbon
⅓ yard fiberfill batting
quilting thread
quilting needle
2 circular brackets (for hanging holder)

Note: Use ¼" seam allowance unless otherwise indicated. From white fabric, cut out a 6" x 5½" block (A), a 9" x 7½" block (B), and a 9¼" x 11¾" block (C). From green fabric, cut out two 1¾" x 8" strips (D), two 1¾" x 6" strips (E), and a 9¼" x 11¾" block (F). Transfer apple and holly patterns to fabrics and cut out.

Center apple on block A, and glue wrong side down. With fabric marker, lightly trace holly branch and apple stem as indicated on pattern. Glue holly leaves wrong side down as indicated on pattern. Pin piece of tear-away backing under block A. Using a machine satin stitch, appliqué apple, branch, and leaves to block A. Remove backing and clip strings.

Stitch a strip E to top of block A, right sides facing. Press seam open. Repeat for bottom. Stitch a strip D to one side of block

A, right sides facing. Press seam open. Repeat for other side. Pin raw edge of lace to top raw edge of strip E, with scallops towards center, and tack in place.

Cut eight 11" lengths from ribbon. Allowing each piece to extend 8", pin one piece to top edge just below lace, and pin another ribbon ¾" from bottom edge. Repeat for other side.

Using block B as a pattern, cut out a piece of batting. Place block B on block A, right sides together, and place batting on block B. With ribbon ends towards center, and leaving an opening for turning, stitch block. Remove pins from ribbon ends and turn. With white thread, quilt around apple, branch, leaves, and edge of block A. Close opening and set block aside.

Using pattern guide and water soluble pen, trace the word GREETINGS onto block C as shown in photograph (top). Pin piece of tear-away backing to top back of block C. Using machine satin stitch, embroider word. Remove backing; cut threads.

Using front block ribbon placement as guide, pin ribbon ends in place. Using block C as a pattern, cut out a piece of batting. Place blocks C and F right sides facing with batting on top of block F. Leaving an opening for turning, stitch block. Remove pins from ribbon, and turn. Close opening.

With white thread, topstitch around edge of just completed block F. Place previously finished block on this block and line up bottom edges exactly. Pin together. With green thread, topstitch blocks together along bottom edge. Tie ribbons into bows and trim ends. Tack circular brackets to top back edges for hanging.

APPLIQUÉ A SHIMMERING GARLAND OF HOLLY

Dazzle a fashionable female with a pullover that shines with moiré holly leaves and shimmers with silver sequined berries.

You begin with a purchased top. Buy ¼ yard of 44"-wide satin moiré that has washing instructions compatible with the garment's. Then fuse double-sided web fabric to the wrong side of the moiré (use a backing sheet if the web fabric does not come backed). Transfer the holly leaf pattern from page 147 to the web side of the moiré 18 times (or more, if needed), and cut out the leaves. Arrange them around the pullover's neck, pin in place, and iron to fuse.

Practicing on scraps to adjust the tension, machine-zigzag a narrow satin stitch over raw edges of each leaf, using thread that matches the moiré. Sew first any leaves overlapped by others. Machine straight-stitch leaf veins with dark green thread. Knot loose threads on wrong side of garment. Finally, sew sequins in groups of 3 among the leaves.

STRANDS OF COUNTRY GEMS

Whimsical necklaces featuring a frisky lad and lass on swings, brightly painted hearts, and a menagerie of farm animals bring to mind the sights and sounds of busy country life.

Painted wooden cutouts and perky craft beads are simply knotted on cord to make this cute-as-can-be jewelry. For variety, use ribbon instead of cord. Or make the strand long and full enough to garland a tabletop tree.

Once you see how easy these necklaces are, you can try even more combinations. Use other patterns from this book by sizing them to suit your fancy.

Materials:
patterns on pages 148 and 149
scraps of ⅜" thick wood
jigsaw
scrap of ¼"-thick wood
2 small craft sticks
drill with ⁵⁄₃₂" bit
sandpaper
wood sealer
1" sponge brush
acrylic paints (black, white, red, dark brown, flesh, burnt umber)
fine-tipped paintbrush
varnish
heavy string
masking tape
45" (2 mm) cord per necklace
beads

For each necklace, trace patterns onto $3/8$"-thick wood, and cut out with jigsaw. For swings, cut $5/8$" x 2" rectangles from $1/4$"-thick wood. For cow's legs, cut craft sticks into 4 ($1\frac{1}{4}$"-long) pieces with rounded ends as feet. Drill $5/32$" holes where indicated on patterns, $1/4$" from short ends of swings and $3/16$" from flat ends of cow's legs. Sand wood with the grain, and wipe off with a lint-free cloth. Seal wood on all sides.

Following photos, use sponge brush to apply the base coat. Paint details with fine-tipped brush. For cheeks and eyes, swirl wooden end of brush in place. Shade pink hearts and big cow's nose and udder with red paint blended into pink. Antique the pig and cows and stain swing with diluted burnt umber paint. When all paint is dry, apply 2 coats of varnish.

Use heavy string to tie cow's legs to body, as shown in photo. To string necklace, make a masking tape "needle" by wrapping $2\frac{1}{2}$" of masking tape around one end of cord. Cut tape to a point; then thread through drilled holes, tying knots on each side of cutouts and beads to hold in place. Knot and fray loose ends as shown in photos.

ANGELIC RAG DOLL

Can ''down-to-earth'' apply to an angel? This sweet-faced innocent seems to possess that quality, with her corn-husk wings, raffia hair, and simple cotton dress. Nestled in a fringed raffia and rag heart wreath, clutching her very own braided raffia and rag heart wreath, she is a folksy door decoration, ready to charm friends with a homespun welcome.

And this design is actually three decorations in one. The angel is a basic rag doll that you can dress in many different ways (even as a boy!) for any season. Leave off the wings, substitute yarn for hair, and she's a soft plaything. The big heart wreath can stand alone as a decoration. And the little hearts make ideal ornaments or, by stringing several together, a country garland.

ANGEL

Materials (for body and dress):
patterns on pages 144-145
¼ yard (36"-wide) unbleached muslin
stuffing
embroidery floss (pink, blue)
red crayon
¼ yard (36"-wide) cotton print fabric
thread to match fabrics
1 yard (½"-wide) crocheted lace
1½ yards (¼"-wide) green satin ribbon
excelsior (packing material) for hair
dried corn husks for wings

BODY: Fold muslin in half, short ends together. Transfer body patterns to muslin, leaving 1" between pieces. Do not cut out. Stitch along outlines through both layers of fabric, leaving open where patterns indicate. Cut out pieces, ¼" from stitching lines. Clip curves and corners, and turn.

Mark face and arm positions on the body. Stuff all pieces to within ½" from openings. Baste leg openings closed. Turn body opening under ¼", insert legs, and pin in place. Stitch across body to secure.

For arms, gather around openings. Tuck raw edges to the inside and stitch arms to body.

Embroider eyes and mouth and add blush to the cheeks by lightly coloring with a red crayon.

DRESS: *Note:* Use ¼" seam allowances unless otherwise indicated.

Transfer dress patterns to cotton print fabric and cut out. Cut out a strip of fabric 1½" x 3½" for the neck facing and a rectangle 6½" x 18" for the skirt. Mark the neck opening on the wrong side of the bodice. Center the neck facing over the neck opening, right sides together, and pin in place. On wrong side of bodice, stitch around the neck opening line, ⅛" from both sides and ends. Cut through both fabric layers along the marked line, clip corners, and turn facing inside bodice. Iron.

For sleeves, gather shoulders, adjust to fit bodice, and stitch, right sides together. Gather sleeve edges to fit angel's wrist. On one side only, sew sleeve and bodice side seam, right sides together. Leave other side seam open.

For skirt, turn 1 long edge under ¼" for hem. Weave ¼"-wide green ribbon through openings in crocheted lace as shown in photo. Pin top edge of crocheted lace ¼" above hem fold. (Lace will extend beyond fabric.) Stitch to attach lace and hem skirt bottom. Pin a second row of lace ¼" above first and stitch top and bottom edges to skirt. Just above the lace, make two ¼" tucks, 1" apart.

Gather skirt top to fit bodice. With right sides together, sew skirt to bodice. Sew remaining side seam from sleeve edge to skirt bottom. Dress the doll.

For hair, stitch sprigs of excelsior along top center of head. For wings, if dried corn husks are too narrow or wrinkled for pattern, soak them in lukewarm water for 10 minutes, lay flat, and weight with a book to dry. Transfer the wing pattern to the corn husks and cut out with scissors. Stitch wings to angel's back.

FINISHING TOUCHES: Stitch angel to large raffia and rag wreath (back of neck to V in wreath). Tie several small braided hearts to the bottom of the large wreath with raffia.

RAFFIA AND RAG HEART WREATHS
Materials (for small and large wreaths):
scraps of cotton fabric
raffia
11" wire heart form (or wire coat hanger) for large wreath

SMALL BRAIDED HEART WREATHS: You will need 2 (1" x 18") strips of cotton fabric and 6 strands of raffia. Turn raw edges of fabric to the inside and tie the fabric strips and raffia together ½" from one end. Braid, tightening tension, to curve slightly as you go. After 6", tie ends together and cut, leaving ½" excess. Repeat this process; then tie both curved braids together at the top and bottom to form a heart.

Stitch a heart wreath to the angel's hands, and make a few of the ornaments to hang from the large wreath.

LARGE RAFFIA AND RAG WREATH: Cut raffia into 8" strips. Grouping 6 to 8 strips at a time, attach raffia to the wire heart form (or a wire hanger bent into a heart shape) as for fringe. Bend raffia strips in half, fold the loop around the wire form, and pull loose ends through the loop on the other side. Continue attaching raffia strips until wreath is full.

Rip fabric scraps into 1"-wide strips; then cut in 6" lengths. Attach a fabric strip between raffia knots, in same manner used to attach raffia.

CROCHET A PILLOW FULL OF TULIPS

Encourage a rest-filled holiday with this double crochet pillow. Though work time is minimal, the result is a gift of beauty as well as comfort. The red tulips are certain to liven up a winter interior and serve as a reminder that spring is on the way.

Materials:
chart on page 152
sport-weight yarn in the following
    amounts: 2 oz. light green, 2 oz. dark
    green, 1 oz. red
crochet hooks in sizes F and H (or size to
    obtain gauge)
tapestry needle
12" pillow form

GAUGE: With F hook, 15 dc and 8 rows = 3"

TAPESTRY CROCHET: Pattern is worked in double crochet (dc). To change colors, work in first color until 2 loops (lps) remain on hook. Pull new color through the 2 lps to complete stitch. Yarn not in use is laid across stitches (sts) of row below to be encased in the new stitches.

PILLOW FRONT: With F hook and light green yarn, chain (ch) 61. Dc in 2nd ch from hook and in each ch across. Ch 2, turn. Starting at row 2 of chart, work across in dc (60 sts, counting ch 2 at beginning of row as 1 dc). Continue to work in dc following chart, until rows 1 through 16 have been completed twice. Work 1 row of light green and fasten off yarn. (*Note:* If desired, the partial flowers on rows 10 through 16 can be omitted.)

PILLOW BACK: With dark green, work same number of rows and sts as front, omitting tapestry pattern.

FINISHING: Sew front and back together on 3 sides. Insert pillow form and sew remaining side. To make cording, with H hook and 3 strands of red held together, crochet a chain 48" long. Sew this cord around the pillow at seams with "bump" side out and "chain" side toward pillow. Finished pillow measures 12" square.

KNIT A HEATHERY AFGHAN

A soft heathery houndstooth afghan extends an invitation for winter comfort that's hard to resist. Knitted in stockinette stitch with rich wool yarn, this throw is a remarkably versatile decorating accent, blending into a wide range of styles. It's a natural for the man on your list, but, as shown here, it can lavishly complement quilts, lace, and dried flowers.

Materials:
100-gram balls knitting worsted (100% virgin wool): 5 balls dark gray, 6 balls beige
size 15 circular 36" needle (or size needed to obtain gauge)

GAUGE: 4 sts = 1"; 4 rows = 1" in St st.
FINISHED SIZE: 40" x 60" (excluding fringe)
PATTERN STITCH: Multiple of 4 sts
Row 1: K 2 light, *1 dark, 3 light*, 1 dark, 1 light
Row 2: P *1 light, 3 dark*
Row 3: K *1 light, 3 dark*
Row 4: P 2 light, *1 dark, 3 light*, 1 dark, 1 light

Note: Entire afghan is worked in St st. Always carry yarn loosely across back of afghan. Do not twist. On purl rows, always bring both strands of yarn to front of work after the first stitch.

Using 1 strand of gray and 1 strand of beige, cast on 162 sts. With double strand of yarn (1 gray and 1 beige), knit the first and last stitch on each row, working the pattern stitch in between.
Example:
Row 1: K 1 st (double yarn), k 2 light, *1 dark, 3 light*, rep between *s to last 3 sts; k 1 dark, 1 light , k last st with double yarn.
Repeat the 4 pattern rows for 60", ending with Row 4. Bind off loosely.
FINISHING: To fringe, cut two 17"-long strands of yarn, one of each color, to knot through every st.

Standard Knitting Abbreviations
st(s)—stitch(es)
St st—Stockinette stitch (k 1 row, p 1 row)
k—knit
p—purl
*—repeat instructions between asterisks to the end of the row or to instructions for last stitches of row

PRETTY PASTEL PONY

Mobile enough to keep up with active children, pull toys have long been a favorite with youngsters. This pretty pony is a good start for the beginning woodworker because the few pattern pieces are easy to cut and assemble. Painting is minimal, allowing many different color schemes.

Materials:
patterns on page 153
14" of 1 x 8 pine
jigsaw
drill with ⅛", ¼", and ⅜" bits
C clamp
sandpaper
9" of ¼" doweling
wood glue
acrylic paints: yellow, rose, dusty blue,
  brown, and white
paintbrushes
1"-long (¼") wood screw
1 yard (⅛"-wide) dusty blue satin ribbon
½" wooden bead

Transfer horse, wheels, and a 3" x 7½" rectangle (base) to wood. Cut out with jigsaw. Drill a ⅛" hole through top of base ¼" from short edge, for ribbon pull. Center horse on base with front feet 1¼" from front edge, and mark placement. Drill ¼" hole through base where front feet will be attached. On long ¾" side of base, measure 1" from front and mark. On same side, measure 1" from back and mark. Secure base in C clamp, and drill ⅜" holes through base for axles (dowels). (To avoid splitting the wood, drill through only until point of bit appears. Turn work over, place point of bit in small hole and finish drilling.) Drill a ¼" hole in center of each wheel. Sand all surfaces.

Cut two 4⅛" pieces from doweling. Put dowels through the ⅜" holes in base. Place a wheel on each dowel end and secure with glue. Dilute blue and yellow paints with small amount of white paint and water. Paint horse with a thin coat of yellow. Paint base, wheels, mane, and tail with a thin coat of blue. Let dry. Add more white to blue paint, and use for accents in mane and tail as shown in photograph. Use brown paint for harness and eyes. Let dry.

Use rose paint to apply freehand stars to horse: one on one side, two on the other. Place screw through ¼" hole from bottom of base and into front feet of horse. Thread a piece of ribbon or string through hole at front of base for pull. (Do not use wooden bead on pull if gift is for a small child.)

TOP BILLING

Some people dream of seeing their name in lights. The next best way to give top billing to family luminaries is with this star-spangled photo display. The shiny stars studding the mat are cut from mylar (a mirrored film), scored, and folded to shape.

The handsome leading man, highlighted here by a dazzling and dimensional constellation, has infinite star quality, but don't be surprised if all your local celebrities demand a showcase of stellar magnitude, too. You may have to make a galaxy of frames for the family gallery.

Materials:
patterns on page 152
blue mat board (or desired color)
5-mil mylar (mirrored plastic film, available by the yard at retail display and art supply stores)
craft knife and sharp blades
straightedge
craft glue
cotton swabs
frame with a ½" rabbet (recess on back of frame)
glass and corrugated cardboard to fit frame
masking tape

Depending on the size of the photo that you wish to frame, you can buy a precut mat, have your local framing shop prepare one, or cut it yourself. (Sample dimensions for a 5" x 7" photo mat: outer dimensions—8" x 10", opening dimensions—4½" x 6½".)

Transfer patterns to mylar. (You can also make stars from paper, and you might want to practice with paper first.) Cut out stars using a craft knife and a straightedge. Lightly score (draw blade along surface only) from star center to the 5 points, as indicated by *broken* lines on pattern. Turn star over and lightly score from star center to arm intersections, as indicated by *dotted* lines on pattern. Fold and pinch along scored lines. (Fold edge should be toward scored side.)

To attach stars to mat, apply a drop of glue to the backs of points. Place star on mat and hold until glue is almost dry. (Wipe any excess glue away with moistened cotton swab.) Repeat for other stars. Cut ¼"-wide, 4"-long strips of mylar. Place at an angle on the mat as shown in photo, taping ends on the back of the mat.

To avoid crushing stars under glass, cut ¼" strips of mat board, 2 the length of the mat, and 2 the width of the mat. Insert glass in frame; then glue strips to inside of frame, just behind glass. Insert mat into frame, resting on strips. Tape photo in place behind mat. Insert cardboard backing and secure with masking tape.

TALK TO THE ANIMALS

All these puppets need is a child's imagination to bring them to life. High-tension springs and a pull cord allow the dog puppet to bark and the pig to oink, and scraps of suede or fabric finish the puppets with ears.

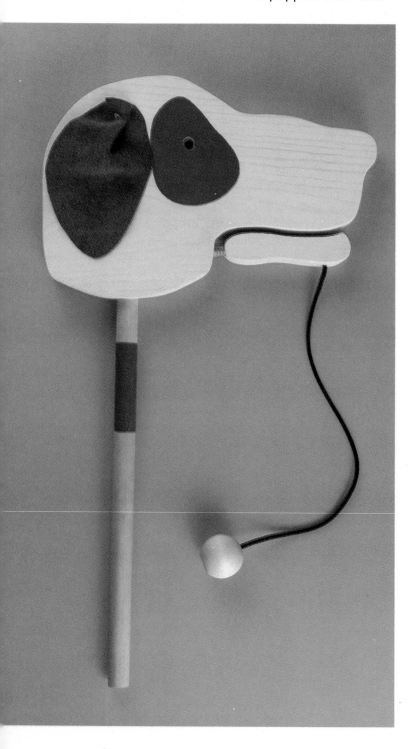

Materials (for both puppets):
patterns on pages 150 and 151
1½ feet 1 x 8 white pine
jigsaw
19″ of ½″ doweling
drill with ⅛″, ¼″, ¹⁷⁄₆₄″, and ½″ bits
sandpaper
wire cutters
¹⁷⁄₆₄″ x 2″ high-tension spring
fast-drying epoxy glue
acrylic paints (red, white, brown)
masking tape
scraps of suede, leather, or felt (pink, brown) for ears
4 small brass carpet tacks
24″ thin black braided cord
2 (1″) round wooden knobs

Following wood grain direction on patterns, transfer patterns to wood and cut out. (Each lower jaw can be cut out along with the head.) Cut doweling in half.

Note: Drilling is more easily completed by starting with smaller-size bits. Using pattern indications, work as follows: With ⅛″ bit, drill holes directly through jaws and centers of knobs for cord; with ¼″ bit, drill holes through heads for eyes; with ½″ bit, drill ½″-deep holes into bases of heads; with ¹⁷⁄₆₄″ bit, drill ¼″-deep holes for springs. Sand all wood pieces.

Cut spring in half. Insert ¼″ of each end of spring into head and jaw, and glue. Glue one end of dowel into base of head.

Mix red and white paints and water for pig puppet. Paint each puppet with respective color as shown in photograph. (Try to match ear and paint colors as closely as possible.) Paint the corresponding color around a 2″ area of dowel 1″ below base of head by masking off area with masking tape. Let dry and remove tape. Transfer ear pattern to suede or fabric and cut out. Fold on lines shown. Using brass tacks, attach ears to each side of head as marked. (If tack is too long, cut extra length off with wire cutters.) Thread cord ends through jaw and wooden knob, knotting and gluing at each end of cord. Knob should hang even with end of dowel.

YOUR CHRISTMAS KITCHEN

From Thanksgiving to New Year's, there are over 100 regular meals (not to mention treats, parties, and after-shopping snacks!). To spice up your repertoire for the holiday season, try the exciting new recipes on the following pages. And don't be surprised if some of these dishes become family favorites, specially requested for Christmases to come.

THE TWELVE DAYS OF CHRISTMAS: A RECIPE COLLECTION

A playful game of free association with the verses of "The Twelve Days of Christmas" stimulated ideas for the holiday recipes and decorations found on the following pages. For example, with "a partridge in a pear tree" in mind, we cooked up Pear Eggnog Muffins. And when we considered "eight maids a-milking," we concocted a creamy milk punch.

On this lyrical list of recipes, there's a bit of everything you'll need for your holiday cooking—food gifts, party dishes, meals, sweet treats—plus a couple of ideas for fancy packaging and table decorations.

1 *On the first day of Christmas, my true love sent to me, a partridge in a pear tree.*

Left: Sweetened with pear chunks, moistened with eggnog, and spiced with dark rum—a basket of Pear Eggnog Muffins makes a great food gift. For a festive look, cook the muffins in foil cups.

PEAR EGGNOG MUFFINS
3 cups all-purpose flour
1 cup firmly packed brown sugar
1 tablespoon plus 1 teaspoon baking powder
½ teaspoon salt
½ teaspoon ground nutmeg
2 medium pears, peeled, cored, and chopped
1 cup commercial eggnog
⅓ cup plus 2 tablespoons butter or margarine, melted
¼ cup dark rum
1 egg, lightly beaten

Combine flour, sugar, baking powder, salt, and nutmeg in a large bowl; make a well in center of dry ingredients. Combine chopped pears, eggnog, butter, rum, and egg, stirring until well blended. Add eggnog mixture to dry ingredients, stirring just until moistened.

Spoon batter into greased muffin pans, filling two-thirds full. Bake at 400° for 15 minutes or until a wooden pick inserted in the center comes out clean. Serve immediately. Yield: 22 muffins.

2 **On the second day of Christmas, my true love sent to me, two turtledoves.**

Above: Your true love will coo like a turtledove with one melt-in-the-mouth bite of this Triple Nut Sweetheart Fudge Candy, layered in chocolate and nuts.

TRIPLE NUT SWEETHEART FUDGE CANDY

2 (8-ounce) packages semisweet chocolate
¼ cup butter
½ cup pecan halves, lightly toasted
½ cup slivered almonds, lightly toasted
½ cup chopped walnuts, lightly toasted
6 ounces white chocolate, coarsely chopped
Additional white chocolate, melted

Melt semisweet chocolate and butter in top of double boiler over simmering water. Remove from heat, and spread ½ cup melted chocolate mixture in a waxed paper-lined 6-inch heart-shaped pan; chill until firm. Measure out and reserve ½ cup melted chocolate mixture. Combine remaining melted chocolate mixture, pecans, almonds, and walnuts in a small bowl. Spread half of chocolate-nut mixture evenly over chocolate layer in pan. Set aside remaining chocolate-nut mixture.

Melt white chocolate in top of double boiler over simmering water; remove from heat, and cool slightly. Pour white chocolate evenly over chocolate-nut layer. Spread remaining chocolate-nut mixture evenly over white chocolate. Top with reserved melted chocolate mixture. Cover and chill several hours or overnight.

Invert candy onto platter; remove waxed paper; drizzle additional melted white chocolate over surface of candy in a decorative pattern. Bring to room temperature before serving. To serve, cut candy with a sharp knife. Yield: about 2 pounds.

3 On the third day of Christmas, my true love sent to me, three French hens.

Below: On a cold winter's night, this hearty French Hen Pie, a variation on the classic potpie, will warm your loved ones from the inside out. The Savory Pie Pastry is filled with hen, egg, onions, and celery. Sliced ham brushed with mustard adds tang.

FRENCH HEN PIE

1 (6- to 6½-pound) baking hen
4 stalks celery, cut into 1-inch pieces
1 small onion, sliced
Savory Pie Pastry (recipe follows)
¾ pound thinly sliced ham, divided
¼ cup coarse-grain mustard
2 cloves garlic
1 cup loosely packed parsley sprigs
2 eggs
1 teaspoon salt, divided
½ teaspoon dried thyme leaves
½ teaspoon freshly ground pepper, divided
1 small onion, chopped
¼ cup butter
2 cups soft whole wheat breadcrumbs
1 tablespoon butter, melted

Place first 3 ingredients in an 8-quart Dutch oven; add water to cover. Bring to a boil; cover, reduce heat, and simmer 45 minutes or until hen is tender. Cool hen completely in broth. Drain hen, discarding broth, celery, and onion. Bone hen, separating white and dark meat. Set aside.

Prepare Savory Pie Pastry. Roll two-thirds of pastry to ¼-inch thickness on a lightly floured surface; fit into a 9-inch springform pan. Trim overhang to 1 inch, reserving excess pastry. Wrap excess in plastic wrap and refrigerate.

Arrange half of ham on pastry; brush with mustard. Cover and set aside.

With food processor running, drop garlic through feed tube, and process until minced. Add the white meat; process until coarsely ground. Add parsley, eggs, ½ teaspoon salt, thyme, and ¼ teaspoon pepper; process just until well blended. Spread mixture evenly over ham layer.

Sauté onion in butter in a small skillet until tender. Set aside. Chop dark meat, and combine with the sautéed onion mixture, the whole wheat breadcrumbs, remaining salt, and pepper in a large bowl. Spread mixture over white meat layer. Arrange remaining ham on hen layers.

Roll out remaining pastry to a 10-inch circle (¼-inch thick); drape over ham layer, leaving a 1-inch overhang at edge of pan. Turn pastry edges under and flute. Roll excess pastry to ⅛-inch thickness on a lightly floured surface; cut into decorative shapes and place on pie. Bake at 400° for 55 minutes. Brush melted butter over pie, and bake 5 additional minutes. Cool pie on a wire rack for 30 minutes. Remove side of pan; cut pie into wedges. Yield: 10 servings.

Savory Pie Pastry:
3½ cups all-purpose flour
1 teaspoon salt
1 teaspoon sugar
1 cup shortening
2 egg yolks
⅔ cup cold water

Combine flour, salt, and sugar in a large mixing bowl; stir well. Cut in shortening with a pastry blender until mixture resembles coarse meal.

Combine yolks and water in a small mixing bowl, stirring well. Sprinkle water mixture over flour mixture, stirring until dry ingredients are moistened. Turn dough out on a lightly floured surface, and knead 4 or 5 times. Yield: enough pastry for one 9-inch springform pan.

4
On the fourth day of Christmas, my true love sent to me, four calling birds.

Left: When you go calling on friends, leave behind a bird's nest box filled with cookies, candies, or even potpourri. And you can put a feather in your cap when you make it yourself. Simply cover a round wooden box in pretty fabrics or paint, glue on mosses and bits of dried flowers in the shape of a nest, and then wire or glue on the birds (available at most import shops). For a lacy border beneath the lid, place a doily inside the box, and let it spill over the edge.

5 *On the fifth day of Christmas, my true love sent to me, five golden rings.*

Opposite: This golden ring fits all sizes. Nuts, apricots, raisins, chocolate morsels, and a generous portion of liqueur flavor a Golden Chocolate Chip Fruitcake.

GOLDEN CHOCOLATE CHIP FRUITCAKE

3 cups chopped pecans or walnuts
1½ cups chopped dried apricots
1½ cups golden raisins
1 cup Cointreau or brandy
Additional Cointreau or brandy
¾ cup butter
1¼ cups sugar
4 eggs
2⅔ cups all-purpose flour
1½ teaspoons baking powder
¾ teaspoon freshly grated nutmeg
½ teaspoon salt
1 (12-ounce) package semisweet chocolate
    mini-morsels
1 cup apricot preserves, melted
Dried apricots, slivered (optional)
Walnut halves (optional)

Combine first 4 ingredients; cover and let stand at room temperature overnight.

Drain nut mixture, reserving liqueur. Add additional Cointreau to reserved liqueur to equal ½ cup. Set nut mixture and liqueur aside. Cream butter in a large mixing bowl; gradually add sugar, beating until light and fluffy. Add eggs, one at a time, beating well after each addition.

Combine flour, baking powder, nutmeg, and salt; mix well. Measure out 1 cup flour mixture; add to reserved nut mixture and chocolate morsels, tossing to coat. Add remaining flour mixture to creamed mixture, beating at low speed just until dry ingredients are moistened. Add dredged nut mixture and reserved ½ cup liqueur; stir just until well combined. Spoon batter into a greased and floured Bundt pan. Bake at 300° for 1½ hours or until a long wooden pick inserted in the center comes out clean. Cool

cake completely in pan on a wire rack.

Place a triple thickness of cheesecloth on a large piece of aluminum foil. Remove cake from pan, and place on cheesecloth. Generously brush cake with Cointreau, and wrap with cheesecloth. Brush cheesecloth with Cointreau, and wrap snugly with aluminum foil. Refrigerate 2 weeks, unwrapping and brushing cake with Cointreau weekly.

Before serving, place cake on a serving platter; brush with apricot preserves. Garnish with slivered apricots and walnut halves, if desired. Yield: one 9-inch cake.

6 *On the sixth day of Christmas, my true love sent to me, six geese a-laying.*

Above: With this recipe for Six Eggs au Gratin, you won't score a goose egg in a best dish contest. Hard-cooked eggs (chicken eggs are fine!) are topped with a peppery cheese sauce and sliced olives and served with buttered tortillas cut in wedges. For a ladies' holiday brunch or a post-shopping dinner, this dish is quick and tasty. (Recipe on next page.)

SIX EGGS AU GRATIN

¼ cup chopped onion
2 cloves garlic, minced
1 tablespoon olive oil
¼ cup half-and-half
1 cup (4 ounces) shredded Cheddar
   cheese
½ teaspoon crushed dried red pepper
¼ cup sliced ripe olives, divided
6 hard-cooked eggs, quartered
Paprika
Hot buttered flour tortillas

Sauté onion and garlic in olive oil 5 minutes; cool slightly, and transfer mixture to a blender container. Add half-and-half, cheese, and red pepper; process until smooth. Stir in 3 tablespoons olives.

Arrange eggs in the bottom of a shallow 1-quart casserole or au gratin dish. Pour sauce over eggs; cover and bake at 375° for 15 minutes or until thoroughly heated. Garnish with remaining olives and paprika. Serve with tortillas. Yield: 6 servings.

---

7 On the seventh day of Christmas, my true love sent to me, seven swans a-swimming.

Below: A swan can swim across your table, too, for a fantasy centerpiece. This shimmery scene belies simple, inexpensive materials. For the swan, coat a plastic bird container with spray glue, place in a bag with iridescent confetti, and shake to cover. Set the swan a-swimming on a mirror lake. Treat bare branches the same as the swan, and insert them in florists' foam to create a glittery forest around the lake. Hide the foam and fill the swan with iridescent baubles.

8

**On the eighth day of Christmas,
my true love sent to me,
eight maids a-milking.**

*Right: So sinfully rich it may make maids blush,
Creamy Milk Punch is thick with ice cream and spiked
with bourbon. Before serving, sprinkle with freshly
grated nutmeg.*

CREAMY MILK PUNCH
1 pint vanilla ice cream
2 cups half-and-half or milk
¼ cup bourbon
2 tablespoons sugar
¼ teaspoon vanilla extract
Freshly grated nutmeg

Combine ice cream, half-and-half, bourbon, sugar, and vanilla in container of an
electric blender; cover and process until
smooth. Pour into punch cups, and sprinkle
with nutmeg. Serve punch immediately.
Yield: 1 quart.

9

**On the ninth day of Christmas,
my true love sent to me,
nine drummers drumming.**

*Left: Set the scene for good vibrations with a striking
centerpiece or buffet arrangement of drums. Collect
drums (real ones, toys, tins, or decorations like those
shown here), or fashion your own from cardboard
cereal containers covered with pretty papers and trims.
You can even use a drum with an open end for a fresh
flower container. Add other musical instruments, sheet
music, ribbons, or other baubles, and arrange on softly
draped fabric.*

103

10 *On the tenth day of Christmas, my true love sent to me, ten pipers piping.*

Above: Honey Walnut Torte features light layers flavored with ground walnuts and sandwiched with Honey Vanilla Buttercream. Pipers piped a pattern of melted chocolate that contrasts with the buttercream, and crystallized violets flower the top. Serve this lovely dessert with piping hot coffee to follow a fine meal or to solo as a sweet treat when friends gather.

HONEY WALNUT TORTE

¼ cup fine, dry breadcrumbs
1 tablespoon vanilla extract
2 teaspoons grated lemon rind
6 eggs, separated
½ cup plus 1 teaspoon sugar, divided
2 cups chopped walnuts, ground
3 tablespoons red currant jelly, melted
 and divided
Honey Vanilla Buttercream (recipe
 follows)
2 (1-ounce) squares semisweet chocolate,
 melted and cooled
Crystallized violets (optional)

Note: To make ground walnuts light and dry—not oily or pasty—grind in a food processor, using the start/stop technique.

Grease and flour a 15- x 10- x 1-inch jellyroll pan, and line with waxed paper; grease and flour waxed paper. Set aside. Combine breadcrumbs, vanilla, and grated lemon rind in a small bowl; stir well.

Combine egg yolks and ½ cup sugar in a large mixing bowl; beat until thick and pale. Gently fold in breadcrumb mixture and ground walnuts. Beat egg whites (at room temperature) until soft peaks form. Add remaining sugar, and beat until stiff peaks form. Stir ½ cup of beaten egg whites into yolk mixture; gently fold remaining egg whites into yolk mixture.

Pour batter into prepared pan, and bake at 350° for 15 minutes or until cake springs back when lightly touched in center. Cool in pan 10 minutes. Loosen cake around edges, and invert onto a wire rack; remove waxed paper, and cool completely. Cut cake across width into 4 equal strips. Place 1 cake layer on serving platter; spread 1 tablespoon melted jelly on top of cake layer. Spread ⅓ cup Honey Vanilla Buttercream over jelly. Repeat procedure twice, and top with remaining cake layer. Spoon remaining Honey Vanilla Buttercream into a pastry bag fitted with a No. 7 or 8 tip. Pipe in vertical rows, up sides and across top of cake. Using a small spatula, spread buttercream evenly over entire surface of torte.

Spoon melted chocolate into a pastry bag fitted with a No. 2 round tip. Pipe chocolate on top of cake in a decorative pattern. Garnish with crystallized violets, if desired. Yield: 10 servings.

Honey Vanilla Buttercream:

1½ cups unsalted butter, softened
2 teaspoons lemon juice
1 teaspoon vanilla extract
½ cup honey

Cream butter at high speed of an electric mixer until light and fluffy (about 5 minutes). Add lemon juice and vanilla; beat well. Gradually add honey in a thin stream until well blended. Yield: about 2⅓ cups.

11 *On the eleventh day of Christmas, my true love sent to me, eleven ladies dancing.*

Above: Eyes will dance when dinner guests discover the lady's slipper orchid, nature's fairy shoe, in its delectable debut as a favor. This dainty flower is available at many florists' shops during the holidays. Simply place the stem in a water vial or small glass container and set atop a package on the plate.

12 On the twelfth day of Christmas, my true love sent to me, twelve lords a-leaping.

Left: Keep those athletic lords a-leaping throughout the holidays by substituting slimming ingredients for a few fat-laden ones. The calories for this Exercise Lover's Spice Cheesecake are 243 per serving. (A traditional cheesecake has 484 per serving.)

EXERCISE LOVER'S SPICE CHEESECAKE

1 teaspoon margarine
1 tablespoon plus 2 teaspoons zwieback toast crumbs
4 (8-ounce) packages Neufchâtel cheese, softened
½ cup skim milk
¾ cup plus 2 tablespoons firmly packed brown sugar
3 eggs
2 teaspoons pumpkin pie spice
½ cup finely chopped pecans, toasted

Grease an 8-inch springform pan with margarine. Sprinkle bottom and sides of pan with zwieback crumbs; set aside.

Combine cheese, milk, and sugar in a large bowl; beat at medium speed of an electric mixer until smooth. Add eggs and pumpkin pie spice, beating just until blended. Pour into prepared pan.

Bake at 325° for 1½ hours or until firm. Cool completely in pan on a wire rack; chill thoroughly. Remove sides of springform pan, and place cheesecake on a serving platter. Garnish with chopped pecans. Yield: 16 servings (about 243 calories per serving).

A VERY SPECIAL CHRISTMAS DINNER

ORANGE-GRAPEFRUIT CHRISTMAS SALAD
MINTED VEGETABLE SALAD
PINEAPPLE-GLAZED HAM
ROAST TURKEY AND
SPINACH-SAUSAGE STUFFING
BURGUNDY-GLAZED CARROTS
FESTIVE BUTTERNUT SQUASH SAUTÉ
BRUSSELS SPROUTS IN
SHERRIED MUSTARD SAUCE
BROCCOLI IN GREEN ONION BUTTER
CREAMY CHOCOLATE RASPBERRY DESSERT
CRANBERRY SHERBET

For many families, the holiday season culminates in the big family dinner on Christmas Day. The feverish planning is over, and gifts have been lovingly distributed. It is a time to be together, to appreciate each other, and to express thanks. And, yes, it is a time to share a delicious meal, partaking of time-honored foods. This menu includes the traditional turkey *and* the traditional ham (so that everyone gets his favorite meat). There are also savory salads, a variety of spiced and sauced vegetables, and tempting desserts.

ORANGE-GRAPEFRUIT CHRISTMAS SALAD
3 medium grapefruit
4 medium oranges
1 small head romaine lettuce
1 small head Boston lettuce
Creamy Horseradish Dressing (recipe
    follows)

Using a sharp knife and working over a small bowl to collect juices, peel grapefruit and oranges, being careful to remove all white pith. Measure out and reserve 2 tablespoons juice for dressing. Cut the fruit into ½-inch slices; set aside.

Stack 4 to 5 lettuce leaves on a chopping board. Slice the stack into ½-inch shreds. Repeat shredding procedure with remaining lettuce. Place lettuce on a large serving platter. Arrange grapefruit and orange slices on lettuce. Serve with Creamy Horseradish Dressing. Yield: 10 to 12 servings.

Creamy Horseradish Dressing:
Reserved 2 tablespoons citrus juice
1 tablespoon prepared horseradish
¼ teaspoon salt
¼ teaspoon white pepper
¾ cup sour cream

Combine first 4 ingredients in a small bowl; stir in sour cream, and chill thoroughly. Serve with fruit salads. Yield: 1 cup.

MINTED VEGETABLE SALAD
8 small zucchini (2 pounds), cut into
    julienne strips
2 tablespoons olive oil, divided
½ cup minced onion
1 clove garlic, minced
¼ cup white wine vinegar
1 tablespoon dried mint flakes
½ teaspoon dried basil leaves
¼ teaspoon salt
¼ teaspoon pepper
1 (8¾-ounce) can whole kernel corn,
    drained and rinsed
Lettuce leaves
Tomato roses (optional)

Sauté zucchini in 1 tablespoon oil in a large skillet until crisp-tender. Remove the

Opposite: With a spread like this, there may not be room on the plate for the first round of servings. Even so, there are bound to be lots of second helpings. Clockwise from bottom: Orange-Grapefruit Christmas Salad with Creamy Horseradish Dressing, Burgundy-Glazed Carrots, Brussels Sprouts in Sherried Mustard Sauce, Pineapple-Glazed Ham, Festive Butternut Squash Sauté, Roast Turkey overflowing with Spinach-Sausage Stuffing, a side dish of stuffing, and Broccoli in Green Onion Butter.

zucchini from skillet with a slotted spoon, and set aside. Add remaining olive oil, onion, and garlic to skillet; sauté until tender. Stir in vinegar, mint, basil, salt, and pepper; simmer 2 minutes. Remove from heat, and cool to room temperature.

Combine onion mixture, reserved zucchini, and corn in a large bowl; cover and chill 8 hours or overnight.

To serve, transfer the zucchini mixture onto a lettuce-lined serving platter. Garnish with tomato roses, if desired. (Peel tomatoes in a continuous strip and roll peel into flower shape.) Yield: 10 to 12 servings.

PINEAPPLE-GLAZED HAM
1 (8-ounce) can unsweetened pineapple
    tidbits, undrained
1 (10- to 12-pound) fully cooked ham
2 cloves garlic, thinly sliced
1 (4-ounce) package crystallized ginger
    slices, cut in half crosswise
2½ cups Chablis or other dry white wine
1 (16-ounce) jar pineapple preserves
1 teaspoon dry mustard
½ teaspoon ground ginger
Green and purple grapes (optional)
Celery leaves (optional)

Drain pineapple, reserving juice. Trim outer layer of skin from ham, leaving ¼-inch layer of fat. Score fat in a diamond pattern. Make about 20 (2-inch-deep) slits in ham. Stuff slits with pineapple, garlic, and ginger.

Place ham on rack, fat side up, in a large roasting pan. Pour wine over the ham; cover, and refrigerate overnight, basting the ham occasionally.

Insert meat thermometer, making sure it does not touch fat or bone. Bake ham, covered with aluminum foil, at 350° for 2½ hours or until meat thermometer registers 140°. Remove from oven, and cool slightly.

Melt preserves in a small saucepan. Stir in dry mustard, ground ginger, and reserved pineapple juice. Brush surface of ham with preserves mixture.

Bake, uncovered, at 400° for 20 minutes,

basting occasionally with preserves mixture. Transfer ham to a serving platter; cool. Garnish with grapes and celery leaves, if desired. Brush with any remaining preserves mixture. Yield: 20 to 24 servings.

ROAST TURKEY AND SPINACH-SAUSAGE STUFFING
1 (12- to 14-pound) turkey
½ teaspoon salt
½ teaspoon freshly ground pepper
Spinach-Sausage Stuffing (recipe follows)
½ cup butter or margarine, melted
2 cups water
Additional melted butter or margarine
Fresh spinach leaves
Pecan halves
Apple wedges

Remove giblets and neck from turkey; reserve for other use, if desired. Rinse turkey with cold water; pat dry. Sprinkle salt and pepper over surface and in cavity of turkey.

Fill cavity with Spinach-Sausage Stuffing; close skin over cavity with skewers, and truss. Tie ends of legs to tail with string or tuck them under flap of skin around tail. Lift wingtips up and over back so they are tucked securely.

Brush entire bird with ½ cup melted butter; place breast side up on rack in a roasting pan. Pour 2 cups water in bottom of pan. Insert meat thermometer in breast or meaty part of thigh, making sure it does not touch bone. Bake on lowest oven rack at 325° until meat thermometer registers 185° (about 3½ to 4½ hours); baste turkey frequently with additional melted butter. (If turkey gets too brown, cover lightly with aluminum foil.)

When turkey is two-thirds done, cut the cord or band of skin holding the drumsticks, to ensure that insides of thighs are cooked. Turkey is done when drumsticks move easily. Transfer to serving platter; let stand 15 minutes before carving. Garnish with spinach, pecan halves, and apple wedges. Yield: 20-24 servings.

Spinach-Sausage Stuffing:

½ pound bulk pork sausage
2 pounds fresh spinach, torn
½ cup butter or margarine
2 cups chopped celery
1 medium onion, chopped
6 cups crumbled cornbread
1 cup chopped unsalted pecans, cashews,
  or peanuts
½ cup cold water
½ teaspoon salt
1 teaspoon poultry seasoning
½ teaspoon freshly ground pepper

Cook sausage in a large Dutch oven over medium heat until browned, stirring to crumble. Drain, reserving 1 tablespoon drippings in Dutch oven. Place sausage in a large bowl; set aside. Place spinach in Dutch oven. Cook spinach, covered, over high heat

Above: The carving of the holiday roast, a responsibility often passed from father to son, is a job that makes mouths water in anticipation. For best results, allow the meat to cool for at least 15 minutes before carving. To steady the meat while cutting, use a large two-tined fork. The knife blade should be long, flexible, and very sharp. (A sharpener will help.) Carve across the grain of the meat in thin slices. To keep the meat from drying out, cut from one side and slice only as much as needed at a time.

3 to 5 minutes or until spinach wilts. Drain and set aside.

Melt butter in a large saucepan; add celery and onion, and sauté until tender. Add reserved spinach, sautéed vegetables, and remaining ingredients to sausage, stirring well. Spoon into turkey cavity. Spoon remaining stuffing into a greased baking dish; bake at 325° for 30 minutes or until lightly browned around edges. Yield: 11 cups.

BURGUNDY-GLAZED CARROTS

⅓ cup Burgundy or other dry red wine
¼ cup currants
Additional Burgundy
1 tablespoon butter
1½ tablespoons sugar
3 tablespoons lemon juice
¼ cup red currant jelly
2½ pounds baby carrots, peeled and
   steamed

Combine Burgundy and currants in a small bowl. Cover and let stand at room temperature overnight. Drain, reserving Burgundy. Add additional Burgundy to equal ⅓ cup.

Melt butter in an 8-quart Dutch oven; add sugar, and cook over medium heat until sugar melts. Add reserved Burgundy, lemon juice, and jelly. Cook, stirring frequently, until mixture thickens (about 10 minutes).

Add carrots and currants, stirring gently to coat. Cook an additional 10 minutes, stirring frequently, until carrots are glazed. Spoon carrot mixture onto a serving platter, and serve immediately. Yield: 10 to 12 servings.

FESTIVE BUTTERNUT SQUASH SAUTÉ

¼ cup butter or margarine
2 (2-pound) butternut squash, peeled and
   cut into ½-inch cubes
½ cup firmly packed dark brown sugar
¼ cup maple syrup
2 tablespoons water
½ teaspoon grated orange rind
½ teaspoon ground cinnamon
¼ teaspoon salt
1 cup chopped dates
Toasted flaked coconut

Melt butter in a large Dutch oven; stir in squash. Cook, stirring frequently, over medium heat until tender.

Combine next 7 ingredients in a large bowl; stir well. Stir in squash mixture. Spoon into a greased 12- x 8- x 2-inch baking dish. Bake, uncovered, at 350° for 30 minutes. Sprinkle with coconut, and bake 5 additional minutes. Yield: 12 servings.

BRUSSELS SPROUTS IN SHERRIED MUSTARD SAUCE

2 pounds fresh Brussels sprouts, washed
¼ cup butter or margarine, melted and
   divided
½ cup minced onion
¼ cup chicken broth
¼ cup dry sherry
1¼ cups whipping cream
2 tablespoons Dijon mustard
¼ teaspoon freshly ground pepper
½ cup finely chopped walnuts
⅓ cup fine dry breadcrumbs

Cut stems from Brussels sprouts, and slash bottom of each sprout with a shallow X. Cook sprouts in boiling salted water 12 minutes or until tender; drain and place in a 2-quart casserole. Set aside.

Sauté onion in 2 tablespoons butter in a large skillet; stir in broth and sherry. Bring to a boil. Boil until mixture reduces by half. Stir in whipping cream; boil, stirring frequently, until mixture thickens (about 5 minutes). Stir in mustard and pepper.

Spoon mustard sauce over Brussels sprouts. Cover and bake at 325° for 15 minutes. Combine remaining 2 tablespoons butter, walnuts, and breadcrumbs. Sprinkle the breadcrumb mixture over the Brussels sprouts. Bake, uncovered, an additional 5 minutes. Yield: 12 servings.

BROCCOLI IN GREEN ONION BUTTER

3 (1-pound) bunches fresh broccoli
Green Onion Butter (recipe follows)
¾ cup chopped pecans
1 large carrot, peeled and chopped

Trim off large leaves and tough ends of lower stalks of broccoli. Separate into flowerets, leaving 2 inches of stalk attached. Cook broccoli, covered, in a small amount of boiling water 5 minutes or until crisp-tender. Drain and set aside.

Melt Green Onion Butter in a medium skillet over low heat; add pecans and carrot, and sauté until carrot is tender. Combine broccoli and melted butter mixture in a large bowl. Arrange broccoli-carrot mixture on a platter. Serve hot. Yield: 10 to 12 servings.

Green Onion Butter:
½ cup butter, softened
3 green onions with tops, minced (about ½ cup)
1 large clove garlic, minced
¼ teaspoon freshly ground pepper
Dash of hot sauce

Cream butter; add remaining ingredients, beating well. Spoon butter mixture into a small crock or bowl. Cover and refrigerate overnight for flavors to blend. Serve with hot baked potatoes or use to sauté fresh vegetables. Yield: 1½ cups.

CREAMY CHOCOLATE RASPBERRY DESSERT
1 (14.1-ounce) package brownie mix
12 (1-ounce) squares semisweet chocolate
¼ cup plus 2 tablespoons butter or margarine
4 eggs
½ cup sugar
1 tablespoon unflavored gelatin
1½ teaspoons coffee powder
¼ cup water
1½ cups whipping cream, whipped
Raspberry Honey Glaze (recipe follows)
Additional whipped cream
Grated chocolate (optional)

Prepare brownie batter following package directions; spoon into a lightly greased 9-inch springform pan. Bake at 350° for 25 minutes or until done. Cool completely on a wire rack. Cover and refrigerate.

Melt chocolate in top of a double boiler over simmering water. Remove top of double boiler; add butter to chocolate, one tablespoon at a time, beating with a wire whisk until smooth. Set aside.

Beat eggs and sugar in a small mixing bowl until thick and pale. Gradually add chocolate mixture, beating constantly at low speed of an electric mixer until well blended. Combine gelatin and coffee powder in a small saucepan; stir in water. Cook over low heat, stirring constantly, until gelatin dissolves. Beat into chocolate mixture. Let stand until mixture has cooled completely. Gently fold in whipped cream. Pour into brownie crust; cover and refrigerate overnight.

Gently spread Raspberry Honey Glaze over top of chocolate dessert; spoon or pipe whipped cream around outside edge of dessert. Garnish with grated chocolate, if desired. Chill. Yield: 12 servings.

Raspberry Honey Glaze:
2 (10-ounce) packages frozen raspberries in syrup, thawed and undrained
2 tablespoons honey
¼ teaspoon vanilla extract

Process raspberries in blender or food processor until smooth. Press mixture through a sieve, discarding seeds.

Combine raspberry puree and honey in a small saucepan. Bring to a boil; reduce heat and simmer 10 minutes, stirring frequently, or until mixture is the consistency of jam. Remove from heat, and stir in vanilla. Cool to room temperature. Yield: ¾ cup.

CRANBERRY SHERBET
1½ cups cranberry juice cocktail
½ cup orange juice
1⅓ cups sugar
2 cups buttermilk
1 cup whipping cream

Combine cranberry juice, orange juice, sugar, buttermilk, and whipping cream in a large bowl; stir well. Freeze for several hours, stirring 2 to 3 times during freezing process until mixture reaches the consistency of a sherbet.

Scoop sherbet mixture into a food processor fitted with a steel chopping blade. Process just until smooth. Serve immediately or store in an airtight container in the freezer. Yield: ½ gallon.

PARTY DISHES WITH FLAIR AND FLAVOR

In a season when every party hostess presents a bountiful sampling of outstanding taste sensations, you can excel with the dishes featured here. These recipes have rich, exotic combinations of ingredients that your guests are sure to rave about.

APPLE CHEESE WEDGES
½ cup slivered almonds, toasted
2 cups loosely packed fresh parsley sprigs
1 teaspoon dried basil
½ teaspoon salt
¼ cup olive oil
1½ cups (6 ounces) shredded Cheddar cheese, divided
4 ounces cream cheese, softened
2 small apples, cored and cut into ½-inch pieces
2 tablespoons lemon juice
6 English muffins, split and toasted

Position knife blade in food processor bowl. Add toasted almonds; cover, and pulse 6 times or until finely chopped. Add parsley, basil, salt, olive oil, 1 cup shredded Cheddar cheese, and cream cheese to food processor bowl; process about 15 seconds or until smooth.

Sprinkle apple slices with lemon juice, and toss lightly. Spread cheese mixture on English muffin halves. Cut each muffin half into four wedges; place wedges on a baking sheet. Top each muffin wedge with apple. Sprinkle remaining ½ cup shredded cheese over wedges. Broil 3 to 5 minutes or until cheese is melted. Yield: 4 dozen.

Opposite: Party foods simply must be sampled when prepared in appealing and manageable servings and handsomely displayed. Clockwise from bottom right: Apple Cheese Wedges, Feta-Filled Cherry Tomatoes, Dilled Shrimp Canapés, and Bacon-Pepper Breadsticks.

FETA-FILLED CHERRY TOMATOES
2 pints cherry tomatoes
1¼ cups finely crumbled feta cheese
1 (2¼-ounce) can sliced ripe olives, drained and finely chopped
⅓ cup pine nuts, toasted
3 green onions, minced
2 tablespoons olive oil
1 tablespoon capers
1 tablespoon minced fresh parsley
½ teaspoon dried oregano
1 clove garlic, minced

Remove stems from tomatoes, and cut a thin slice from the top of each. Scoop out pulp and discard, leaving shells intact. Invert tomato shells on paper towels to drain; set aside.

Combine remaining ingredients, stirring well. Spoon cheese mixture into tomato shells. Chill until ready to serve. Yield: 4 dozen.

CHEESE AND VEGETABLES IN SPICY LEMON MARINADE
½ pound fresh Brussels sprouts
1 small head cauliflower, broken into flowerets
2 sweet red peppers, seeded and cut into 1-inch cubes
8 ounces cubed Monterey Jack cheese
8 ounces cubed sharp Cheddar cheese
1 (7¾-ounce) can pitted ripe olives, drained
1 (5¾-ounce) jar pimiento-stuffed olives, drained
¾ cup freshly squeezed lemon juice
½ cup olive or vegetable oil
4 cloves garlic, minced
3 dried red chilies, seeded and finely chopped
2 tablespoons sugar
1 tablespoon dried basil
¼ teaspoon salt
Spinach leaves

Wash Brussels sprouts thoroughly, and remove discolored leaves. Cut off stem ends,

115

and slash bottom of each sprout with a shallow X. Place sprouts in a small amount of boiling salted water; return to a boil. Cover, reduce heat, and simmer 10 minutes or until tender. Drain well. Combine sprouts and next 6 ingredients in a large bowl; toss gently. Set aside.

Combine lemon juice, oil, garlic, chilies, sugar, basil, and salt in a small saucepan. Bring to a boil; cook over high heat 1 minute. Remove from heat, and let cool slightly. Pour mixture over reserved vegetables, tossing gently. Cover and marinate 8 hours or overnight, stirring occasionally. Before serving, drain the vegetables and arrange on a spinach-lined platter. Serve with wooden picks. Yield: 11 cups.

DILLED SHRIMP CANAPÉS
2 pounds medium shrimp, cooked and peeled
½ cup butter or margarine, softened
2 (3-ounce) packages cream cheese, softened
¼ cup chopped onion
2 teaspoons lemon juice
2 teaspoons soy sauce
½ teaspoon red pepper
¼ teaspoon dried dillweed
1 (8-ounce) loaf party whole wheat bread
Sliced almonds, toasted
Fresh dill sprigs

Measure out and set aside 37 shrimp. Finely chop remaining shrimp, and set aside.

Combine butter and cream cheese in a medium bowl; beat at medium speed of electric mixer just until smooth. Add reserved chopped shrimp, onion, lemon juice, soy sauce, red pepper, and dillweed, beating until well blended. Cover and chill shrimp mixture 30 minutes.

Spread shrimp mixture on each slice of bread. Garnish each slice with a reserved shrimp, toasted almond, and dill sprig. Arrange on serving platter; cover with plastic wrap, and chill up to 2 hours before serving. Yield: about 3 dozen.

MICROWAVE BACON-PEPPER BREADSTICKS
⅔ cup grated Parmesan cheese
3 tablespoons chopped fresh parsley
1 teaspoon lemon-pepper seasoning
¼ teaspoon paprika
⅛ teaspoon red pepper
1 pound sliced bacon
1 (3¼-ounce) package commercial Italian breadsticks

Combine first 5 ingredients in a shallow container. Dredge one side of each bacon slice in cheese mixture. Wrap bacon slices around each breadstick, cheese side against breadstick. Place breadsticks, 8 at a time, on a microwave rack. Cover with paper towels, and microwave at HIGH for 6 to 7 minutes or until bacon is crisp. Dredge hot breadsticks in remaining Parmesan mixture. Serve immediately. Repeat with remaining breadsticks. Yield: about 2 dozen.

MUSHROOM HAM FRITTERS
6 green onions, chopped
8 ounces fresh mushrooms, chopped
2 tablespoons butter or margarine
½ cup milk
2 eggs, beaten
1 cup minced smoked ham
1½ cups all-purpose flour
½ cup grated Parmesan cheese
2 teaspoons baking powder
½ teaspoon salt
½ teaspoon pepper
Vegetable oil
Chutney Mustard (recipe follows)

Sauté onion and mushrooms in margarine until tender. Let cool. Combine milk, eggs, and ham in a large bowl; beat well. Stir in sautéed vegetables. Add dry ingredients, stirring just until moistened.

Carefully drop batter by heaping teaspoonfuls, a few at a time, into deep hot oil (375°). Fry 2 to 3 minutes, turning once, or until fritters are golden brown. Drain well on paper towels. Serve immediately with Chutney Mustard. Yield: about 3 dozen.

Chutney Mustard:
1 (8-ounce) jar chutney
¼ cup dry mustard
1½ teaspoons ground ginger
1½ teaspoons curry powder
2 tablespoons honey

Insert knife blade in food processor bowl. Combine first 4 ingredients in bowl, and process 1 minute, scraping sides of bowl occasionally. Stir in honey. Yield: about 1 cup.

AVOCADO CRAB APPETIZERS
8 ounces fresh crabmeat, drained and flaked
3 tablespoons freshly squeezed lime juice, divided
1 teaspoon grated lime rind
1 small avocado, peeled, seeded, and mashed
1 small tomato, peeled and diced
1 teaspoon minced jalapeño pepper
¼ teaspoon salt
Dash of red pepper
Toasted Pita Triangles (recipe follows)
Pimiento strips

Combine fresh crabmeat, 1 tablespoon lime juice, and lime rind; toss gently. Set aside.
Combine avocado, remaining lime juice, tomato, jalapeño pepper, salt, and red pepper; stir well. Spoon about 1 heaping teaspoon avocado mixture on each toasted Pita Triangle. Top each with about 1 heaping teaspoon of reserved crabmeat mixture. Garnish with pimiento strips. Serve immediately. Yield: 32 appetizers.

Toasted Pita Triangles:
4 (6-inch) pita bread rounds
⅓ cup butter or margarine, melted

Split pita bread rounds in half to form 8 flat discs. Cut each disc into 4 triangles.

Brush each triangle with butter. Place on ungreased baking sheets and bake at 325° for 12 minutes or until crisp. Yield: 32 triangles.

BLACK FOREST CHEESE TARTS
1½ cups all-purpose flour
1 cup sugar, divided
½ cup cocoa
¼ teaspoon salt
½ cup butter or margarine
⅓ cup ice water
1 (16-ounce) can pitted tart cherries, drained
1 (6-ounce) package semisweet chocolate mini-morsels
2 (3-ounce) packages cream cheese, softened
1 (8-ounce) carton commercial sour cream
4 egg yolks
2 teaspoons brandy
Grated chocolate (optional)

Combine flour, ½ cup sugar, cocoa, and salt in a large mixing bowl. Cut in butter with pastry blender until mixture resembles coarse meal. Sprinkle water evenly over surface, stirring with a fork until dry ingredients are moistened. Shape dough into 1-inch balls. Place balls in ungreased 1¾-inch miniature muffin tins; press on bottom and sides to form shells. Bake at 350° for 5 minutes. Cool slightly.
Place one cherry and ½ teaspoon mini-morsels in each shell. Set aside. Combine cream cheese and remaining ½ cup sugar in a medium mixing bowl; beat well. Add sour cream, egg yolks, and brandy, beating just until well blended. Spoon 2 teaspoons cream cheese mixture into each shell. Bake at 350° for 10 minutes. Chill at least 8 hours or overnight. Garnish with grated chocolate, if desired. Yield: 4 dozen.

Tip: Make ice cubes for a party ahead of time and store them in plastic bags in the freezer. Count on 350 cubes for 50 people or about 7 cubes per person.

CHRISTMAS BREADS

Many people make bread only during the holidays. Then it becomes a ritual of loving creation, from the mixing and kneading of fresh, wholesome ingredients; to the magical rise of the dough; to the heavenly yeasty aroma of loaves, buns, and braids browning in the oven.

GRANOLA RYE BUNS

2 packages dry yeast
1 teaspoon sugar
½ cup warm water (105° to 115°)
2 cups rye flour
¾ cup dark corn syrup
½ cup shortening
2 teaspoons salt
2 cups boiling water
7 cups all-purpose flour, divided
1½ cups granola, divided
1 egg, lightly beaten
1 tablespoon water

Dissolve yeast and sugar in warm water; let stand 5 minutes or until bubbly. Combine rye flour, corn syrup, shortening, and salt in a large bowl. Add boiling water, stirring until shortening melts. Add dissolved yeast and 2 cups flour, mixing well. Stir in enough of the remaining flour to make a soft dough. Turn dough out onto a lightly floured surface, and knead 10 minutes or until dough is smooth and elastic.

Shape dough into a ball; place in a greased bowl, turning to grease top. Cover and let rise in a warm place (85°), free from drafts, 40 minutes or until doubled in bulk. Punch dough down; cover and let rest 5 minutes.

Sprinkle half of granola on a lightly floured surface; turn dough out onto granola, and knead until granola is blended into dough. Sprinkle remaining granola over dough, and continue kneading until blended into dough.

Shape dough into 2-inch balls, and place 4 inches apart on lightly greased baking sheets. Combine egg and one tablespoon water, stirring with a fork until well blended. Brush each bun with egg mixture. Let buns rise, uncovered, in a warm place (85°), free from drafts, 30 minutes or until dough is doubled in bulk.

Bake at 400° for 15 minutes or until lightly browned. Cool completely on wire racks. Yield: about 2½ dozen.

OATMEAL CRACKER BREAD

1 package dry yeast
1 tablespoon sugar, divided
½ cup warm water (105° to 115°)
1 cup all-purpose flour
1 cup whole wheat flour
1 cup plus 2 tablespoons regular oats, uncooked, divided
½ teaspoon salt
2 tablespoons butter or margarine, cut into small pieces
½ cup milk
1 egg, beaten
2 tablespoons butter or margarine, melted

Dissolve yeast and 1 teaspoon sugar in water; let stand 5 minutes or until bubbly. Combine remaining 2 teaspoons sugar, flour, 1 cup oats, salt, and butter in a food processor fitted with a steel chopping blade; process 15 seconds. With processor running, gradually add yeast mixture and milk through feed tube in a slow steady stream. Process 60 seconds to knead dough. Shape dough into a ball; place in a greased bowl, turning to grease top. Cover and let rise in a warm place (85°), free from drafts, 1 hour or until doubled in bulk.

Punch dough down; cover and let rest 5 minutes. Divide dough in half. Place one half on a large, lightly greased baking sheet, and roll into a 14-inch circle. Using a sharp knife, score dough into 16 wedges, being careful not to cut through the dough. (These indentations must remain clearly visible in the dough. If they subside quickly, let the dough rest 5 additional minutes, and score again.) Prick each wedge of dough 2 or 3 times with the tines of a fork. Brush beaten egg over entire surface of dough; sprinkle with 1 tablespoon oats, pressing gently to make them adhere. Repeat procedure with remaining dough, egg, and oats.

Bake at 400° for 15 minutes or until lightly browned and crisp. Remove from oven, and carefully break into wedges along scored lines. Brush melted butter on each wedge, and cool completely on wire racks. Yield: 32 wedges.

CINNAMON BUTTERFINGERS
1 cup butter, softened
¾ cup firmly packed brown sugar
1 teaspoon vanilla extract
2¼ cups all-purpose flour
1½ teaspoons ground cinnamon, divided
¾ cup sifted powdered sugar

Cream butter in a large mixing bowl; gradually add brown sugar, beating until light and fluffy. Add vanilla, beating well. Gradually add flour and 1 teaspoon cinnamon, stirring until well blended. Shape dough into a

Below: Ellen de Lathouder of Birmingham, Alabama, passes on her family recipe for Twist-Top Yeast Bread to daughter Ann Marie. Ellen's great-grandparents immigrated to Chicago from Bohemia, and they brought the recipe with them. When Ellen's mom married an Alabama man, she won over her southern mother-in-law with this pretty and delicious bread. She shared her recipe and, in turn, learned the secrets of successful southern biscuits and cornbread.

disc; wrap well and chill at least 1 hour.

Shape level teaspoonfuls of dough into 2-inch fingers. Place 1 inch apart on ungreased baking sheets. Bake at 300° for 25 to 30 minutes. Transfer to wire racks, and cool completely. Combine powdered sugar and remaining cinnamon, mixing well. Roll cookies in sugar mixture. Yield: about 5½ dozen.

TWIST-TOP YEAST BREAD

1 package dry yeast
½ cup plus 1 teaspoon sugar, divided
¼ cup warm water (105° to 115°)
1 cup milk, scalded
¼ cup butter or margarine
2 eggs, lightly beaten
5 to 6 cups all-purpose flour, divided
1 teaspoon salt
Melted butter
Glaze (recipe follows)
Red and green candied cherries (optional)

Dissolve yeast and 1 teaspoon sugar in warm water; let stand 5 minutes or until bubbly. Combine scalded milk and butter in a large mixing bowl, stirring until butter melts. Add eggs and remaining sugar, stirring with a whisk until well blended. Stir in yeast mixture. Add 2 cups flour and the salt, mixing well. Add enough of remaining flour to make a stiff dough. Turn dough out onto a floured surface, and knead 10 minutes or until dough is smooth and elastic.

Shape dough into a ball; place in a greased bowl, turning to grease top. Cover and let rise in a warm place (85°), free from drafts, 1 hour or until doubled in bulk. Punch dough down; cover and let rest 5 minutes. Turn dough out onto a floured surface, and knead 5 minutes.

Divide dough into 2 equal portions; set one aside. Divide one portion into 3 equal pieces. Roll each piece into an 18-inch rope. Braid ropes together, pinching ends to seal. Carefully transfer large dough rope to a greased baking sheet; set aside.

Pinch off and set aside a 4-inch-diameter ball of dough from reserved portion. Divide remaining dough into 3 equal pieces. Roll each piece into an 18-inch rope. Braid ropes together, pinching ends to seal. Carefully place braided dough on top of larger braid. Gently pinch together the two braided ropes, and brush edges with water to seal. (If the two braids are not pinched together evenly around the edge of the top braid, the bread will be lopsided.)

Divide reserved 4-inch ball of dough in half. Roll each half into an 18-inch rope; loosely twist the two ropes together. Place twisted rope on top of small braid, brushing edges with water and pinching to seal. Let loaf rise in a warm place (85°), free from drafts, 1 hour or until doubled in bulk.

Bake at 350° for 30 minutes or until golden brown. Brush with melted butter, and cool completely on a wire rack. Drizzle glaze on loaf, and decorate with candied cherries, if desired. Yield: 1 loaf.

Glaze:
2 cups sifted powdered sugar
2 tablespoons milk
1 teaspoon vanilla extract

Combine all ingredients, stirring until smooth. Yield: about 1 cup.

CRANBERRY DATE BREAD

1 cup fresh or frozen cranberries, thawed
⅓ cup water
¾ cup sugar, divided
1 (8-ounce) package chopped dates
1 cup chopped walnuts or pecans
1 cup boiling water
⅓ cup shortening
2 cups all-purpose flour
2 teaspoons baking powder
¾ teaspoon salt
1 egg, beaten
1 teaspoon vanilla extract

Combine cranberries, water, and ¼ cup sugar in a small saucepan; bring to a boil. Reduce heat, and simmer 3 minutes or until cranberries just begin to pop. Remove from heat, and cool to room temperature.

Combine dates, walnuts, boiling water, and shortening in a small bowl; stir until shortening melts. Combine flour, baking powder, salt, and remaining ½ cup sugar in a large bowl; make a well in center of dry ingredients. Add cranberry mixture, date mixture, egg, and vanilla, stirring just until moistened. Spoon mixture into a greased 8½- x 4½- x 3-inch loafpan.

Bake at 350° for one hour and 5 minutes or until a wooden pick inserted in center comes out clean. Cool in pan 10 minutes; remove bread from pan, and cool completely on a wire rack. Wrap loaf in plastic wrap, and let stand overnight before serving. Yield: 1 loaf.

CARROT CAKE BREAD
3 cups all-purpose flour
1¾ cups sugar
2 teaspoons ground cinnamon
1 teaspoon soda
1 teaspoon baking powder
1 teaspoon salt
2 cups grated carrot (about 3 medium carrots)
1 cup vegetable oil
3 eggs, lightly beaten
2 teaspoons vanilla extract
Cream Cheese-Orange Glaze (recipe follows)

Combine flour, sugar, cinnamon, soda, baking powder, and salt in a large bowl; stir in grated carrot. Combine oil, eggs, and vanilla in a small mixing bowl; add to flour mixture, stirring just until dry ingredients are moistened. Spoon batter into 2 greased 8½- x 4½- x 3-inch loafpans.

Bake at 350° for 50 to 55 minutes or until a wooden pick inserted in center comes out clean. Cool in pans 5 minutes; remove from pans, and cool completely on wire racks. Place loaves in an airtight zip-top plastic bag, and refrigerate overnight before serving. Drizzle the Cream Cheese-Orange Glaze over the loaves before serving. Yield: 2 loaves.

Cream Cheese-Orange Glaze:
1 cup sifted powdered sugar
½ (3-ounce) package cream cheese, softened
1 tablespoon milk
1 tablespoon orange juice concentrate, undiluted

Combine all the ingredients in a medium mixing bowl; beat at low speed of an electric mixer until the mixture is smooth. Yield: ⅔ cup.

CRISP BLUE CHEESE WAFERS
1¾ cups all-purpose flour
¾ cup finely chopped pecans
8 ounces blue cheese, crumbled
½ cup butter or margarine, cut into ½-inch pieces
2 egg yolks
1 teaspoon pepper

Combine all ingredients in a large bowl; mix with hands until dough is smooth. Divide dough in half; shape each half into a roll, 1½ inches in diameter. Wrap dough rolls in waxed paper, and chill 4 hours or overnight.

Cut dough into ¼-inch slices; place on ungreased baking sheets. Bake at 425° for 10 minutes or until lightly browned. Transfer to wire racks, and cool completely. Store wafers in an airtight container. Yield: about 4½ dozen.

SKILLET COFFEE CAKE
¾ cup raisins or currants
½ cup cream sherry
1¼ cups all-purpose flour
½ cup whole wheat flour
¼ cup firmly packed dark brown sugar
2 teaspoons baking powder
¼ teaspoon salt
¾ cup butter or margarine, divided
¼ teaspoon soda
⅔ cup buttermilk
2 tablespoons honey

Combine raisins and sherry in a small saucepan; bring to a boil. Remove from heat. Cover and let stand overnight.

Combine flour, brown sugar, baking powder, and salt in a large bowl, mixing well. Cut in ½ cup butter with a pastry blender until mixture resembles coarse meal.

Dissolve soda in buttermilk. Add buttermilk mixture and raisin mixture to flour mixture, stirring with a fork just until dry ingredients are moistened. Turn dough out on a lightly floured surface; knead 2 to 3 times. With floured fingers, pat dough into an 8-inch circle. Cut circle into 8 wedges using a floured sharp knife.

Place 3 tablespoons of remaining butter in a 9-inch cast-iron skillet; cook over medium heat until butter melts. Tilt skillet so that butter coats the entire inner surface. Place dough wedges in a single layer in skillet. Bake at 450° for 15 minutes or until golden brown.

Melt remaining 1 tablespoon butter in a small saucepan over low heat; stir in honey. Remove from heat, and brush warm glaze over hot cake wedges. Serve immediately. Yield: one 9-inch coffee cake.

ORANGE-CHOCOLATE PASTRIES
1 (17¼-ounce) package frozen puff pastry sheets
Sugar
1 egg, lightly beaten
½ cup sugar
Grated rind of 1 medium orange
1 (1-ounce) square semisweet chocolate, finely grated

Thaw pastry sheets according to package directions; unfold on a lightly sugared surface. Roll one sheet to a 14- x 12-inch rectangle, and brush lightly with beaten egg. Combine ½ cup sugar and orange rind, stirring until well blended. Sprinkle half of sugar mixture evenly over pastry, leaving a 1-inch margin; sprinkle with half of grated chocolate. Roll up short ends of pastry, jellyroll fashion, to meet in center.

Using a sharp knife or kitchen shears, cut pastry rolls into ½-inch slices. Place slices on lightly greased baking sheets, 2 inches apart. Repeat procedure with remaining pastry, sugar mixture, and grated chocolate.

Bake at 400° for 10 minutes or until lightly browned. Transfer to wire racks, and cool completely. Yield: 2 dozen.

ONION BATTER BREAD
3½ cups all-purpose flour, divided
2 packages dry yeast
2 tablespoons sugar
½ (2.62-ounce) package dry onion soup mix
½ cup milk
½ cup water
½ cup vegetable oil
2 eggs

Combine 2 cups flour, yeast, sugar, and onion soup mix in a large mixing bowl; set aside. Combine milk, water, and vegetable oil in a small saucepan; cook over medium heat until mixture is very warm (120° to 130°). Add to flour mixture, and beat at low speed of an electric mixer until moistened. Add the eggs, and beat for 3 minutes at medium speed.

Stir in enough of remaining flour, using a wooden spoon, to make a stiff batter. Spoon batter evenly into 2 greased 1-pound coffee cans. Let rise in a warm place (85°), free from drafts, 30 minutes or until batter is doubled in bulk.

Bake at 375° for 25 minutes or until golden brown. Cool in cans 10 minutes; remove bread from cans, and cool completely on wire racks. Yield: 2 loaves.

Tip: Sifting flour, unless it's cake flour, is no longer necessary. Simply stir the flour, gently spoon it into a dry measure, and level the top. Powdered sugar, however, should be sifted to remove the lumps.

ONE-DISH MEALS FOR BUSY DAYS

Between shopping and attending special holiday events, it may be difficult to find the time to cook. The solution? One-dish meals. The recipes offered here are hearty and easy to fix, and for quick preparation, there are several microwave conversions.

STUFFED ACORN SQUASH

3 medium acorn squash (about 3¼ pounds)
1 (5¼-ounce) can pineapple tidbits, undrained
½ pound ham, cut into ½-inch cubes
½ cup raisins
½ cup coarsely chopped walnuts
Pineapple-Cheese Sauce (recipe follows)

Cut squash in half lengthwise; scoop out seeds. Place squash, cut sides down, in a baking dish large enough to hold them in a single layer; add water to equal 1 inch.

Cover loosely with aluminum foil, and bake at 400° for 45 minutes or until easily pierced with a fork. Remove from oven, and drain off water. Arrange squash halves, cut sides up, in baking dish; set aside.

Drain pineapple, reserving ⅓ cup juice for Pineapple-Cheese Sauce. Combine pineapple, ham, raisins, and walnuts in a medium bowl; stir well, and spoon mixture evenly into squash halves.

Return to oven, and bake an additional 15 minutes or until thoroughly heated. Serve immediately with Pineapple-Cheese Sauce. Yield: 6 servings.

Pineapple-Cheese Sauce:

1½ tablespoons butter or margarine
1 tablespoon all-purpose flour
½ cup half-and-half
1 cup (4 ounces) shredded Cheddar cheese
⅓ cup pineapple juice

Melt butter in a small saucepan over low

Above: After a busy day, plan a cozy, relaxing supper in front of a warming fire. This tasty Vegetable Corn Chowder takes only about half an hour to prepare, and served with French bread, it's a satisfying meal.

heat; add flour, stirring until smooth. Cook 1 minute, stirring constantly. Gradually add half-and-half; cook over medium heat, stirring constantly, until mixture is thickened and bubbly. Add cheese, and stir just until melted.

Remove from heat; stir in reserved pineapple juice. Yield: about 1⅓ cups.

Microwave Conversion:

Prepare squash as directed above. Arrange squash, cut side down, in a circular pattern on a glass platter (omit water). Cover with heavy-duty plastic wrap, and microwave at HIGH for 13 to 16 minutes, rearranging squash and rotating platter halfway through cooking time. Drain off accumulated juices.

Turn squash, cut sides up, on platter, and spoon ham mixture into squash halves. Re-cover and microwave at HIGH for 1 to 2 minutes or until thoroughly heated. Serve immediately as directed above.

To microwave sauce, place butter in a 4-cup glass measure. Microwave at HIGH for 45 seconds to 1 minute or until butter melts. Add flour, and beat with a wire whisk until well blended. Microwave at HIGH for 45 seconds to 1 minute or until bubbly. Stir in half-and-half; microwave at HIGH for 1½ to 2 minutes, stirring after 1 minute. Stir in cheese, and microwave at HIGH for 30 seconds; stir until cheese melts. Stir in the pine-apple juice.

FETTUCCINE WITH ITALIAN SAUSAGE AND MUSHROOMS

½ pound hot Italian sausage
1 tablespoon butter or margarine
1 tablespoon olive or vegetable oil
1 medium onion, chopped
1 medium-size green or red bell pepper, seeded and cut into ¼-inch strips
½ pound fresh mushrooms, sliced
⅔ cup half-and-half or whipping cream
1 tablespoon Worcestershire sauce
¼ teaspoon freshly ground pepper
½ (12-ounce) package fettuccine, cooked
¼ cup freshly grated Parmesan cheese

Brown sausage in a large Dutch oven, stir-ring to crumble. Drain sausage on paper towels, and set aside. Drain drippings, and wipe out Dutch oven with a paper towel.

Add butter and oil to Dutch oven; cook over low heat until butter melts. Add onion, bell pepper, and mushrooms; sauté until tender. Stir in half-and-half, Worcestershire sauce, and pepper; bring to a simmer. Sim-mer 5 minutes or until liquid thickens. Re-move from heat; stir in reserved sausage. Add cooked fettuccine, and toss gently.

Transfer mixture to a serving platter. Sprin-kle with freshly grated Parmesan cheese, and serve immediately. Yield: 4 servings.

MOROCCAN SHRIMP

2 (14½-ounce) cans tomato wedges, undrained
¼ pound fresh mushrooms, sliced
1 medium onion, diced
3 tablespoons olive oil
2 teaspoons ground cumin
1 teaspoon dried basil leaves
½ teaspoon freshly ground pepper
1½ cups chicken broth
1 pound medium shrimp, peeled and deveined
1½ cups uncooked couscous

Combine first 7 ingredients in a small Dutch oven; bring to a boil. Cover, reduce heat, and simmer 10 minutes. Add chicken broth and shrimp; bring to a boil, stirring oc-casionally. Boil 2 to 3 minutes or until shrimp begin to turn pink. Stir in couscous, and immediately remove from heat. Cover and let stand 5 minutes. Serve immediately. Yield: 6 to 8 servings.

SPINACH SAUTÉ WITH CHICKEN

4 chicken breast halves, skinned and boned
⅓ cup Italian-style fine, dry breadcrumbs
½ teaspoon paprika
¼ teaspoon garlic powder
¼ teaspoon dried basil
¼ teaspoon salt
2 tablespoons olive oil
1 tablespoon butter or margarine
1 pound fresh spinach, torn
1 cup (4 ounces) shredded Swiss or mozzarella cheese

Place each chicken breast half between 2 sheets of waxed paper. Flatten chicken to ¼-inch thickness, using a meat mallet or rolling pin; set aside.

Combine breadcrumbs and next 4 ingre-dients in a shallow dish, stirring well. Dredge chicken pieces in crumb mixture, and set aside. Place olive oil in a large skillet over medium heat. Add chicken, and cook about 4 minutes on each side or until lightly brown. Remove chicken from skillet; keep warm.

Melt butter in a skillet over low heat. Add spinach, and sauté just until tender. Divide spinach in skillet into 4 equal portions. Place a chicken breast half on top of each portion. Sprinkle each portion with cheese; cover and cook 1 minute or until cheese melts. Serve immediately. Yield: 4 servings.

SWEET-AND-SPICY CHICKEN

2 tablespoons soy sauce
2 tablespoons sherry
2 boneless chicken breast halves, skin removed and cut into 1-inch pieces
2 teaspoons peanut or sesame oil
1 red or green bell pepper, cut into ½-inch strips
¼ pound fresh snow peas, trimmed
1 clove garlic, minced
½ cup chicken broth
2 tablespoons firmly packed brown sugar
½ tablespoon cornstarch
¼ teaspoon dried red pepper flakes
2 to 3 cups hot cooked rice
½ cup chopped roasted cashews

Combine soy sauce and sherry; pour over chicken in a small shallow dish. Cover and let stand at room temperature 1 hour.

Drain chicken, reserving marinade. Sauté chicken in oil in a large skillet until lightly browned. Remove chicken using a slotted spoon; set aside. Stir in bell pepper, snow peas, and garlic; cook, stirring frequently, over medium-high heat until vegetables are crisp-tender. Remove from skillet, and set aside.

Combine reserved marinade, chicken broth, brown sugar, cornstarch, and red pepper flakes in a small bowl, stirring well to dissolve cornstarch. Pour into skillet, and bring to a boil. Cook over high heat 1 minute or until thickened, stirring constantly.

Return chicken and vegetables to skillet; cook, stirring constantly, until hot. Serve chicken mixture over rice, and sprinkle with cashews. Yield: 4 servings.

Microwave Conversion:

Marinate chicken as above.

Drain chicken, reserving marinade. Place chicken in a 1-quart casserole; cover with heavy-duty plastic wrap and vent. Microwave at HIGH for 2 to 3 minutes or until done, stirring twice. Remove chicken, and set aside.

Combine bell pepper, snow peas, garlic, and oil in casserole, tossing lightly. Cover with heavy-duty plastic wrap and vent. Microwave at HIGH for 2 to 3 minutes or until crisp-tender, stirring once.

Combine reserved marinade, chicken broth, brown sugar, cornstarch, and red pepper flakes in a small bowl; stir until well blended. Cover with heavy-duty plastic wrap and vent. Microwave at HIGH for 1 to 1½ minutes or until thickened.

Combine chicken, vegetables, and thickened sauce in casserole, stirring well. Recover with heavy-duty plastic wrap and vent. Microwave at HIGH for 1½ to 2 minutes, stirring every 30 seconds, until sauce boils. Serve as directed above.

VEGETABLE CORN CHOWDER

4 slices bacon, cut into 1-inch pieces
1 medium onion, chopped
3 ribs celery, thinly sliced
2 medium carrots, shredded
1½ tablespoons all-purpose flour
1½ cups milk
1½ cups beef broth
½ teaspoon dried thyme leaves
¼ teaspoon dried marjoram leaves
¼ teaspoon salt
¼ teaspoon freshly ground pepper
2 medium boiling potatoes, peeled and cubed
1 (12-ounce) can whole kernel corn, drained

Cook bacon in a large saucepan until crisp; drain on paper towels, and set aside. Reserve 2 tablespoons drippings in saucepan. Sauté onion, celery, and carrots in drippings until tender. Reduce heat to low. Sprinkle flour over sautéed vegetables, and stir until smooth. Cook, stirring constantly, 1 minute.

Stir in next 7 ingredients. Cover and simmer 15 minutes or until potatoes are tender. Stir in corn and bacon; cook over medium heat until hot. Yield: 8 servings.

Microwave Conversion:

Place bacon in a 3-quart casserole. Cover with paper towels, and microwave at HIGH for 5 minutes or until crisp. Drain bacon on paper towels, and set aside. Reserve 2 tablespoons of drippings in casserole. Stir in onion, celery, and carrots; cover with heavy-duty plastic wrap and vent. Microwave at HIGH for 3 to 4 minutes or until vegetables are tender. Sprinkle flour over vegetables and stir until smooth. Add next 7 ingredients, stirring well. Microwave, uncovered, at HIGH for 10 to 12 minutes or until potatoes are tender, stirring every 3 minutes.

Stir in corn and reserved bacon; microwave at HIGH for 1 to 2 minutes or until thoroughly heated. Let stand 5 to 10 minutes before serving.

QUICK-BAKE FLOUNDER AND VEGETABLES
2 tablespoons butter or margarine
8 ounces fresh mushrooms, sliced
4 carrots, thinly sliced
4 green onions, chopped
2 cloves garlic, minced
4 (4-ounce) flounder fillets
¼ cup whipping cream or half-and-half
¼ cup freshly squeezed lemon juice
1 (2-ounce) jar diced pimiento, drained
¼ teaspoon salt
½ teaspoon freshly ground pepper

Cut four 15- x 12-inch pieces of aluminum foil. Fold in half lengthwise, creasing firmly. Unfold foil. Set aside.

Heat butter in a large skillet over medium-high heat. Add mushrooms, carrots, green onions, and garlic; sauté until crisp-tender. Remove vegetables from skillet, and arrange on one half of each foil sheet near the crease. Place a fillet over vegetables on each sheet; set aside.

Add cream, lemon juice, pimiento, salt, and pepper to skillet; bring to a boil. Cook over high heat, stirring frequently, 5 minutes or until mixture reduces to ⅓ cup.

Spoon cream mixture over fillets. Fold over remaining halves of foil. Pleat open edges together to seal. Place pouches on a baking sheet. Bake at 425° for 15 minutes. Serve immediately. Yield: 4 servings.

ONE-DISH STEAK AND RICE
1 cup regular rice, uncooked
1 (1½-pound) flank steak
2 tablespoons mayonnaise, divided
1 medium onion, chopped
2 medium-size green or red bell peppers, cut into 1-inch pieces
2 cloves garlic, minced
1 cup beef broth, diluted
1 cup beer
1 teaspoon ground thyme
½ teaspoon salt
½ teaspoon freshly ground pepper
¼ teaspoon red pepper
Chopped fresh parsley

Place rice in the bottom of a 2-quart casserole; set aside.

Pound steak to ½-inch thickness with a meat mallet or rolling pin. Slice diagonally across the grain into ¼-inch-thick slices. Set aside.

Place 1 tablespoon mayonnaise in a large skillet over high heat. Add onion, peppers, and garlic; sauté until tender. Remove vegetables from skillet. Spoon evenly over rice.

Place remaining mayonnaise in skillet. Add steak pieces to skillet; brown steak on all sides. Remove steak from skillet and arrange evenly over reserved vegetable mixture; reserve pan drippings. Add beef broth, beer, thyme, salt, and pepper to reserved pan drippings. Bring to a boil. Pour beef broth mixture over steak pieces. Cover; bake at 350° for 1 hour or until steak is tender. Sprinkle with parsley. Yield: 6 servings.

PATTERNS

CHUBBY POM-POM SANTA

Instructions are on page 54. Patterns are full-size. Patterns include a ¼" seam allowance.

BOOT
Cut 4.

Leave open for stuffing.

MITTENS
Cut 2; reverse and cut 2.

HEAD
Cut 2.

Nose

Beard Line

Leave open for stuffing.

CAP
Cut 2.

128

Top

Place on fold.

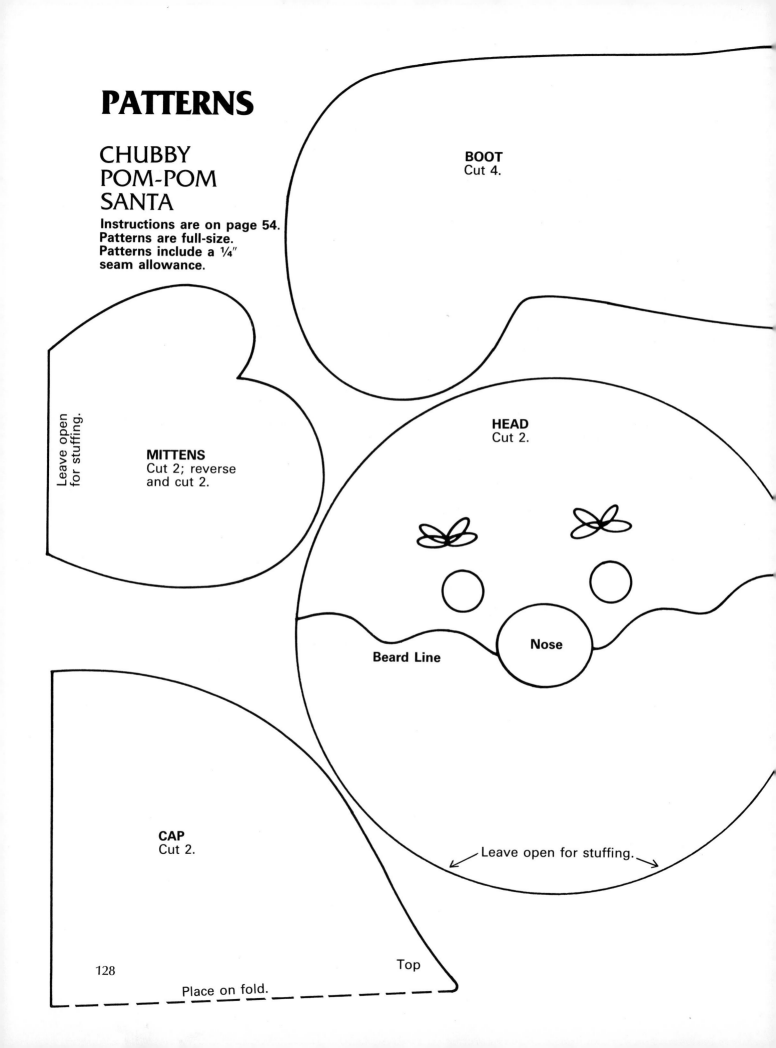

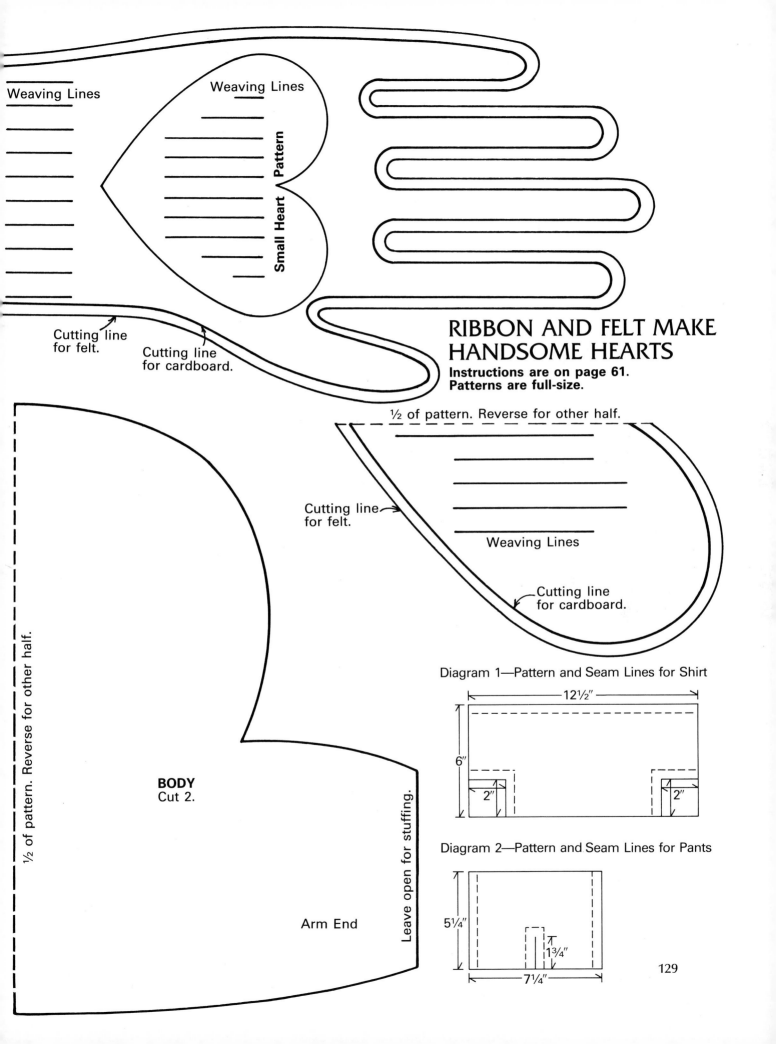

Weaving Lines

Weaving Lines

Small Heart Pattern

Cutting line for felt.

Cutting line for cardboard.

RIBBON AND FELT MAKE HANDSOME HEARTS

Instructions are on page 61.
Patterns are full-size.

½ of pattern. Reverse for other half.

Cutting line for felt.

Weaving Lines

Cutting line for cardboard.

Diagram 1—Pattern and Seam Lines for Shirt

12½″

6″

2″

2″

Diagram 2—Pattern and Seam Lines for Pants

5¼″

1¾″

7¼″

½ of pattern. Reverse for other half.

BODY
Cut 2.

Arm End

Leave open for stuffing.

129

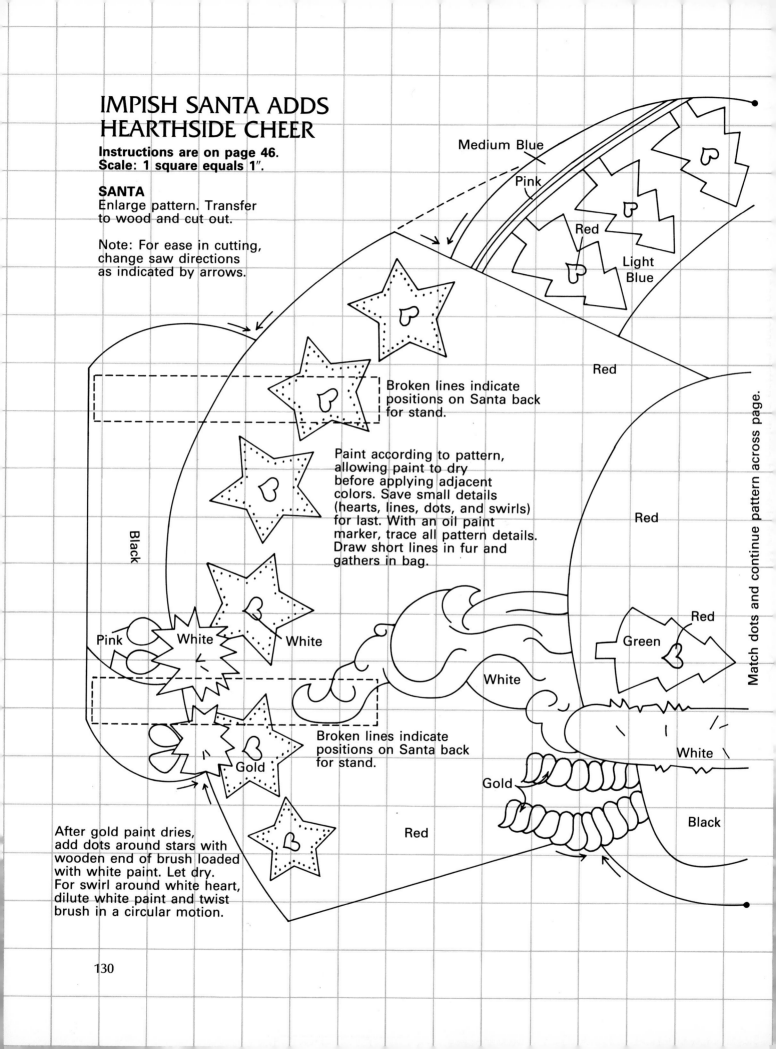

IMPISH SANTA ADDS HEARTHSIDE CHEER

Instructions are on page 46.
Scale: 1 square equals 1".

SANTA
Enlarge pattern. Transfer to wood and cut out.

Note: For ease in cutting, change saw directions as indicated by arrows.

Medium Blue

Pink

Red

Light Blue

Red

Broken lines indicate positions on Santa back for stand.

Paint according to pattern, allowing paint to dry before applying adjacent colors. Save small details (hearts, lines, dots, and swirls) for last. With an oil paint marker, trace all pattern details. Draw short lines in fur and gathers in bag.

Black

Red

Red

Green

Red

Pink   White   White

White

White

Gold

Gold

Broken lines indicate positions on Santa back for stand.

Black

After gold paint dries, add dots around stars with wooden end of brush loaded with white paint. Let dry. For swirl around white heart, dilute white paint and twist brush in a circular motion.

Red

Match dots and continue pattern across page.

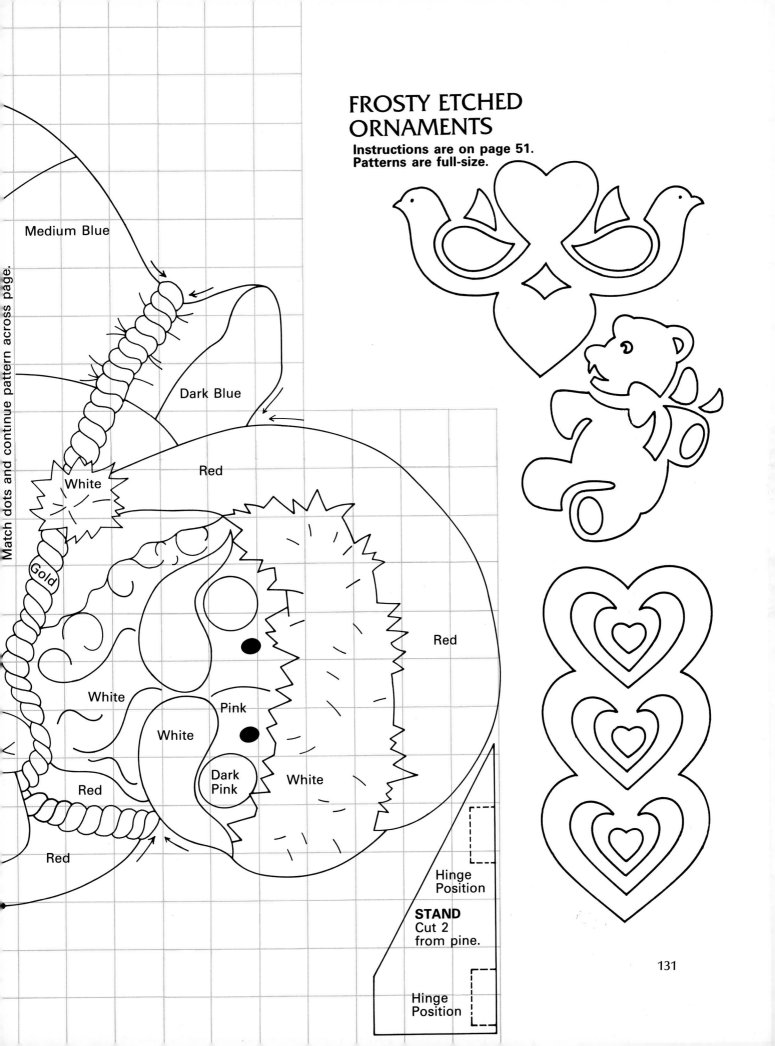

FROSTY ETCHED ORNAMENTS
Instructions are on page 51.
Patterns are full-size.

Match dots and continue pattern across page.

Medium Blue

Dark Blue

White

Red

Gold

White

Red

White

Pink

White

Dark Pink

White

Red

Red

Red

Hinge
Position

STAND
Cut 2
from pine.

Hinge
Position

131

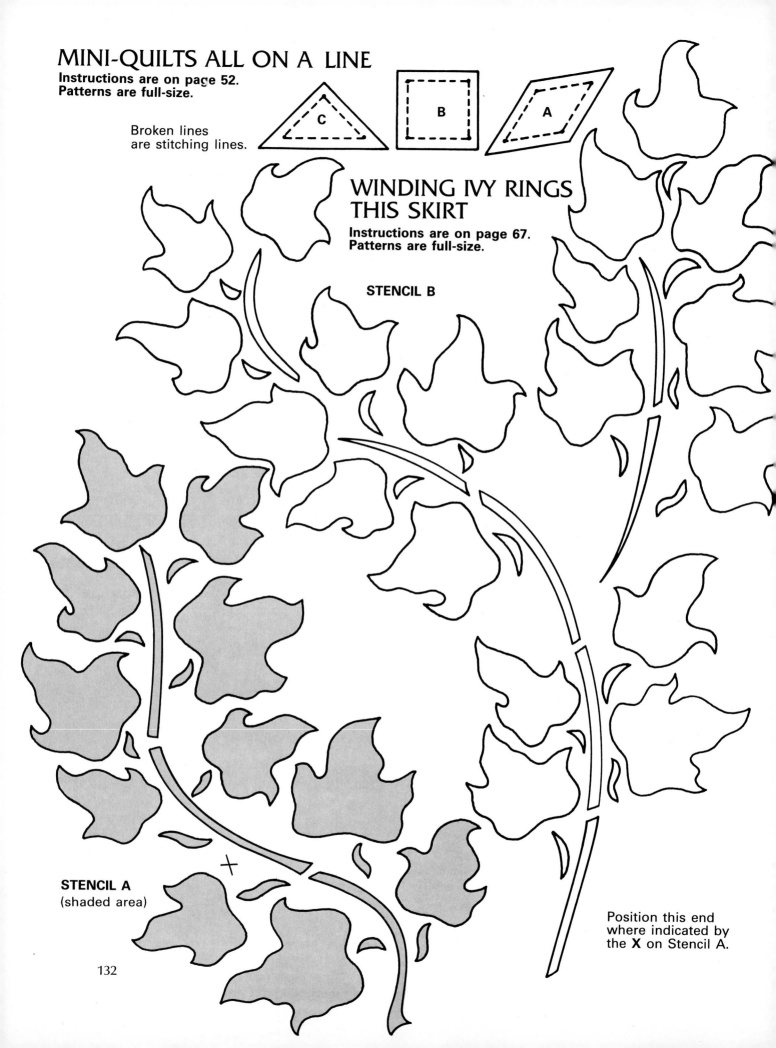

MINI-QUILTS ALL ON A LINE
Instructions are on page 52.
Patterns are full-size.

Broken lines
are stitching lines.

C

B

A

WINDING IVY RINGS
THIS SKIRT
Instructions are on page 67.
Patterns are full-size.

STENCIL B

STENCIL A
(shaded area)

Position this end
where indicated by
the **X** on Stencil A.

132

HOMESPUN STOCKING THREESOME

Instructions are on page 32.
Patterns are full-size.
Patterns include ¼" seam allowance.

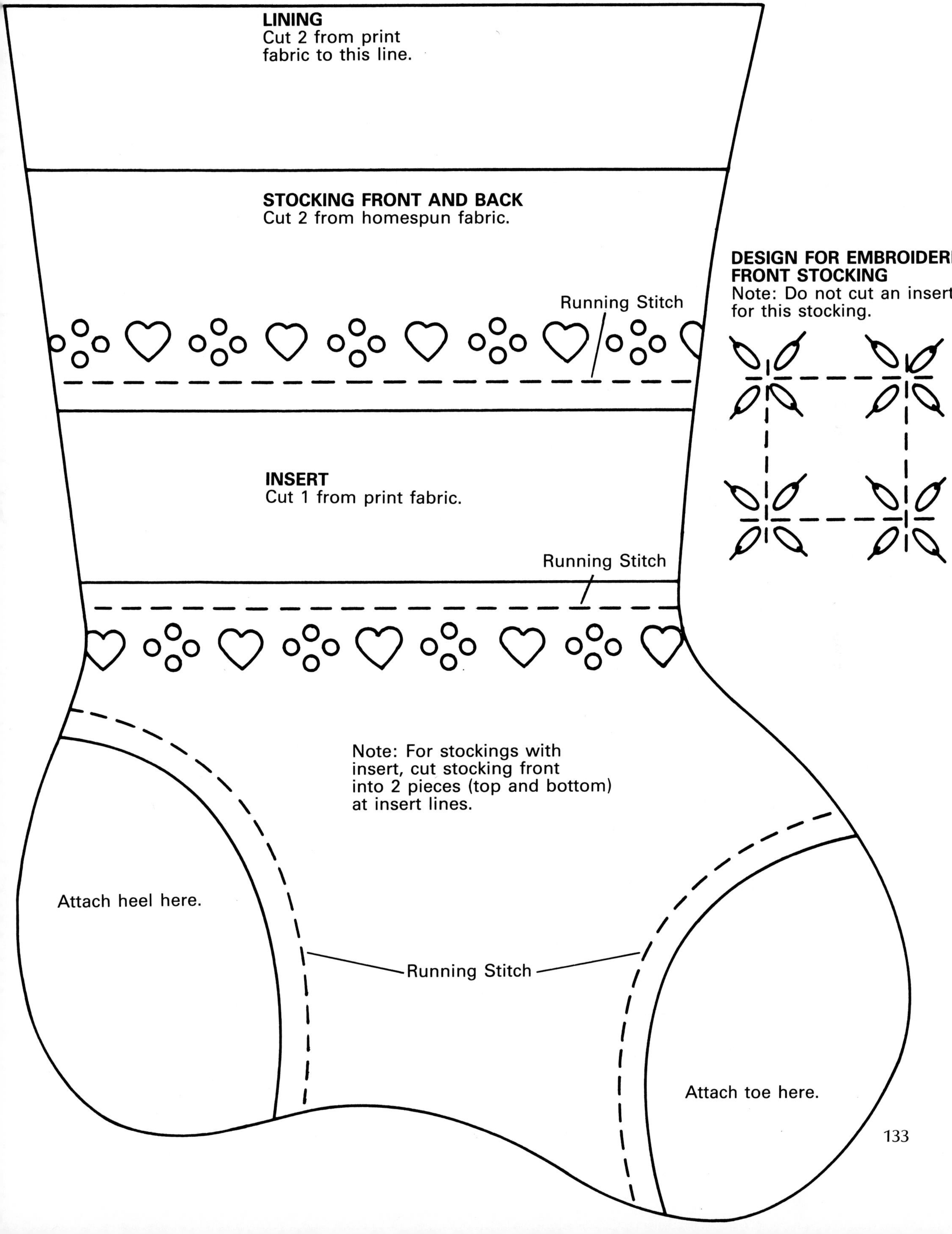

LINING
Cut 2 from print
fabric to this line.

STOCKING FRONT AND BACK
Cut 2 from homespun fabric.

**DESIGN FOR EMBROIDERED
FRONT STOCKING**
Note: Do not cut an insert
for this stocking.

Running Stitch

INSERT
Cut 1 from print fabric.

Running Stitch

Note: For stockings with
insert, cut stocking front
into 2 pieces (top and bottom)
at insert lines.

Attach heel here.

Running Stitch

Attach toe here.

ANGELS IN CROSS-STITCH

Instructions are on page 42.

Color Key
1—pink
2—rose
3—blue
4—yellow
5—flesh
6—gold metallic
7—brown

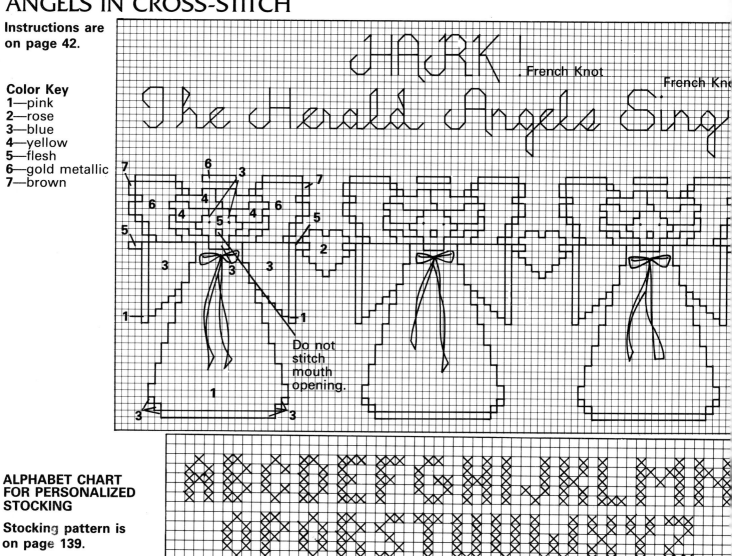

ALPHABET CHART FOR PERSONALIZED STOCKING

Stocking pattern is on page 139.

MAKE THEM FROM SCRAPS

RAGPOINT ORNAMENTS
Instructions are on page 48.

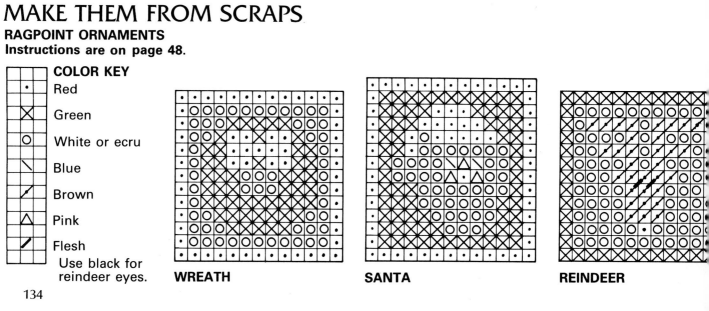

COLOR KEY

•	Red
X	Green
O	White or ecru
\	Blue
/	Brown
△	Pink
/	Flesh

Use black for reindeer eyes.

WREATH   **SANTA**   **REINDEER**

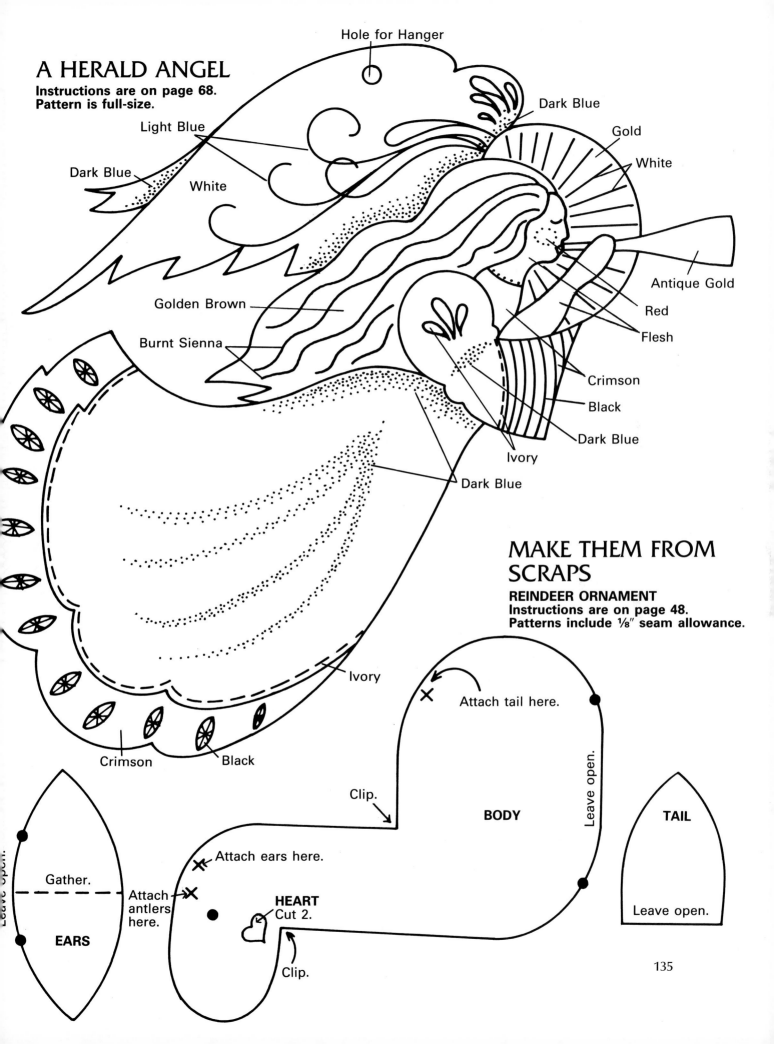

A HERALD ANGEL
**Instructions are on page 68.
Pattern is full-size.**

Hole for Hanger

Dark Blue

Light Blue

Gold

White

Dark Blue

White

Golden Brown

Antique Gold

Red

Flesh

Burnt Sienna

Crimson

Black

Dark Blue

Ivory

Dark Blue

Ivory

Crimson

Black

MAKE THEM FROM SCRAPS

**REINDEER ORNAMENT
Instructions are on page 48.
Patterns include ⅛″ seam allowance.**

Attach tail here.

Leave open.

Clip.

BODY

TAIL

Leave open.

Leave open.

Gather.

Attach ears here.

Attach antlers here.

HEART
Cut 2.

EARS

Clip.

135

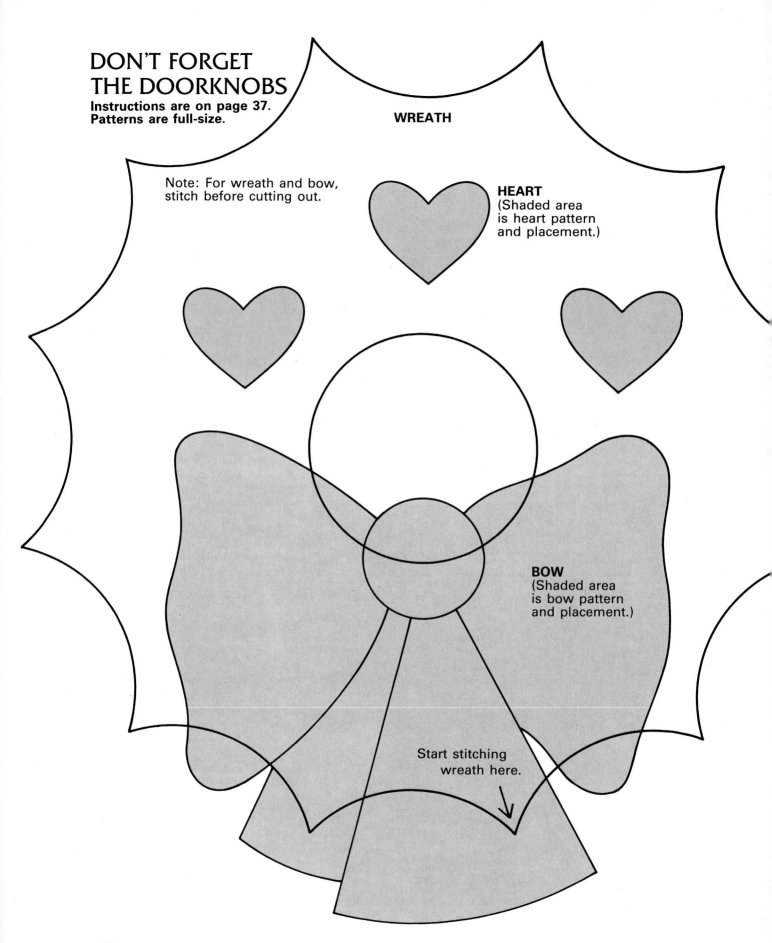

DON'T FORGET THE DOORKNOBS

**Instructions are on page 37.
Patterns are full-size.**

WREATH

Note: For wreath and bow,
stitch before cutting out.

HEART
(Shaded area
is heart pattern
and placement.)

BOW
(Shaded area
is bow pattern
and placement.)

Start stitching
wreath here.

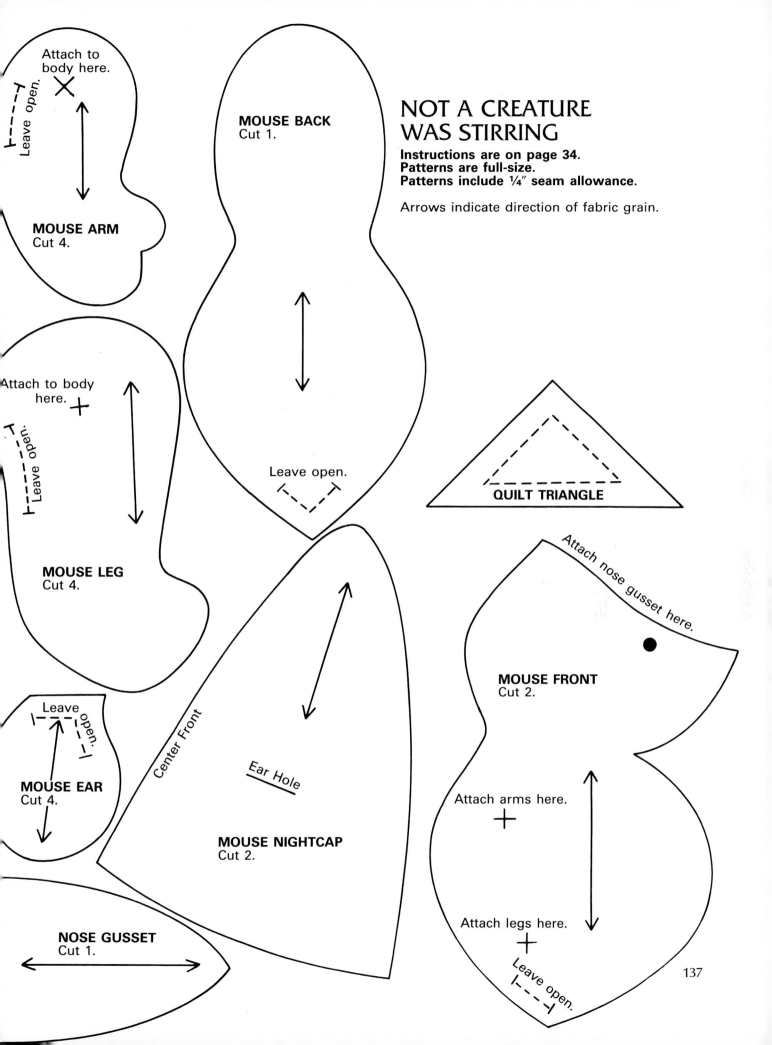

MOUSE ARM
Cut 4.

Attach to body here. X

Leave open.

MOUSE BACK
Cut 1.

Leave open.

NOT A CREATURE WAS STIRRING

Instructions are on page 34.
Patterns are full-size.
Patterns include ¼″ seam allowance.

Arrows indicate direction of fabric grain.

Attach to body here. +

Leave open.

MOUSE LEG
Cut 4.

QUILT TRIANGLE

Attach nose gusset here.

MOUSE FRONT
Cut 2.

Center Front

Ear Hole

Leave open.

MOUSE EAR
Cut 4.

MOUSE NIGHTCAP
Cut 2.

Attach arms here. +

NOSE GUSSET
Cut 1.

Attach legs here. +

Leave open.

137

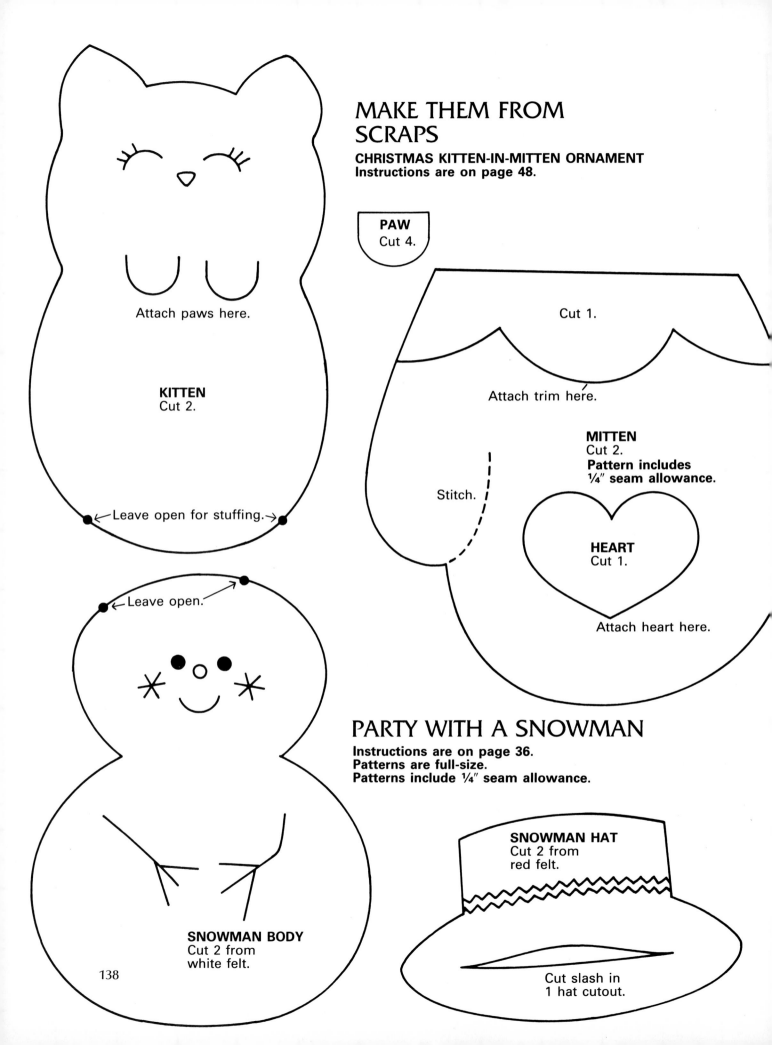

MAKE THEM FROM SCRAPS

CHRISTMAS KITTEN-IN-MITTEN ORNAMENT
Instructions are on page 48.

PAW
Cut 4.

Attach paws here.

KITTEN
Cut 2.

← Leave open for stuffing. →

Cut 1.

Attach trim here.

MITTEN
Cut 2.
Pattern includes
¼″ seam allowance.

Stitch.

HEART
Cut 1.

Attach heart here.

← Leave open. →

PARTY WITH A SNOWMAN

Instructions are on page 36.
Patterns are full-size.
Patterns include ¼″ seam allowance.

SNOWMAN HAT
Cut 2 from
red felt.

SNOWMAN BODY
Cut 2 from
white felt.

138

Cut slash in
1 hat cutout.

For Ribbon Stocking, cut to this line.

For Angels in Cross-Stitch Stocking,
cut to this line.

A RIPPLING RIBBON STOCKING

Instructions are on page 57.
Pattern includes ¼″ seam allowance.
Scale: 1 square equals 1″.

ANGELS IN CROSS-STITCH

**Instructions are
on page 42.
Pattern is full-size.
Pattern includes
¼″ seam allowance.**

139

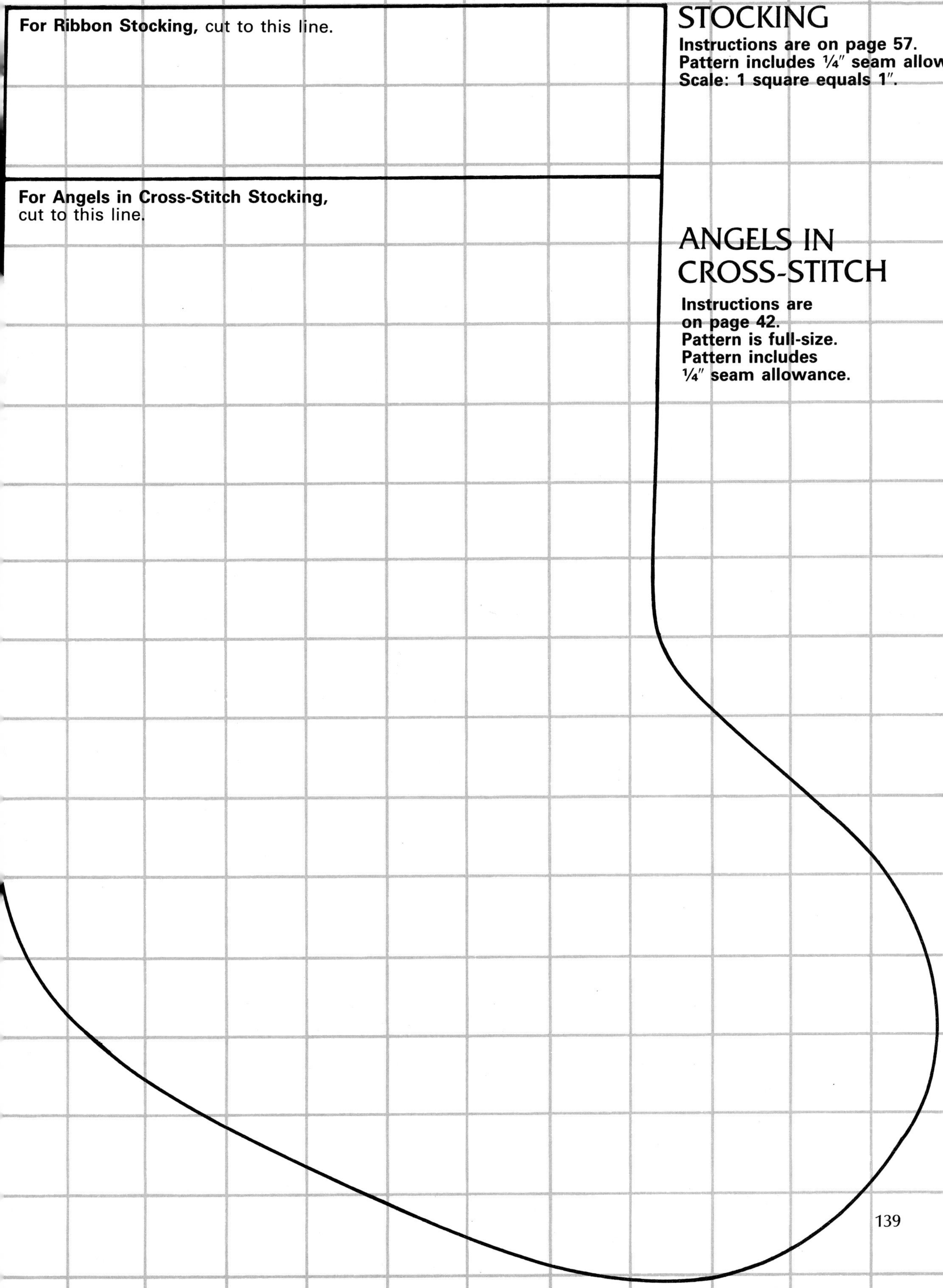

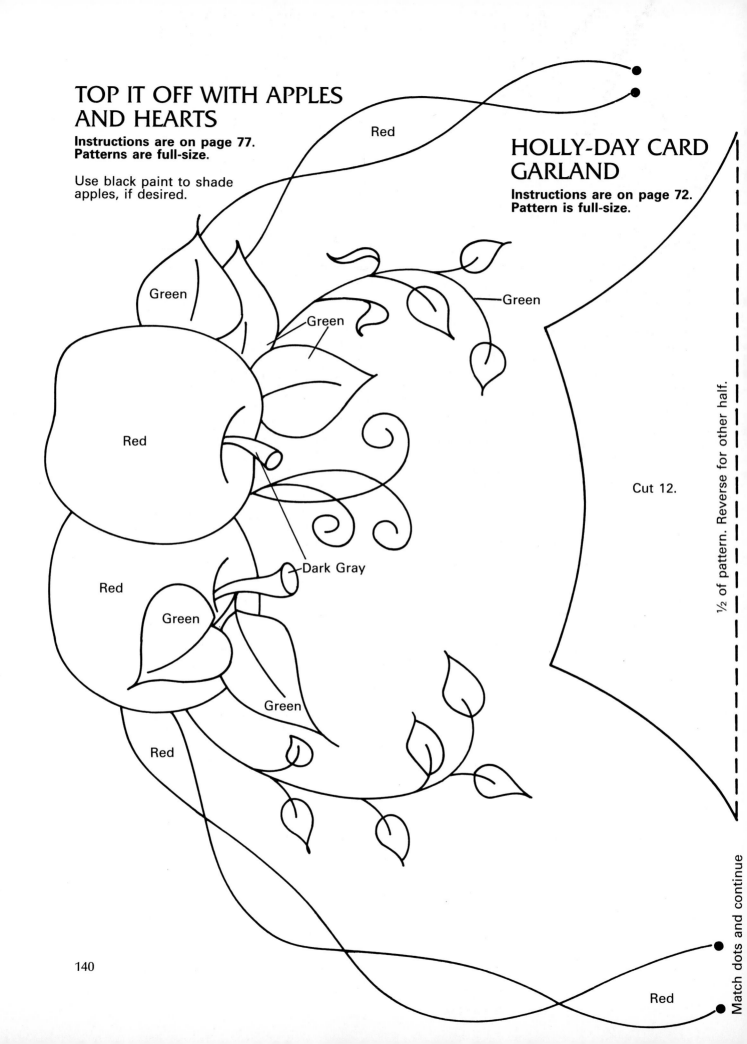

TOP IT OFF WITH APPLES AND HEARTS

**Instructions are on page 77.
Patterns are full-size.**

Use black paint to shade
apples, if desired.

Red

Green

Green

Green

Red

Red

Green

Dark Gray

Green

Red

Red

HOLLY-DAY CARD GARLAND

**Instructions are on page 72.
Pattern is full-size.**

Cut 12.

½ of pattern. Reverse for other half.

Match dots and continue

Red

140

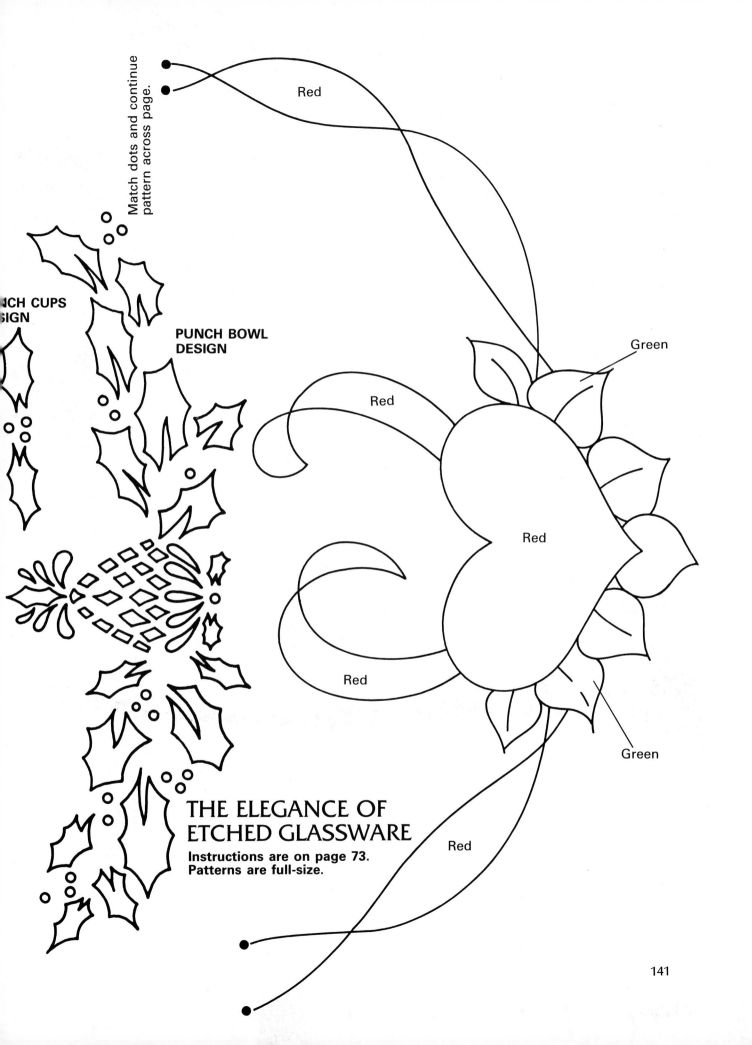

Match dots and continue pattern across page.

Red

NCH CUPS
SIGN

**PUNCH BOWL
DESIGN**

Green

Red

Red

Red

Red

Green

THE ELEGANCE OF
ETCHED GLASSWARE
**Instructions are on page 73.
Patterns are full-size.**

Red

141

KEEPSAKE CHRISTMAS CONTAINERS

Instructions are on page 78.

Color Key

(for all 3 keepers)
Note: Numbers are for DMC floss.

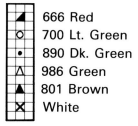

666 Red
700 Lt. Green
890 Dk. Green
986 Green
801 Brown
White

CHRISTMAS QUILT CHART

(Heart 3-Quart Keeper)

Backstitch with red.

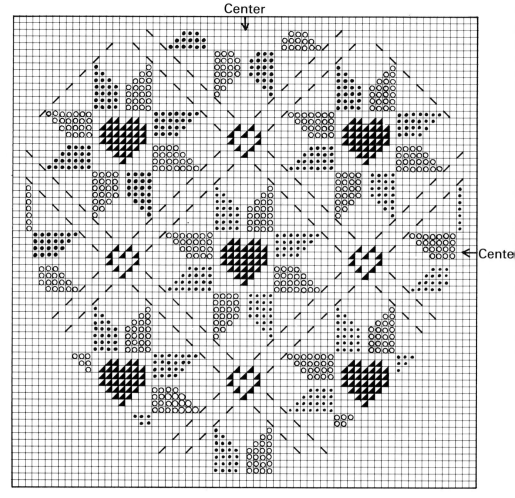

Center

← Center

TO WARM YOU CHART
(Round 3-Quart Keeper)

Backstitch tree trunks with brown, white portions of trees with white, green portions of trees with green.

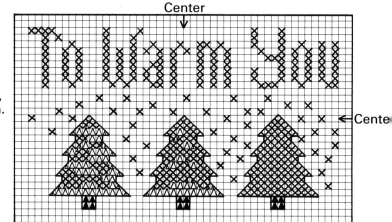

Center

← Center

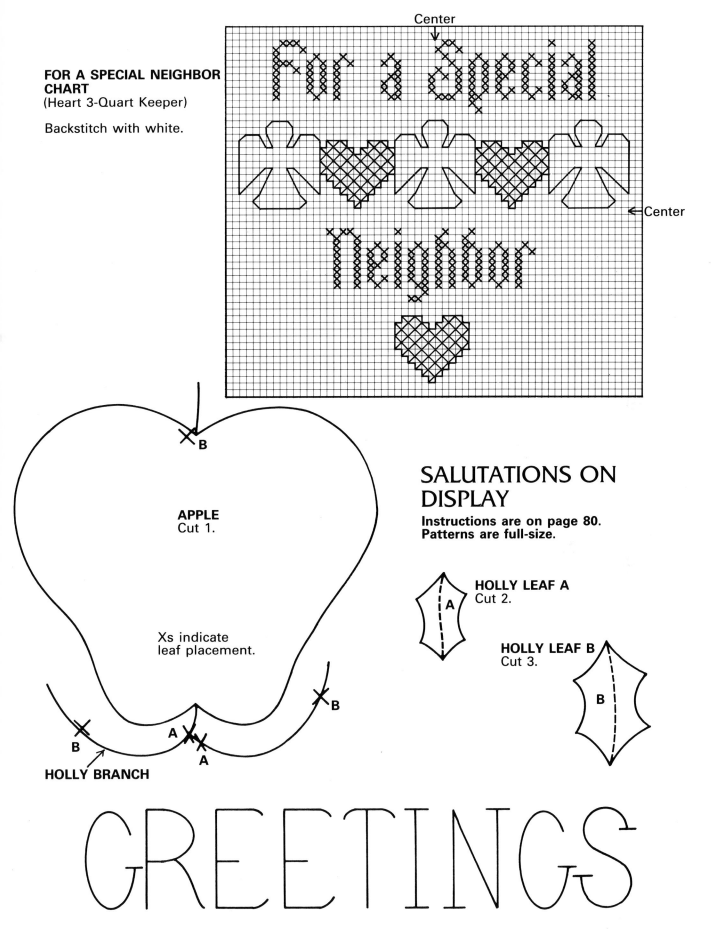

FOR A SPECIAL NEIGHBOR CHART
(Heart 3-Quart Keeper)

Backstitch with white.

Center

Center

APPLE
Cut 1.

Xs indicate
leaf placement.

HOLLY BRANCH

SALUTATIONS ON DISPLAY

**Instructions are on page 80.
Patterns are full-size.**

HOLLY LEAF A
Cut 2.

HOLLY LEAF B
Cut 3.

GREETINGS

143

ANGELIC RAG DOLL

Instructions are on page 85.
Patterns are full-size.

Note: For angel body, legs, and arms, allow 1″ between pattern when transferring to muslin. (Do not cut out.) For sleeve and bodice of dress, ¼″ seam allowances are included.
For skirt, cut a 6½″ x 18″ rectangle.
For neck facing, cut a 1½″ x 3½″ strip.

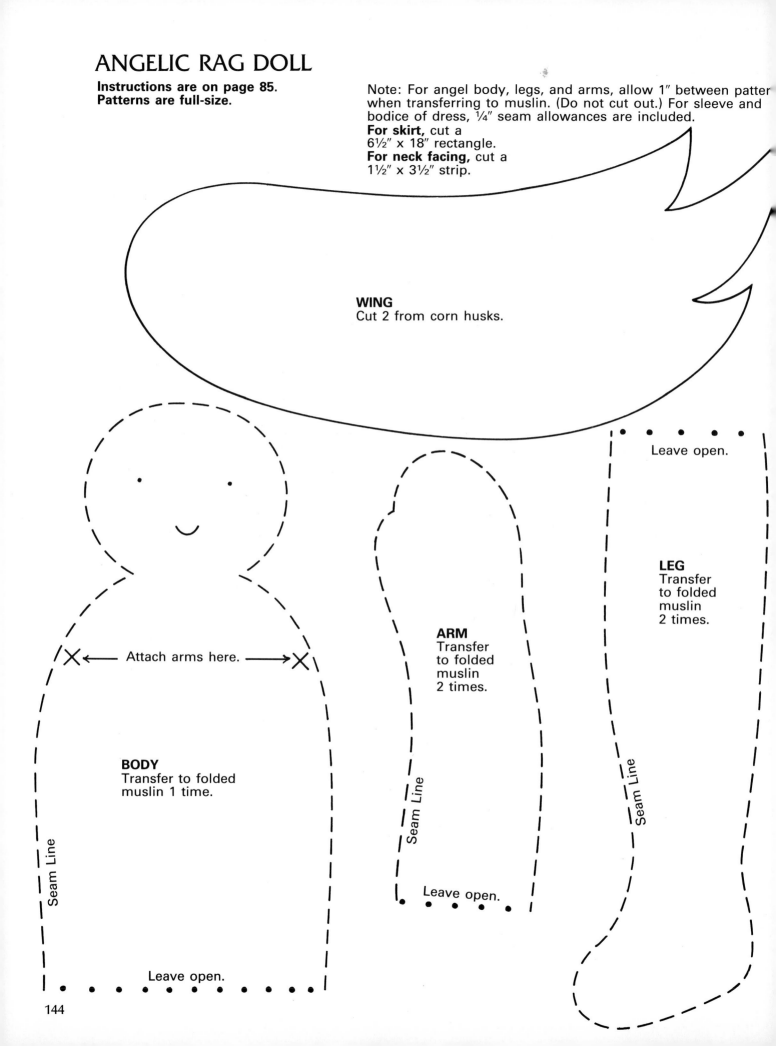

WING
Cut 2 from corn husks.

Attach arms here.

BODY
Transfer to folded muslin 1 time.

Seam Line

Leave open.

ARM
Transfer to folded muslin 2 times.

Seam Line

Leave open.

Leave open.

LEG
Transfer to folded muslin 2 times.

Seam Line

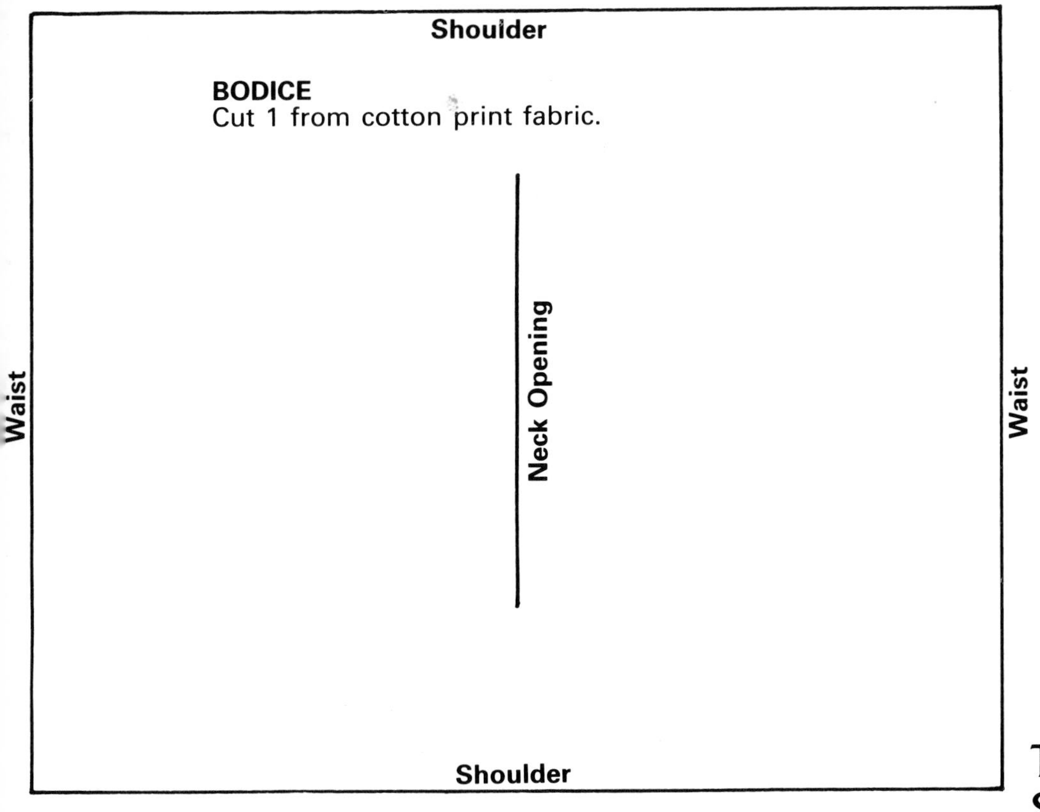

Shoulder

BODICE
Cut 1 from cotton print fabric.

Neck Opening

Waist

Waist

Shoulder

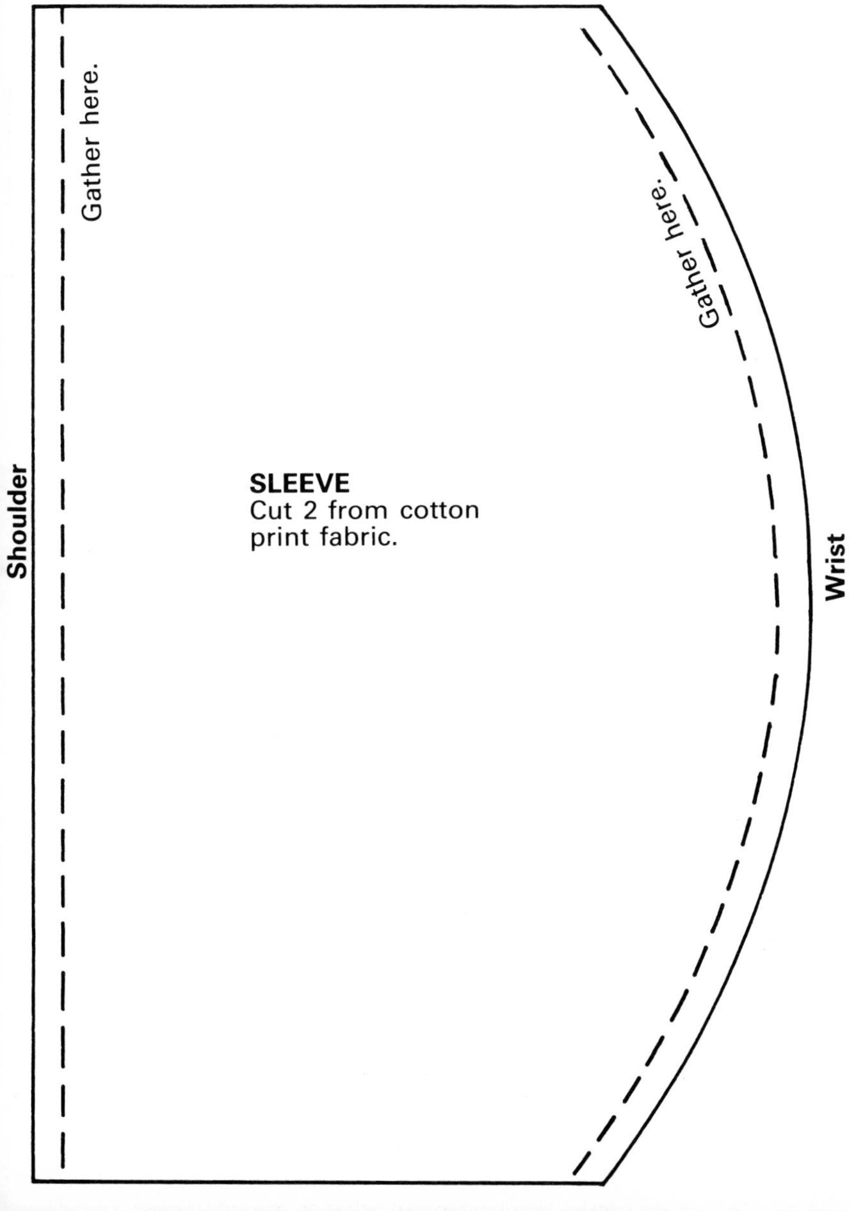

THE KEY TO A SUCCESSFUL BAZAAR

**Instructions are on page 40.
Pattern is full-size.**

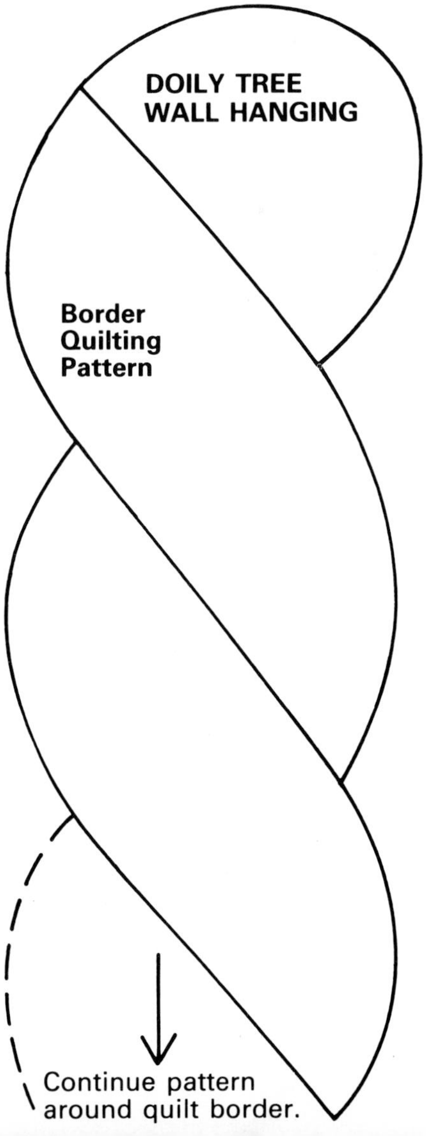

Gather here.

Gather here.

Shoulder

SLEEVE
Cut 2 from cotton
print fabric.

Wrist

**DOILY TREE
WALL HANGING**

**Border
Quilting
Pattern**

145

Continue pattern
around quilt border.

A BIG FAMILY CHRISTMAS IN UTAH

**Project is featured on page 21.
Patterns are full-size.
If desired, enlarge or reduce pattern
for trees in a variety of sizes.**

To paint trees and bases, thin
acrylic paints with water. (Use
2 to 4 contrasting colors as
desired.) Paint all surfaces,
allowing wood grain to show
through. Let dry. Sand lightly
along edges to reveal wood.

TREE
With a jigsaw, cut trees from
1″ pine. Sand.

TREE BASE
With a jigsaw, cut tree bases
from 1″ pine. Sand.

STENCIL PATTERNS
To stencil, cut out designs of
choice from a sheet of plastic.
Stencil designs onto trees, mixing
colors and patterns as desired.

Match dots and continue pattern across the page.

146

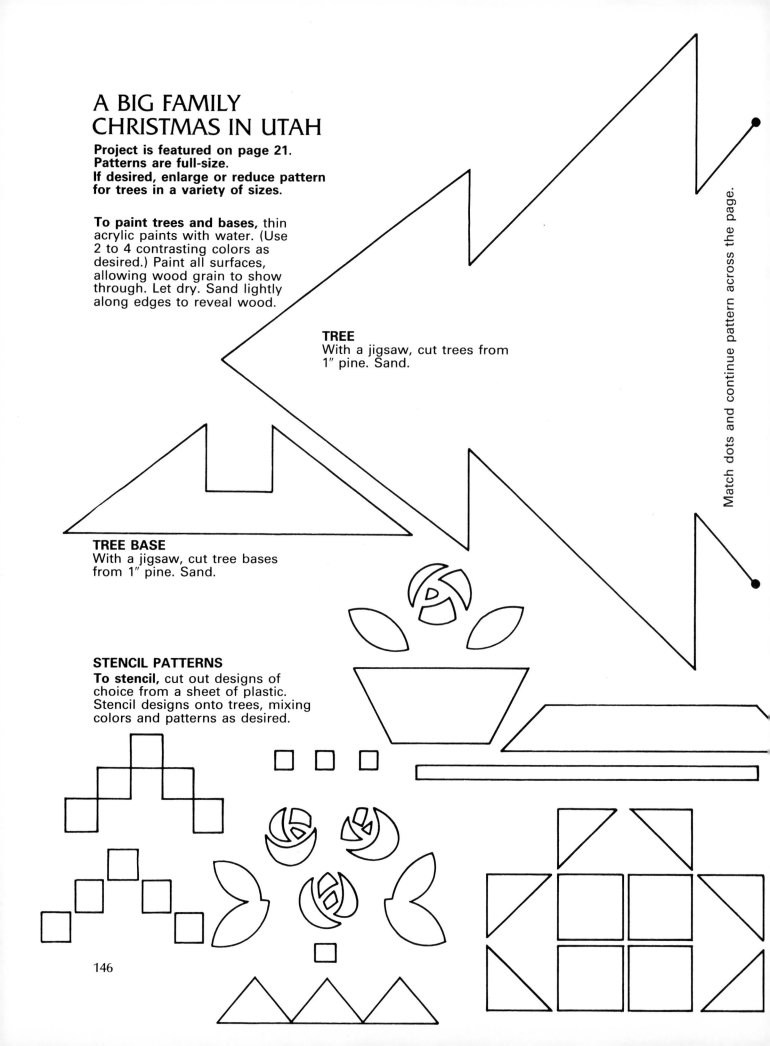

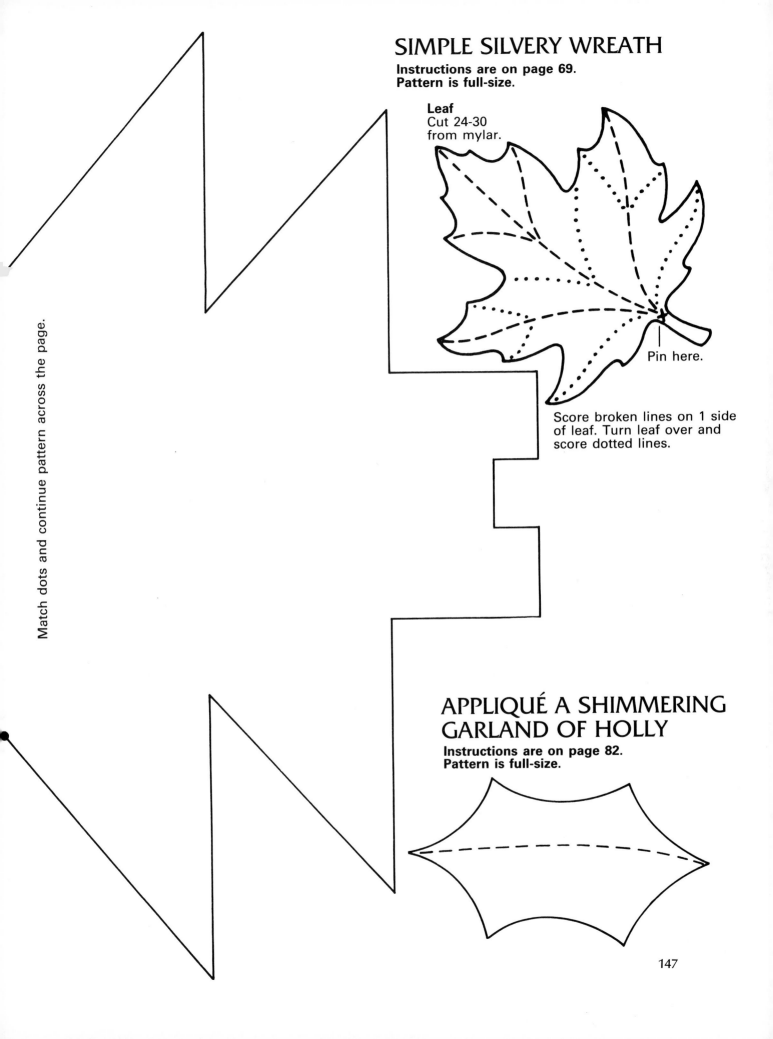

SIMPLE SILVERY WREATH

Instructions are on page 69.
Pattern is full-size.

Leaf
Cut 24-30
from mylar.

Pin here.

Score broken lines on 1 side
of leaf. Turn leaf over and
score dotted lines.

Match dots and continue pattern across the page.

APPLIQUÉ A SHIMMERING GARLAND OF HOLLY

Instructions are on page 82.
Pattern is full-size.

STRANDS OF COUNTRY GEMS

Instructions are on page 83.
Patterns are full-size.
Drill holes where marked with
circles or broken lines.

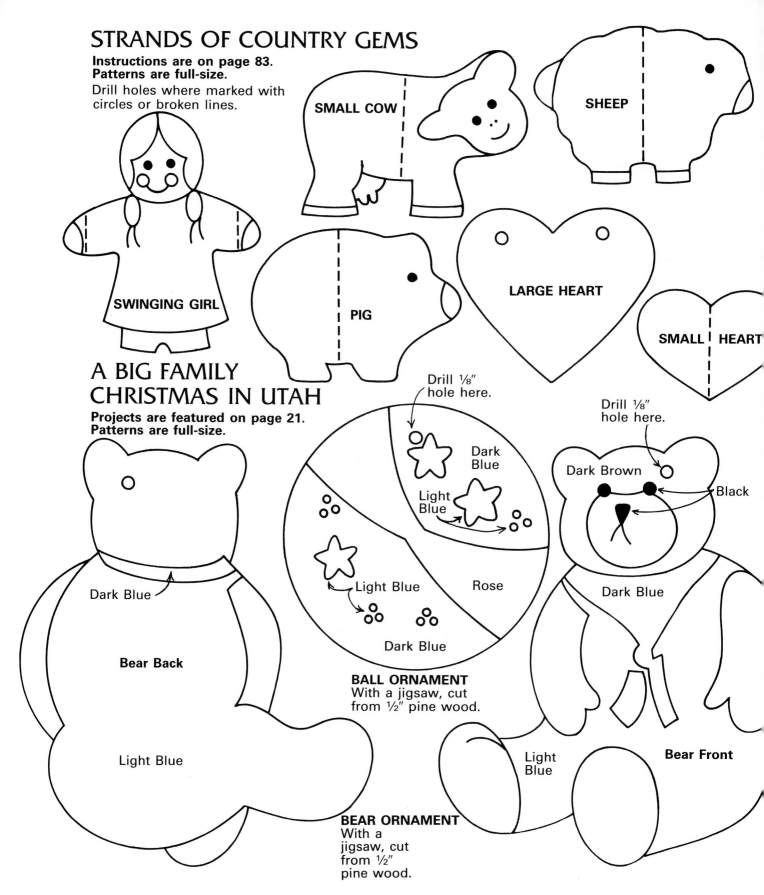

SMALL COW

SHEEP

SWINGING GIRL

PIG

LARGE HEART

SMALL HEART

A BIG FAMILY
CHRISTMAS IN UTAH

Projects are featured on page 21.
Patterns are full-size.

Drill 1/8"
hole here.

Drill 1/8"
hole here.

Dark
Blue

Light
Blue

Dark Brown

Black

Dark Blue

Light Blue

Rose

Dark Blue

Bear Back

Light Blue

Dark Blue

BALL ORNAMENT
With a jigsaw, cut
from 1/2" pine wood.

Dark Blue

Light
Blue

Bear Front

BEAR ORNAMENT
With a
jigsaw, cut
from 1/2"
pine wood.

To paint bears: Sand. Stain all surfaces with mahogany wood stain and let dry. With acrylic paints, paint according to patterns. When dry, sand edges to let wood show through. With liquid embroidery pens, draw face with black; add white details on collar and dark brown details on arms and legs (see photo, page 21).
To paint balls: Sand; then paint details with acrylic paints as indicated on pattern. Sand edges to let wood show through. Add highlights to rose band with a pink liquid embroidery pen (see photo, page 21).

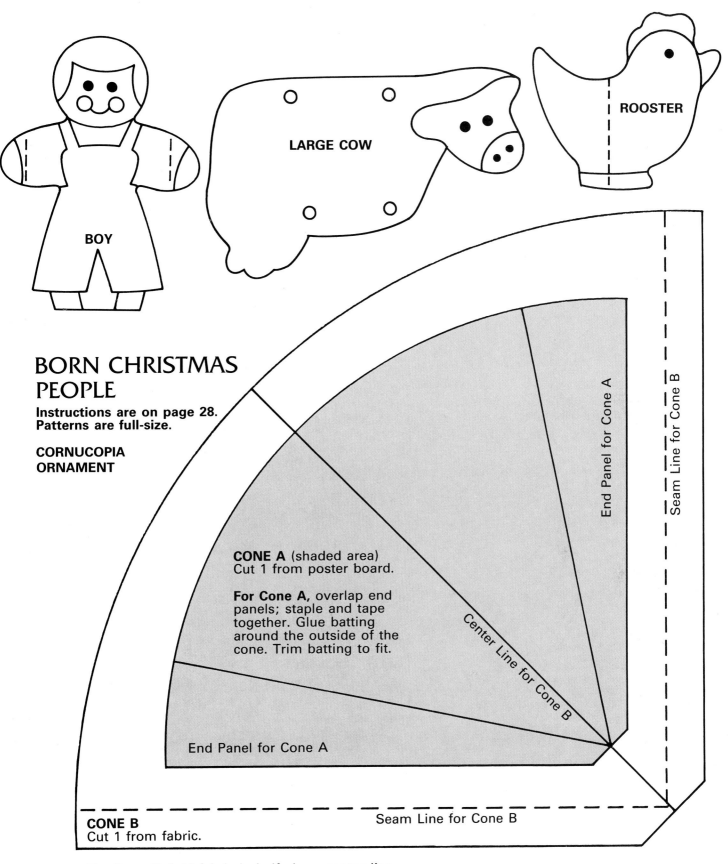

BOY

LARGE COW

ROOSTER

BORN CHRISTMAS PEOPLE

**Instructions are on page 28.
Patterns are full-size.**

**CORNUCOPIA
ORNAMENT**

CONE A (shaded area)
Cut 1 from poster board.

For Cone A, overlap end panels; staple and tape together. Glue batting around the outside of the cone. Trim batting to fit.

End Panel for Cone A

End Panel for Cone A

Center Line for Cone B

Seam Line for Cone B

Seam Line for Cone B

CONE B
Cut 1 from fabric.

For Cone B, fold fabric in half along center line.
Stitch straight edges together with a ⅜″ seam.

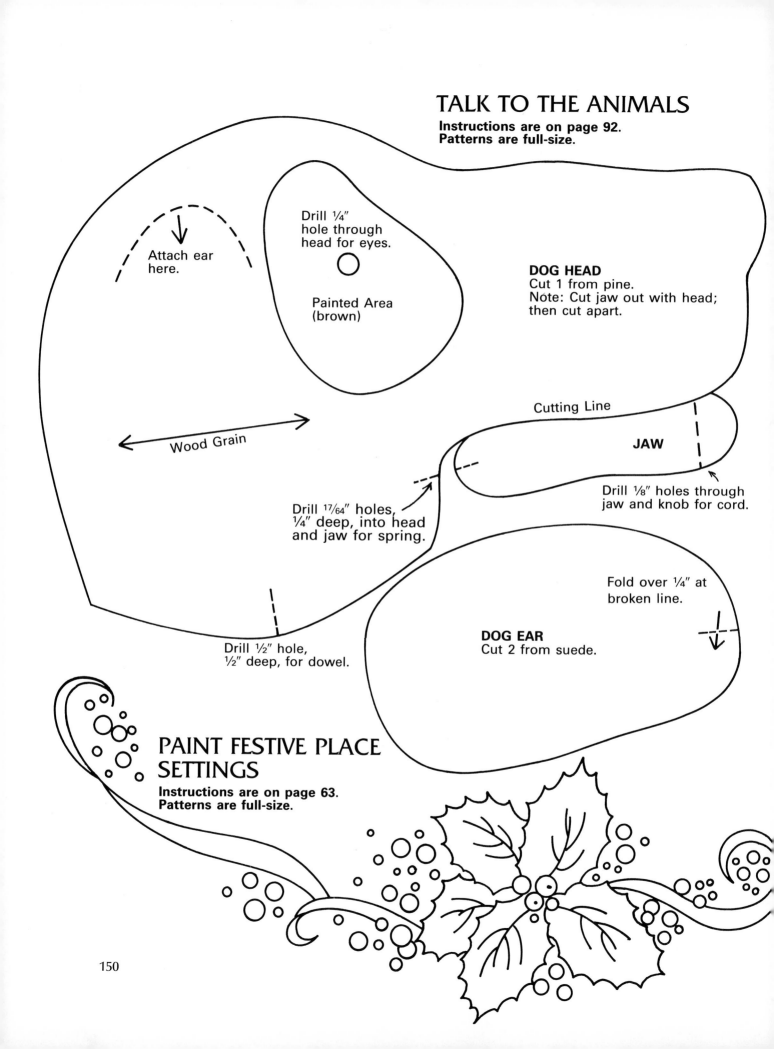

TALK TO THE ANIMALS

**Instructions are on page 92.
Patterns are full-size.**

Drill ¼"
hole through
head for eyes.

Attach ear
here.

Painted Area
(brown)

DOG HEAD
Cut 1 from pine.
Note: Cut jaw out with head;
then cut apart.

Wood Grain

Cutting Line

JAW

Drill ⅛" holes through
jaw and knob for cord.

Drill ¹⁷⁄₆₄" holes,
¼" deep, into head
and jaw for spring.

Fold over ¼" at
broken line.

DOG EAR
Cut 2 from suede.

Drill ½" hole,
½" deep, for dowel.

PAINT FESTIVE PLACE SETTINGS

**Instructions are on page 63.
Patterns are full-size.**

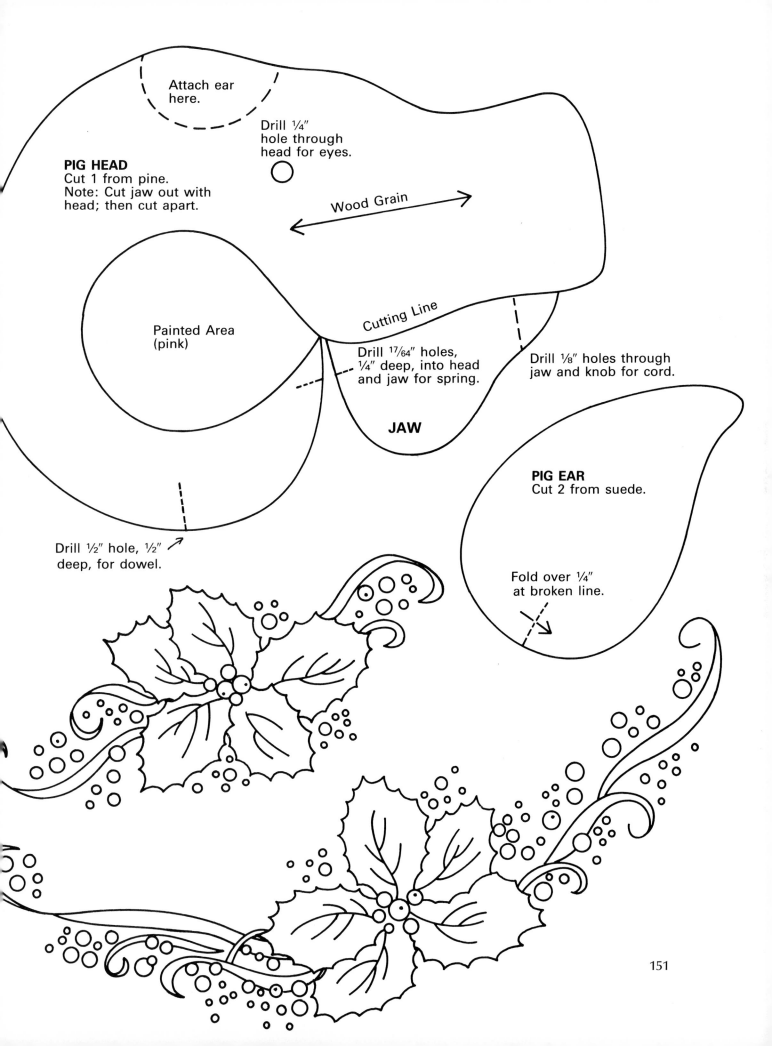

PIG HEAD
Cut 1 from pine.
Note: Cut jaw out with
head; then cut apart.

Attach ear
here.

Drill ¼"
hole through
head for eyes.

Wood Grain

Painted Area
(pink)

Cutting Line

Drill ¹⁷⁄₆₄" holes,
¼" deep, into head
and jaw for spring.

Drill ⅛" holes through
jaw and knob for cord.

JAW

PIG EAR
Cut 2 from suede.

Fold over ¼"
at broken line.

Drill ½" hole, ½"
deep, for dowel.

APRONS FOR CHRISTMAS COOKERY

Instructions are on page 76.

CROSS-STITCH CHARTS

Color Key

Note: Numbers are for DMC floss.

X	666 Red
/	444 Yellow
·	725 Gold
Λ	3326 Pink
O	704 Light Green
◢	701 Dark Green
C	436 Light Tan
•	781 Light Brown
\	433 Medium Brown
■	938 Dark Brown
	414 Gray

For Woman's Apron, backstitch bells and cups with medium brown, steam with gray, and bread slice with dark brown.
For Child's Apron, backstitch straight line of ribbon candy with dark green, dotted line with red, candy wrappers with gray, and gingerbread girl with dark brown.

CROCHET A PILLOW FULL OF TULIPS

Instructions are on page 87.
Crochet Chart

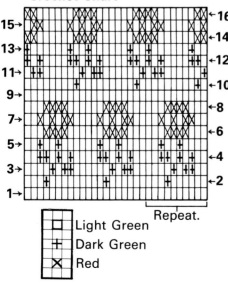

☐	Light Green
+	Dark Green
X	Red

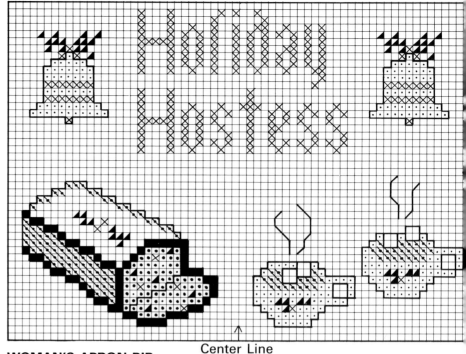

WOMAN'S APRON BIB

Work on 11-count Aida cloth. Design area is 61 squares (width) x 44 squares (height). Use 3 strands of floss to cross-stitch and 2 strands to backstitch.

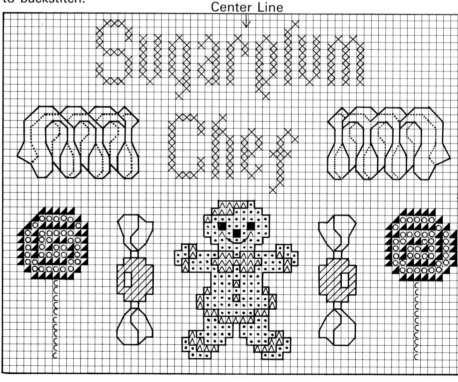

CHILD'S APRON BIB

Work on 11-count Aida cloth. Design area is 61 squares (width) x 47 squares (height). Use 2 strands of floss to cross-stitch and 1 strand to backstitch.

TOP BILLING

Instructions are on page 91.
Patterns are full-size.

Cut out stars along solid lines.
Along broken lines, score on star front.
Along dotted lines, score on star back.

Light Blue

Blue

Blue

Light Blue

PRETTY PASTEL PONY
Instructions are on page 90.
Patterns are full-size.

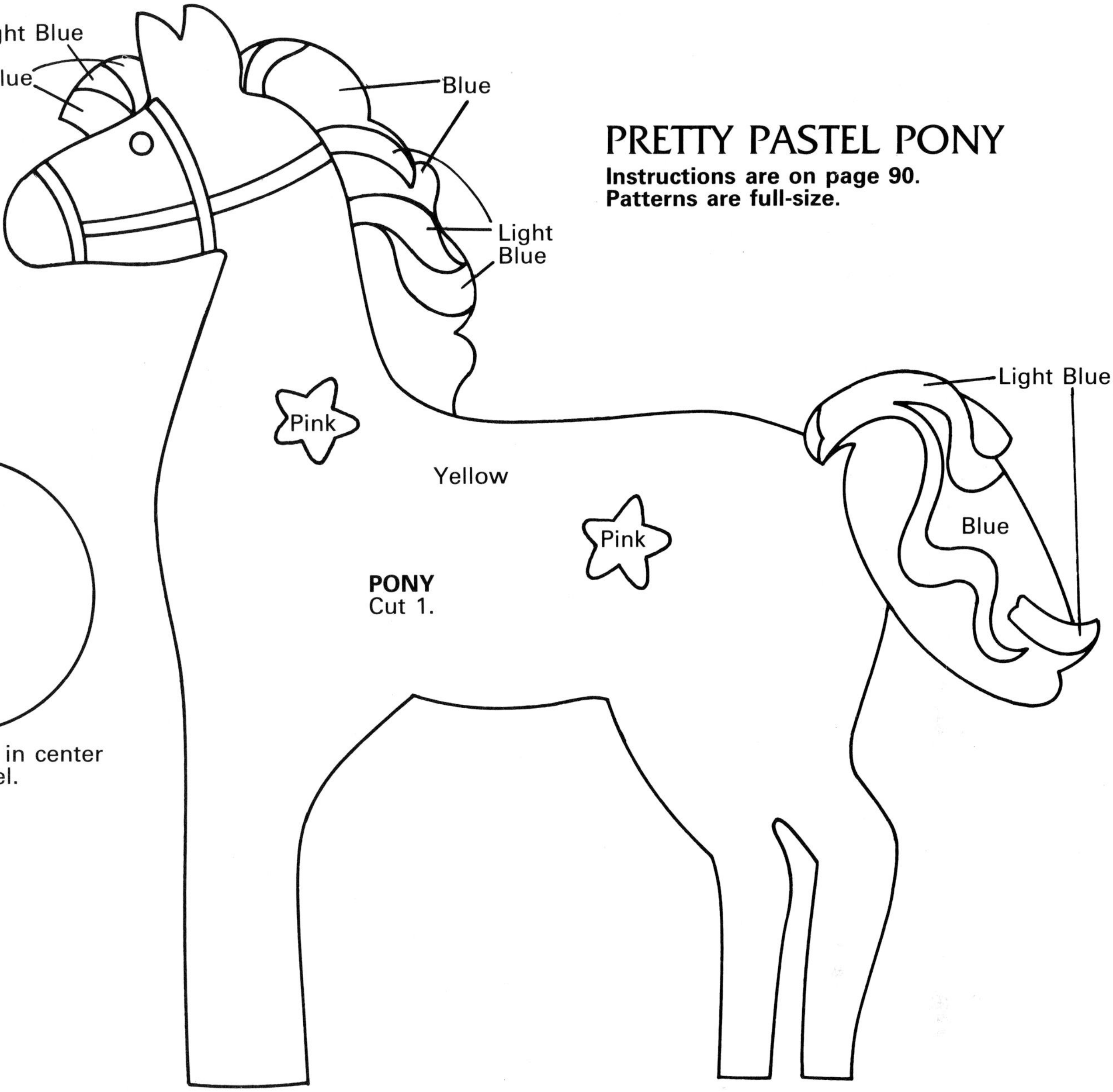

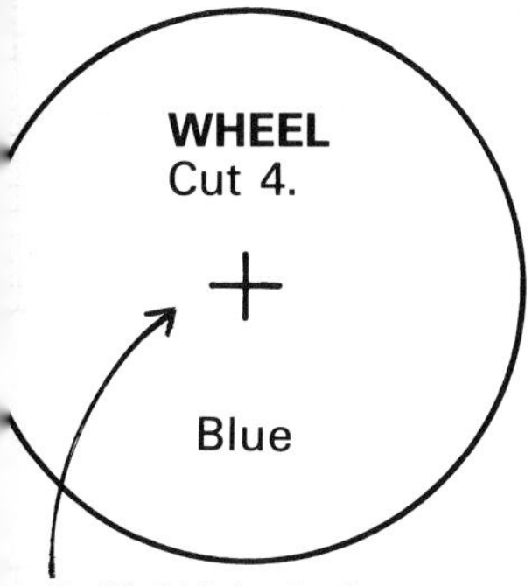

Pink

Light Blue

Light Blue

Yellow

Blue

Pink

WHEEL
Cut 4.

+

Blue

PONY
Cut 1.

Drill ¼" hole in center
of each wheel.

A BIG FAMILY CHRISTMAS
IN UTAH
Projects are featured on pages 22 and 23.
Patterns are full-size.

To stain ornaments, mix 1
package of dark fabric
dye with 2 quarts water. Soak
wooden ornaments in dye. (The wood
grain will show through the dye.)
Let ornaments dry overnight.

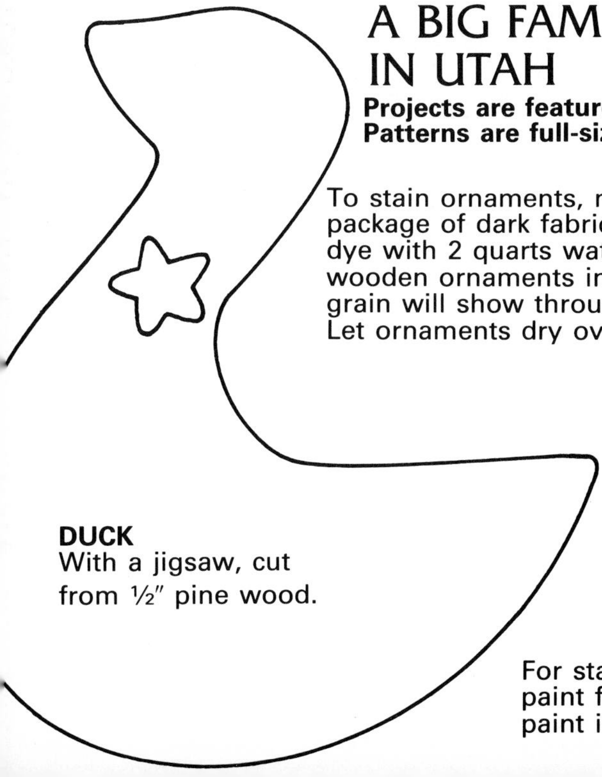

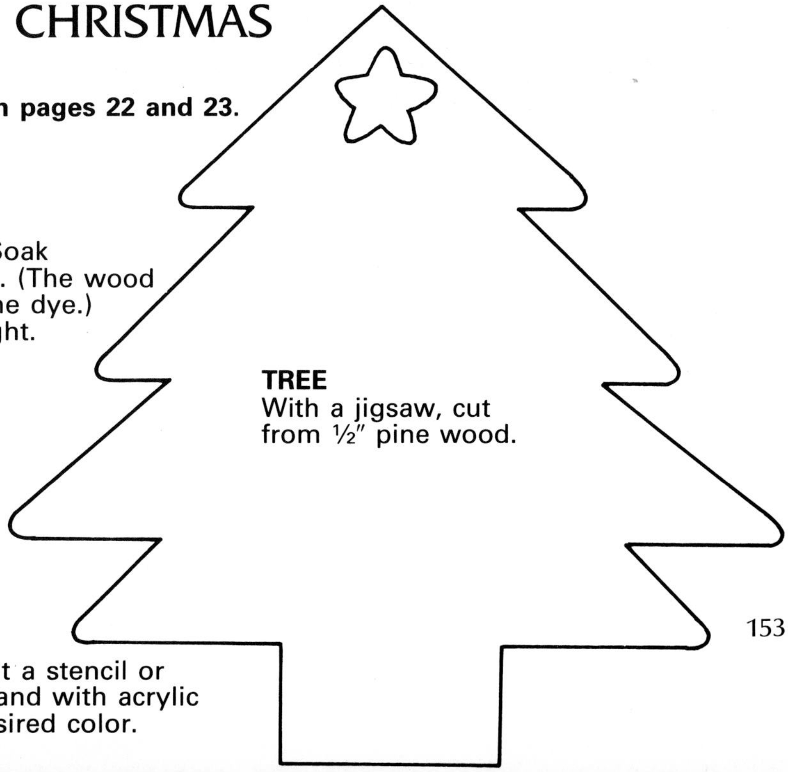

TREE
With a jigsaw, cut
from ½" pine wood.

DUCK
With a jigsaw, cut
from ½" pine wood.

For star, cut a stencil or
paint freehand with acrylic
paint in desired color.

153

CONTRIBUTORS

PHOTOGRAPHERS

PHOTOSTYLISTS

Special thanks to the *Oxmoor House* Test Kitchens staff for preparing recipes.

SPORTS

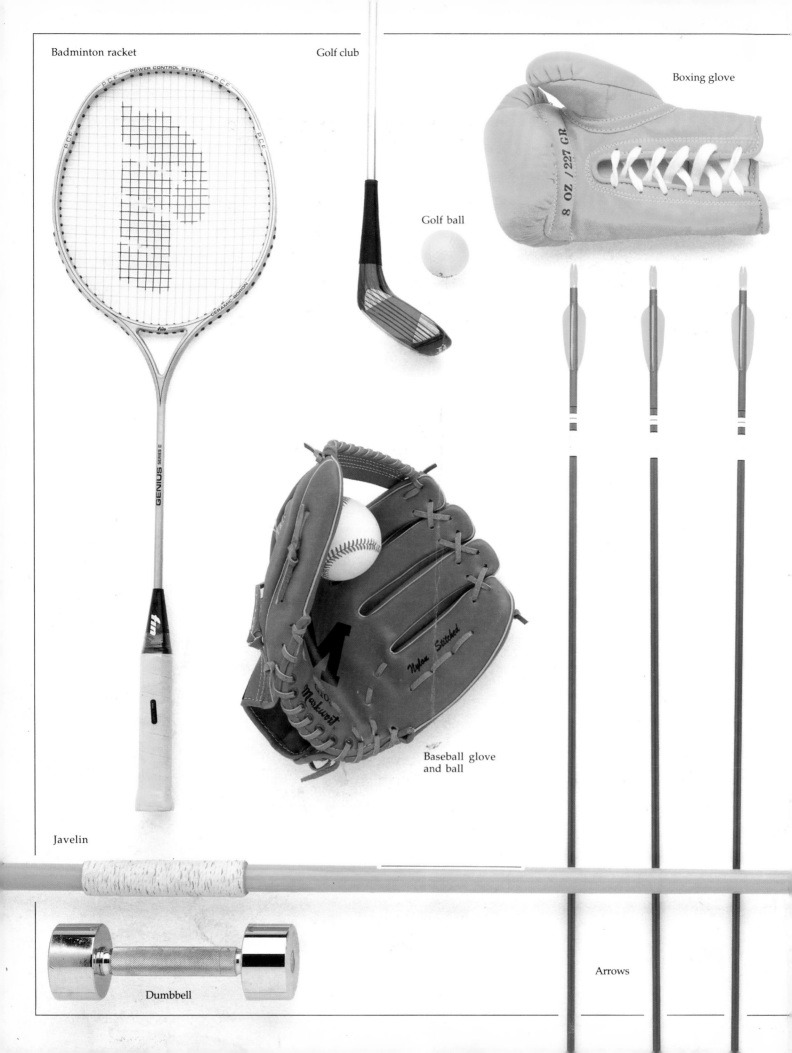

Badminton racket

Golf club

Boxing glove

Golf ball

Baseball glove
and ball

Javelin

Dumbbell

Arrows

Starting
pistol

EYEWITNESS BOOKS

SPORTS

Cricket batting glove

Written by
TIM HAMMOND

Rubber running-track granules

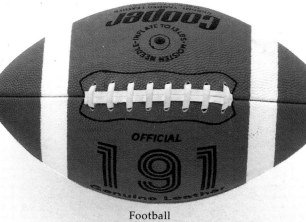
Football

Shuttlecocks

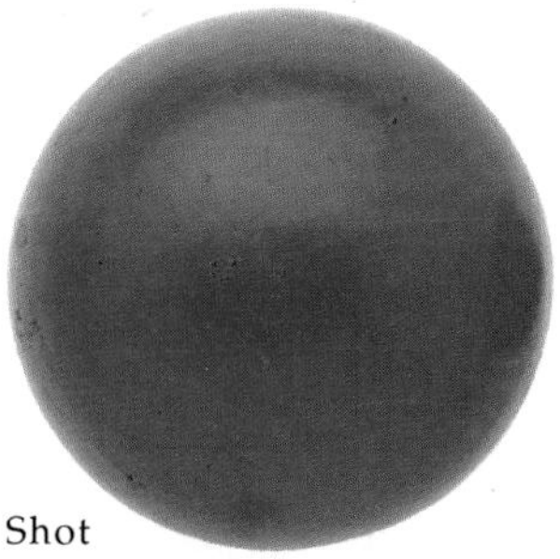

Shot

Relay batons

Stopwatch

ALFRED A. KNOPF • NEW YORK

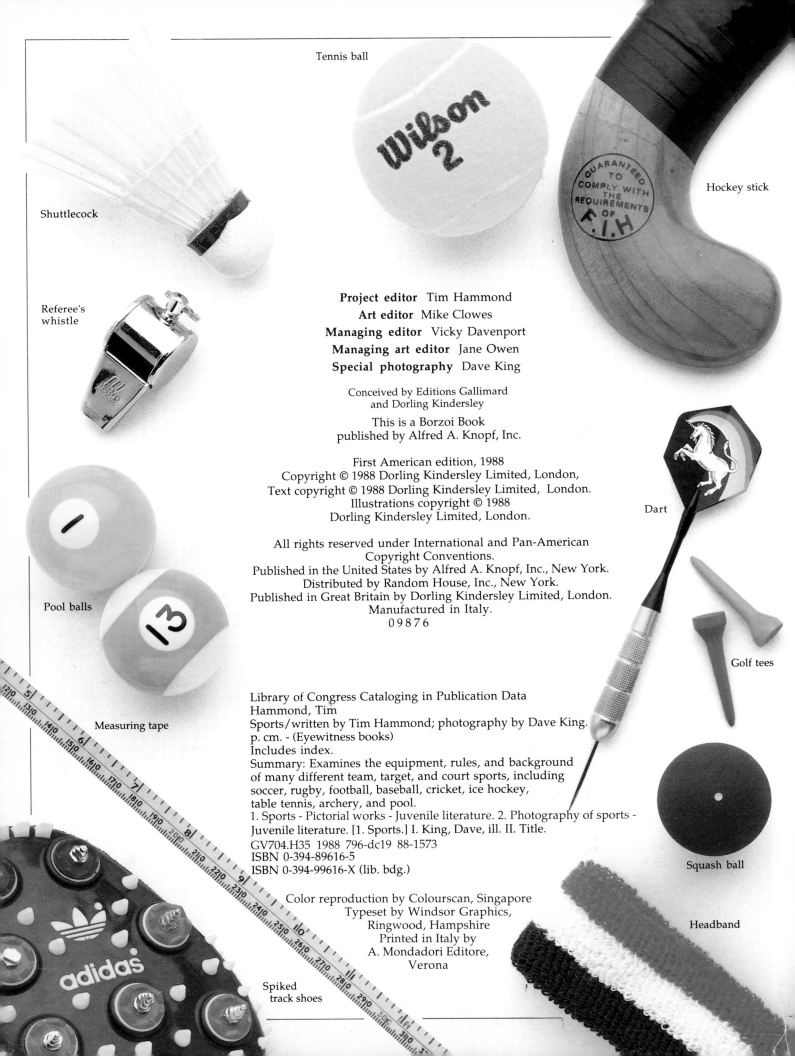

Tennis ball

Shuttlecock

Hockey stick

Referee's whistle

Project editor Tim Hammond
Art editor Mike Clowes
Managing editor Vicky Davenport
Managing art editor Jane Owen
Special photography Dave King

Conceived by Editions Gallimard
and Dorling Kindersley

This is a Borzoi Book
published by Alfred A. Knopf, Inc.

First American edition, 1988
Copyright © 1988 Dorling Kindersley Limited, London,
Text copyright © 1988 Dorling Kindersley Limited, London.
Illustrations copyright © 1988
Dorling Kindersley Limited, London.

Dart

Pool balls

Golf tees

Library of Congress Cataloging in Publication Data
Hammond, Tim
Sports/written by Tim Hammond; photography by Dave King.
p. cm. - (Eyewitness books)
Includes index.
Summary: Examines the equipment, rules, and background
of many different team, target, and court sports, including
soccer, rugby, football, baseball, cricket, ice hockey,
table tennis, archery, and pool.
1. Sports - Pictorial works - Juvenile literature. 2. Photography of sports -
Juvenile literature. [1. Sports.] I. King, Dave, ill. II. Title.
GV704.H35 1988 796-dc19 88-1573
ISBN 0-394-89616-5
ISBN 0-394-99616-X (lib. bdg.)

Measuring tape

Color reproduction by Colourscan, Singapore
Typeset by Windsor Graphics,
Ringwood, Hampshire
Printed in Italy by
A. Mondadori Editore,
Verona

Squash ball

Headband

adidas

Spiked
track shoes

Contents

Soccer shoe studs

Cricket ball

Soccer

SOCCER IS A TEAM SPORT in which players attempt to score goals by kicking or "heading" a ball into the opposing team's goal. Except for the goalkeeper, the players are not allowed to intentionally touch the ball with their hands or arms, unless they are throwing it in from the sideline. Games in which a ball is kicked have been played around the world in various forms for centuries: soldiers in ancient China played "football" as part of their army training - using the head of an enemy warrior as the ball! In 15th-century England, the sport was banned by the king because men preferred it to practicing their archery, and many were so badly injured in the violent matches that they could not fight in the army. Soccer is one of a group of sports - including football and rugby - that grew out of these early "games." It is the most popular sport in the world and is played and enjoyed by millions.

THE FIFA WORLD CUP
The top soccer-playing nations compete for this cup every four years. The original World Cup was kept by Brazil in 1970, after they had won it three times.

Bright-colored fabric can be seen clearly under floodlights

Linesman's flag

THE FIELD OF PLAY
The first soccer matches were played in the streets; there were no time limits - in fact, very few rules at all! Landmarks - such as the gates of the village church - were used as goals. Modern matches are held by teams of 11 players each.

Corner flag

Center circle

Penalty area

Halfway line

Goalpost

Penalty spot

ON THE LINES
Two linesmen patrol the length of the field, assisting the referee. They use flags to signal when the ball goes out of play or when players have broken the rules of the game.

MAN IN THE MIDDLE
The referee starts and stops play by blowing his whistle. Yellow and red cards are held up when a player has committed a serious foul or been thrown out of the game.

"W-M" formation

TEAM FORMATIONS
Each team may organize its defenders, midfield, and attacking players in a different way.

"4-4-2" formation

PLAYING TIME
Two "halves" of 45 minutes each are played. The referee may add on extra time if the game has been delayed.

Red card

Referee's whistle

Yellow card

Soccer fashions

The modern soccer player's clothing has changed greatly from that worn by the first professionals over a hundred years ago. For example, players did not wear numbers on their shirts. Instead, the uniform of each player was different from that of his team-mates, so he could only be identified by the color of his cap or his socks! Perhaps the most noticeable change has been in footwear: the clumsy "armored" shoes of the last century have changed gradually into the flexible and sophisticated modern shoes that are now only a third as heavy.

1880s *above*
At this time it was normal to kick the ball with the toe, so shoes were made with steel or chrome toecaps to protect the kicker's feet. Pads were worn outside the socks to protect shins against stray kicks!

Shoes reached above the ankle

Leather sole

1930s-1950s
Despite the baggy shorts, the player's uniform was now lighter, but the shoes still weighed around 1 lb (500 g) each.

More streamlined shape

Mid 20th-century shoes

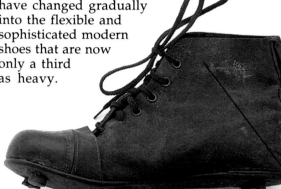

Early 20th-century shoes

Leather studs tacked on to sole

THE GOALKEEPER
The goalkeeper is the only player allowed to handle the ball. His shirt is a different color from the other players'. Many goalkeepers also wear gloves to help them grip the ball, and peaked caps to shade their eyes from the sun.

ARTIFICIAL GRASS
Grass fields get very wet and boggy during the winter, so some teams play on fields made from synthetic materials that are unaffected by the weather. However, artificial fields are more common in football (p. 10).

1980s *below*
Modern soccer shoes weigh only about 8 oz (250 g) or less. The development of such light and flexible shoes went hand-in-hand with changing playing styles; as footballers became more skillful, they needed shoes that allowed them to have better speed and ball control.

Late 20th-century shoes

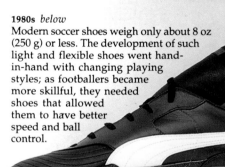

Rubber studs   Aluminum studs   Nylon studs

INTERCHANGEABLE STUDS
Studs of different materials and sizes are suitable for different field conditions - flat rubber studs for hard ground, aluminum for wet and slippery conditions, and nylon when the field is soft but firm.

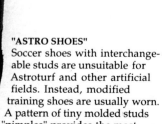

"ASTRO SHOES"
Soccer shoes with interchangeable studs are unsuitable for Astroturf and other artificial fields. Instead, modified training shoes are usually worn. A pattern of tiny molded studs or "pimples" provides the most comfortable shoe and the best grip. This shoe has 73 more "studs" than a normal soccer shoe!

How soccer balls are made

Nowadays soccer balls - as well as the balls used in some other sports - are often made from synthetic materials molded into the correct shape. However, the balls used by professional teams have always been made from leather panels stitched together around a rubber bladder, and the best balls are still made this way. Leather balls have better air resistance, so they don't wobble in flight.

Untreated leather scuffed easily

Final seam had to be laced up

PRE-WAR BALL
Until the 1940s footballs were always tan colored. They were not as waterproof as modern balls, so they became very heavy in wet conditions. The technique for stitching up the final panels of the ball had not yet been invented, so these balls were always laced.

ROUGH AND TUMBLE
The early soccer matches were rowdy affairs, with teams of 100 or more charging through the streets chasing a ball made from an inflated pig's bladder.

Soccer in the Middle Ages

Making a leather ball

Holes punched in panels for stitching

One needle is used at each end of the waxed thread

Maker's name stamped onto panels

MINERVA SUPREME

GUARANTEED HAND SEWN   THE MINERVA® FOOTBALL CO. LTD.   FIFA APPROVED

ENGLAND

Edges cut to fit together perfectly

1 CUTTING THE PANELS
The leather is coated in special paint to make it waterproof, and a strong lining is stuck to the back to make the leather stiffer and keep it from stretching. The firmest leather is used to make the most expensive balls; softer leather stretches more easily and is used for cheaper, practice balls. Two types of panel are cut out, using special knives. There are 18 panels in this type of ball.

Threads twisted together and rubbed with wax

2 STITCHING THE PANELS TOGETHER
Now the stitcher begins to join the leather panels together, using two needles and a special waxed thread made up of five strands. The wax makes the thread waterproof and easier to use. The panels are held together in a special clamp *(see opposite)* gripped between the stitcher's knees so he can have both hands free.

Old-fashioned ball-making tools

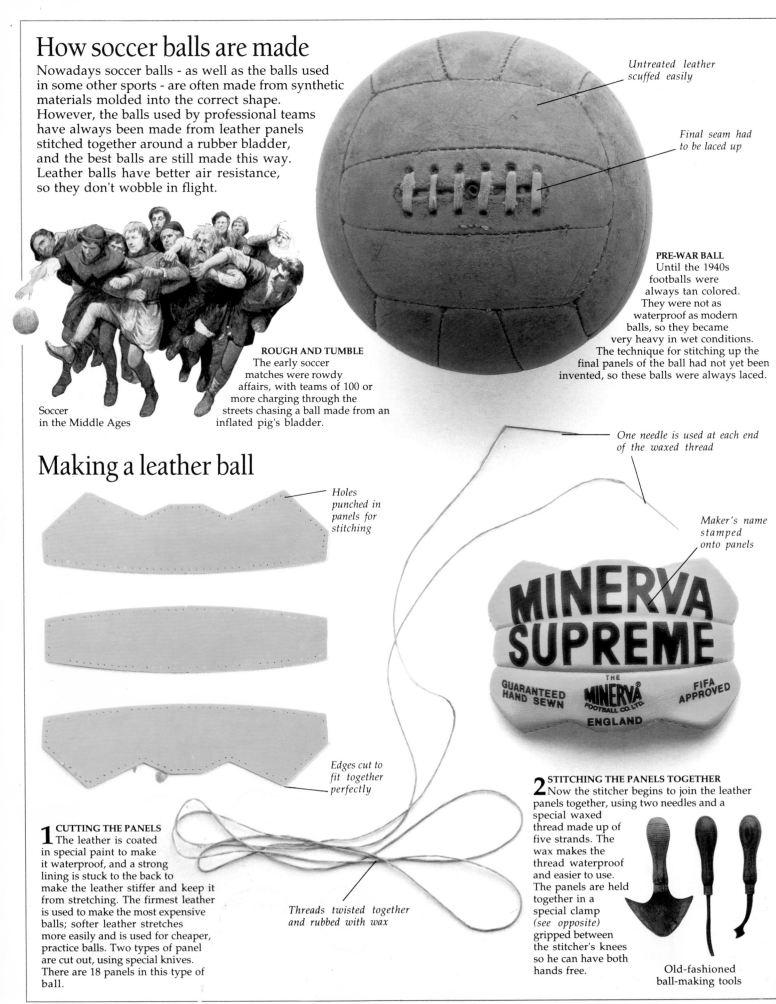

THE STITCHING HORSE
The ball maker sits on a special bench that has a clamp that holds the leather panels tightly while he stitches them together.

These panels are for a rugby ball, (p. 14), which is made in a similar way to a soccer ball

Clamp gripped between knees

Clamp secured by adjustable metal grip

32-PANEL BALL
Balls can be made in several different ways. The main difference is in the number and shape of the panels. This ball is made with a combination of 12 five-sided and 20 six-sided panels.

Bladder valve

Bladder made from latex rubber

5-A-SIDE BALL
A ball like the one shown above is designed for indoor soccer with five or six players on each team. It is slightly smaller than a normal soccer ball and made from soft, feltlike material that has a low bounce ideal for indoor games.

ALTERNATIVE DESIGN
The players in this 1924 match are using a ball made from just 12 panels - the fewer panels there are, the less perfectly round the ball will be.

Finished ball weighs 14-16 oz (400-500 g)

Panels sewn together with ball inside out

3 FORMING THE SHAPE OF THE BALL
The seams on each set of three panels are hammered flat to make the ball as round as possible. With the ball inside out, the panels are then sewn together at right angles to each other. The seams are hammered again to make sure the corners are smooth, and the ball is turned the right way around. The last side of the ball is partly sewn on, leaving enough room for the stitcher to push the rubber bladder into the ball. The air valve of the bladder fits through a hole punched into one of the panels.

The ball will be kicked and headed thousands of times throughout its life

4 THE FINISHED BALL
With the ball the right way out, the stitcher begins the difficult task of sewing up the final seam. He cannot tie off the thread in a knot or it would show on the outside of the ball, so he sews it back into the ball and cuts off the ends as close as he can. The ball is given a thorough inspection to check for any faults and is blown up with air to the correct pressure. Each ball takes about three and a half hours to make.

Football

FOOTBALL IS AN EXCITING SPORT played by two teams of 11 players each; with separate squads for defense and offense, up to 40 men can play for a team during a single game. The tactics can be very complicated, but the object is simple - to score points by crossing the opponents' goal line with the ball (a touchdown) or by kicking the ball between their goalposts. The game is therefore based on each team's attempt to advance up the field toward the other's goal. It was first played in American colleges in the late 19th century and is, without doubt, the team sport with the greatest amount of physical contact. The helmets and huge shoulder pads worn by the players help make this one of the most spectacular of all sports to watch. Canadian football has slightly different rules.

Padded-up football player in full flight

Football helmet

Face mask made from unbreakable plastic coated in rubber

SHOCK ABSORBERS *below*
Inside the helmet, cells filled with air or antifreeze liquid help prevent injury by spreading impact evenly.

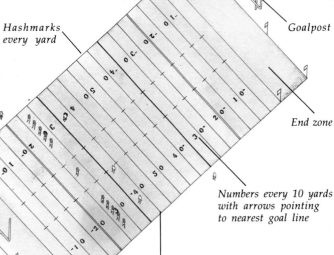

Goal line

Hashmarks every yard

Goalpost

End zone

Numbers every 10 yards with arrows pointing to nearest goal line

Yard lines every 5 yards

THE GRIDIRON
Each team can make four attempts to advance 10 yd (9 m) up the field; each attempt is called a "down." If they succeed, they play another four downs; otherwise their opponents win possession of the ball. The gridiron (field) is marked out in yards to show how far a team has advanced.

HEAD CASES
Every player must wear a proper helmet with a protective face mask. The first "helmets" were made from boiled leather. The modern ones are tough plastic. Most players also use a mouthpiece to protect their teeth.

MODERN WARRIORS
"War paint" was first worn by the Washington Redskins. The players found that painting their cheeks this way helped reduce glare from the sun. Other teams did the same, and face paint is now a common sight.

...AND THE ORIGINAL
The names of many football teams reflect the aggressive nature of the sport. Each game is like a battle, with teams advancing and retreating.

Cincinnati Bengals   Los Angeles Rams   Philadelphia Eagles   New York Jets

San Diego Chargers   Buffalo Bills   Seattle Seahawks   New York Giants

NFL HELMETS
The names of the 28 teams in the National Football League (NFL) are made up of their city name and a nickname. The helmets worn by the teams often bear a logo relating to their nicknames.

Shoulder pads

BROAD SHOULDERS
Shoulder and chest pads can weigh up to 5.5 lb (2.5 kg), depending on the position of the player.

Upper arm pads can be attached to shoulder pads

TACKLE DUMMY
Players build strength and practice their blocking technique on this special piece of equipment.

ARM PADS
The amount of padding worn by each player depends on how fast and agile he must be to do his particular job.

Fingerless gloves give protection and freedom of movement

FOOTBALL SHIRTS
Some players wear tight-fitting shirts that are difficult for opponents to grab. Others wear shirts made of flimsy fabric that simply tears away if pulled. The numbers on the front must be at least 8 in (20 cm) high, and those on the back at least 10 in (25 cm).

Elbow pad

GLOVES
Some players wear gloves to protect their hands and help them grip the ball; others use adhesive tape.

WHAT NUMBER?
Each team is made up of three groups: offense, defense, and special units for kicking. There are no strict rules about numbers, but number 34 is often worn by a running back.

The need for padding

Early forms of football were very dangerous - in 1905, for example, 18 college players were killed and over 150 badly injured. This led to changes in the rules about protective clothing to help make the sport safer. Many players use adhesive tape as a form of protection - some professional teams can use over 300 miles of tape in a season!

RIB PADS *left*
Apart from their helmets and bulky shoulder pads, players wear padding to prevent injuries to the lower parts of their body. The rib pads are like a corset with a hard plastic shell; they tie on to the shoulder pads and lace up at the front.

Straps tie on to shoulder pads

HIP AND GROIN PADS *below*
The protection for the hip area is made up of three separate pads - one for each hip and one for the groin. These are held together by straps that are threaded through each pad and done up at the back.

Rigid plastic covering

Foam-sponge filling

Thigh pads

Leg pads slipped under tight-fitting pants

PANTS *above*
The padding for the hips and legs is worn underneath close-fitting knee-length pants that lace up at the front.

Knee pads

THE BALL

A football is oval in shape, with pointed - rather than rounded - ends that make it easier to throw one-handed. It is made from a rubber bladder, inflated with air and covered in "pebble-grained" leather. In professional football, the home team has to provide 24 footballs for each match.

Pebble-grained leather

Pointed ends

Quarterback preparing to throw

Time out

Touchdown or field goal

Personal foul

Offside or encroaching

Holding

Illegal motion

First down

Pass interference

Missed kick

The kicking technique

Kicking tee

The kicker may use a special tee to support the ball when kicking off

THE PLAYMAKER

The quarterback is the "general" of the team, directing the play and picking out the most suitable receiver of his passes. He has to be quick in mind and body, with a cool head and a strong, accurate throwing arm. Quarterbacks also need to be tough, as they are liable to be tackled or "sacked" by defensive linemen whenever they have the ball.

KICKING THE BALL

Although the name of the game is "football," the ball is kicked only a few times in each match. Special squads are brought on at the various kicking situations: to start or restart play, to kick field goals and touchdown conversions, and to gain ground by punting the ball upfield.

THE "ZEBRAS"

The officials are known as "zebras", because of their striped shirts. The referee uses arm signals to indicate his decisions.

Placekick with holder

Kick-off from tee

Drop kick

Punt

Screw-in studs

Fold-over leather tongue

FOOTBALL FOOTWEAR

Shoes with studs or molded soles are worn depending on field conditions. Some kickers prefer to kick barefoot.

PRIMITIVE PROTECTION

Early padding, like that worn by players in the 1930s, was very different from modern equipment; the leather helmets, which looked like old-fashioned flying hats, were not really very effective.

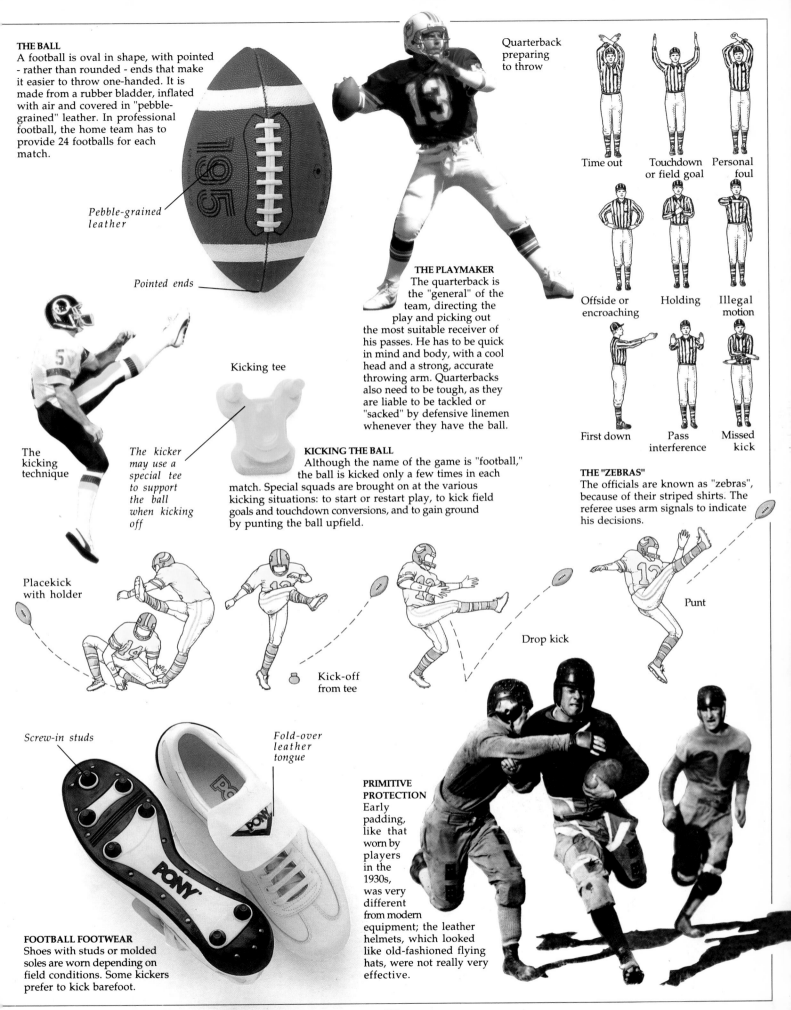

13

Rugby

R UGBY IS A SPORT in which players are allowed to carry, kick, and throw the ball (but they can only throw it backward). Points are scored by touching the ball down over the opponents' goal line (a "try") or by kicking it over the crossbar and between the goalposts. The sport gets its name from Rugby high school in England where it was first played in 1823. The "inventor" of the sport was William Webb Ellis, a pupil at the school, who was the first player to pick up and run with the ball during a soccer game. In 1895 an argument over paying money to players led to a split between rugby clubs in England. Two forms of the sport have existed ever since: the newer, professional (paid) game is known as Rugby League, and has thirteen players per team. The more trad-itional and widely-played amateur (unpaid) version is Rugby Union, with fifteen players on each side. The rules for each are slightly different, but the basic idea behind both sports remains the same.

Scoring a try

TRADITIONAL QUALITY
The company that makes these international match balls was supplying soccer balls to Rugby high school in 1823, when the game was first played there.

Modern leather rugby ball

HUMAN SPIDER
When the teams lock together into a "scrum" (face-off), they look like a giant spider with many legs. The players in the middle of the scrum are the "hookers," who try to heel the ball backward for their team-mates to pick up.

SKY-SCRAPERS AND SIDE-WINDERS *below*
The tallest Rugby Union goalposts in the world are 110 ft (33.5 m) high. Most players today kick the ball soccer-style rather than with the toe of the shoe and are known as "side-winders" because of their curved run-up and kicking action.

High-sided rugby shoe

BOOTING THE BALL *left*
Rugby players may wear soccer shoes or special, high-sided shoes that support the ankles. The longest recorded goal kick was scored in 1932, when the ball was kicked 270 ft (82 m).

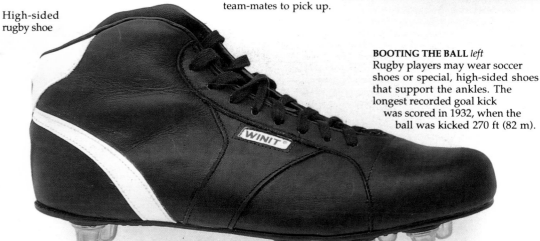

MAORI WARDANCE

The New Zealand national team is known as the All Blacks because of its all-black uniform. The first New Zealand touring team consisted mainly of native Maori players who performed a traditional wardance called a "haka" before each game. This is still a feature of matches played by the modern All · Blacks.

AWARDING CAPS

The practice of giving special caps was introduced at Rugby high school as a way of thanking team members for their efforts. Caps are now awarded in other sports too, when players are chosen to play for their country.

1908 Rugby cap

Rounder-style ball made in 1851

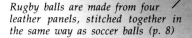

Rugby balls are made from four leather panels, stitched together in the same way as soccer balls (p. 8)

THE EVOLUTION OF THE BALL *left*

Early rugby balls were much rounder than they are today. The modern shape makes the ball much easier to carry and throw.

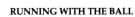

RUNNING WITH THE BALL

One of the most exciting plays in a rugby match is when a player catches the ball and runs the whole length of the field to score a try - hotly pursued by opposing players.

ALTERNATIVE MATERIALS *right*

Over the years, ball makers have tried making balls out of various materials besides the traditional leather. Pig skin, and even camel skin, are excellent materials to work with, but balls made from them were found to be too slippery.

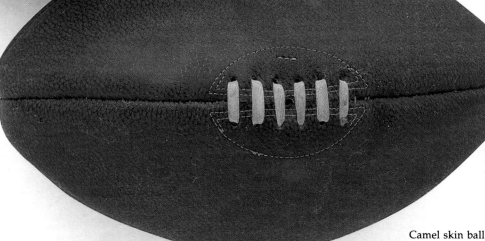

Camel skin ball

Field hockey

FIELD HOCKEY HAS BEEN DESCRIBED in a very simple way as "soccer played with a stick and a cricket ball in place of a soccer ball" and there are, indeed, many ways in which the two sports are alike. Field hockey is played by teams of 11 men or women, and no physical contact is allowed. Ancient Egyptian and Greek wall paintings suggest that games like field hockey were played as far back as the third century B.C., and the Romans are known to have played a game called *paganica*, which used curved sticks and a leather-covered ball. The modern sport is based on the *hurling*, *bandy*, and *shinty* games played in different areas of the British Isles, although the name "hockey" is thought to come from the French word *hoquet*, meaning a "hooked stick."

VICTORIAN PLAYER
Field hockey as it is played today first became popular in England in the late 19th century.

THE GOALKEEPER
The goalie wears extra padding, including a chest protector and a helmet with a face mask, to protect him from shots hit at up to 100 mph (160 kmh).

Goalkeeper's helmet

THE MODERN GAME *left*
Hockey is played indoors and outdoors, at all levels from school- to Olympic-standard, by men and women, and on grass or synthetic fields.

Outdoor stick

25 yd (22 m) line

THE FIELD
Goals can only be scored from inside the opposing team's striking circle. The goals themselves are small - just 12 ft (3.6 m) wide and 7 ft (2.1 m) high .

Striking circle

Halfway line

Penalty spot

TRIBAL GAMES *below*
The earliest form of lacrosse was called *baggataway* and was played by North American Indians as part of their training for war.

Lacrosse ball

Nets made from gut, rawhide, or cord

Plastic net frame

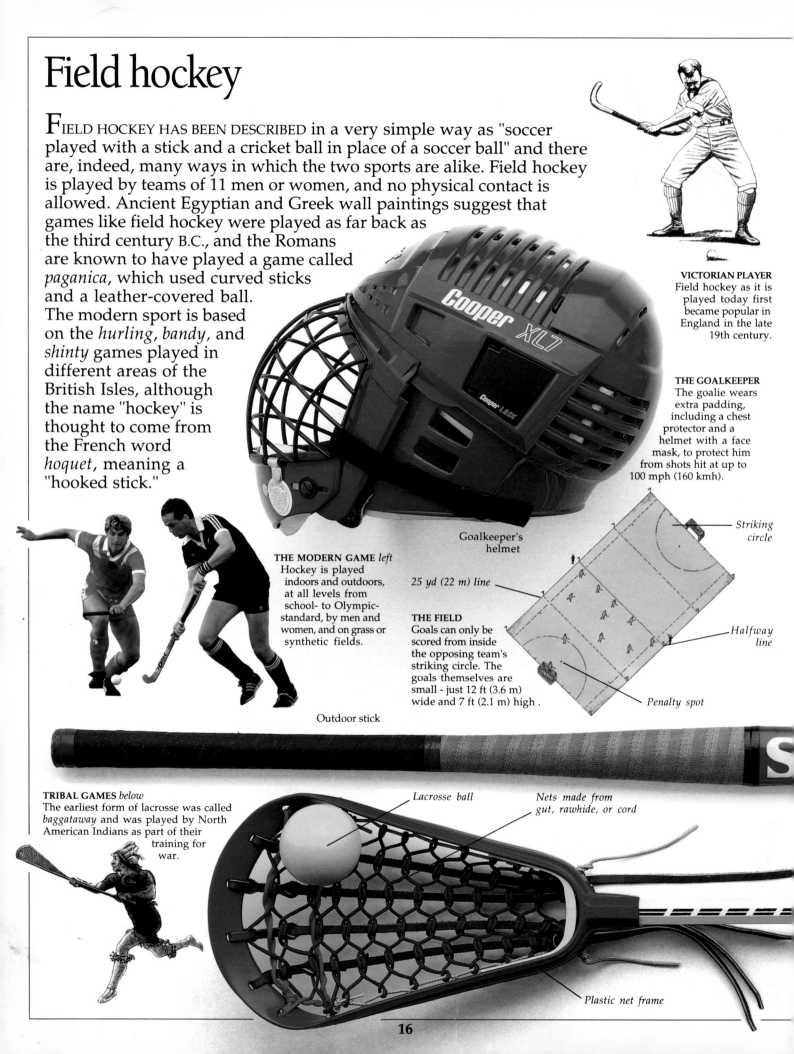

KICKERS
The goalkeeper is the only player allowed to intentionally touch the ball with his feet. He wears special "kickers" outside his shoes, with which he blocks the ball and kicks it clear of his goal.

Rigid palm 2 in (5 cm) thick

Straps fit over normal shoes

Padded toes protect feet against the hard ball

FOOTWEAR
The shoes worn by field hockey players depend on the surface they are playing on. Soccer-style shoes are usually worn on grass, and special multi-studded shoes like these on synthetic fields.

GAUNTLETS
The goalie's gloves are different for each hand. One is flexible, so he can pick the ball up when he has to, and the other has a rigid, padded palm that is used to stop the ball.

Padding extends below the wrist to protect the forearm

Over 60 molded studs on each sole

STICK HEADS *below*
Sticks have a rounded side and a flat face, with which the ball is struck. No part of the stick is allowed to be more than 2 in (5 cm) wide.

Indoor stick

THE BALL
The hard hockey ball is similar in size to a baseball or cricket ball and is usually white.

TYPES OF STICKS *above*
Most modern sticks are made from ash, with a cane handle. The head is steam-bent so that the grain of the wood follows the bend and strengthens the stick. Indoor sticks are lighter and thinner; old-fashioned sticks had a longer curve.

A woman player of 1912

Old-fashioned stick

Lacrosse

This sport is similar to field hockey but uses sticks with nets to throw, catch, and carry the ball. French settlers in North America gave the sport its name - the hooked sticks reminded them of a bishop's staff or *crozier* ("la crosse"). Men's and women's games are played differently.

Women's lacrosse sticks are generally shorter than men's

LACROSSE STICK
Sticks are traditionally made from hickory wood, but many are now made from plastic. The net must be tightly strung so the ball does not become stuck.

INDIAN CROSSE *right*
The type of stick used by the first players varied according to which tribe they came from. Many were decorated with feathers.

Ice hockey

AS ITS NAME SUGGESTS, ice hockey is basically hockey played on ice, and it originated as the winter version of field hockey - played on frozen ponds and lakes. However, there are several other major differences between the modern forms of the two sports: Ice hockey teams have six players who use longer sticks and a hard rubber disk, called a puck, instead of a ball. Modern ice hockey is usually played indoors, where the temperature of the ice is controlled automatically. The ice is cleaned off between each of the three 20-minute periods.

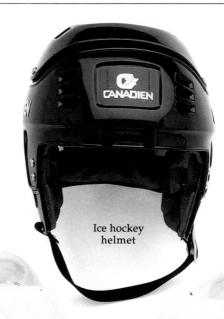

Ice hockey helmet

A modern player in full uniform

SPEEDY SPORT
Ice hockey is the fastest team sport in the world. There is also a great deal of body contact, and the players wear padding to protect them when they crash into the barriers that surround the rink.

Elbow pad

BODY ARMOR
As well as the items shown here, ice hockey players wear special shorts that have thick padding sewn into them to protect the players' legs when they fall on the hard ice. Deliberately tripping an opponent is against the rules, and the offender would be punished by spending time in the penalty box. Depending on how bad the offense was, the penalty lasts from two to ten minutes.

Shoulder and chest padding

GLOVES
The gauntlets worn by skaters players are heavily padded and made from leather or synthetic materials. Rigid fingertip caps provide extra protection. Goalkeepers wear a different kind of glove on each hand - a "catcher" and a "blocker."

FROZEN PUCK
The disk-shaped puck is made from vulcanized (toughened) rubber. It is generally kept frozen before a match so that it keeps its original form as long as possible.

THE RINK

The playing area is divided into defense, neutral, and attacking zones by blue lines. Play is started with a "face-off" in the center circle, when a player from each team competes for the puck dropped by one of the two referees. The game is restarted after a foul by a face-off in the circle nearest to where the foul took place.

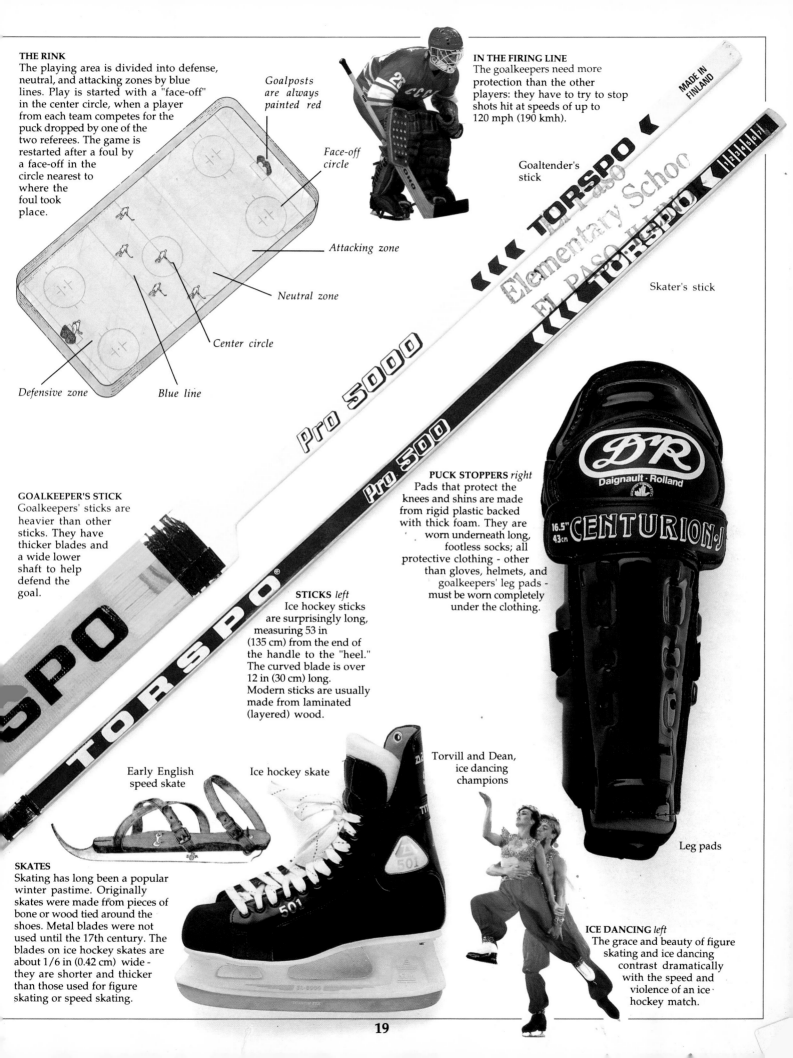

Goalposts are always painted red

Face-off circle

Attacking zone

Neutral zone

Center circle

Defensive zone

Blue line

IN THE FIRING LINE
The goalkeepers need more protection than the other players: they have to try to stop shots hit at speeds of up to 120 mph (190 kmh).

Goaltender's stick

Skater's stick

Pro 5000

Pro 500

GOALKEEPER'S STICK
Goalkeepers' sticks are heavier than other sticks. They have thicker blades and a wide lower shaft to help defend the goal.

PUCK STOPPERS *right*
Pads that protect the knees and shins are made from rigid plastic backed with thick foam. They are worn underneath long, footless socks; all protective clothing - other than gloves, helmets, and goalkeepers' leg pads - must be worn completely under the clothing.

STICKS *left*
Ice hockey sticks are surprisingly long, measuring 53 in (135 cm) from the end of the handle to the "heel." The curved blade is over 12 in (30 cm) long. Modern sticks are usually made from laminated (layered) wood.

Early English speed skate

Ice hockey skate

Torvill and Dean, ice dancing champions

Leg pads

SKATES
Skating has long been a popular winter pastime. Originally skates were made from pieces of bone or wood tied around the shoes. Metal blades were not used until the 17th century. The blades on ice hockey skates are about 1/6 in (0.42 cm) wide - they are shorter and thicker than those used for figure skating or speed skating.

ICE DANCING *left*
The grace and beauty of figure skating and ice dancing contrast dramatically with the speed and violence of an ice hockey match.

Basketball

IN 1891, A CLERGYMAN in America invented the game of basketball when he nailed a peach basket to the balcony at each end of the local gymnasium. The object of the game is to score points by throwing the ball into the "basket" at your opponents' end of the court. Basketball is a nonviolent sport, played indoors, in which the five players on each team throw and bounce the ball, but cannot carry or kick it. Because of the height of the baskets, there are many very tall basketball players - the tallest being 8ft (2.45 m)!

Harlem Globetrotter

The basketball has a circumference of 30-31 in (75-78 cm)

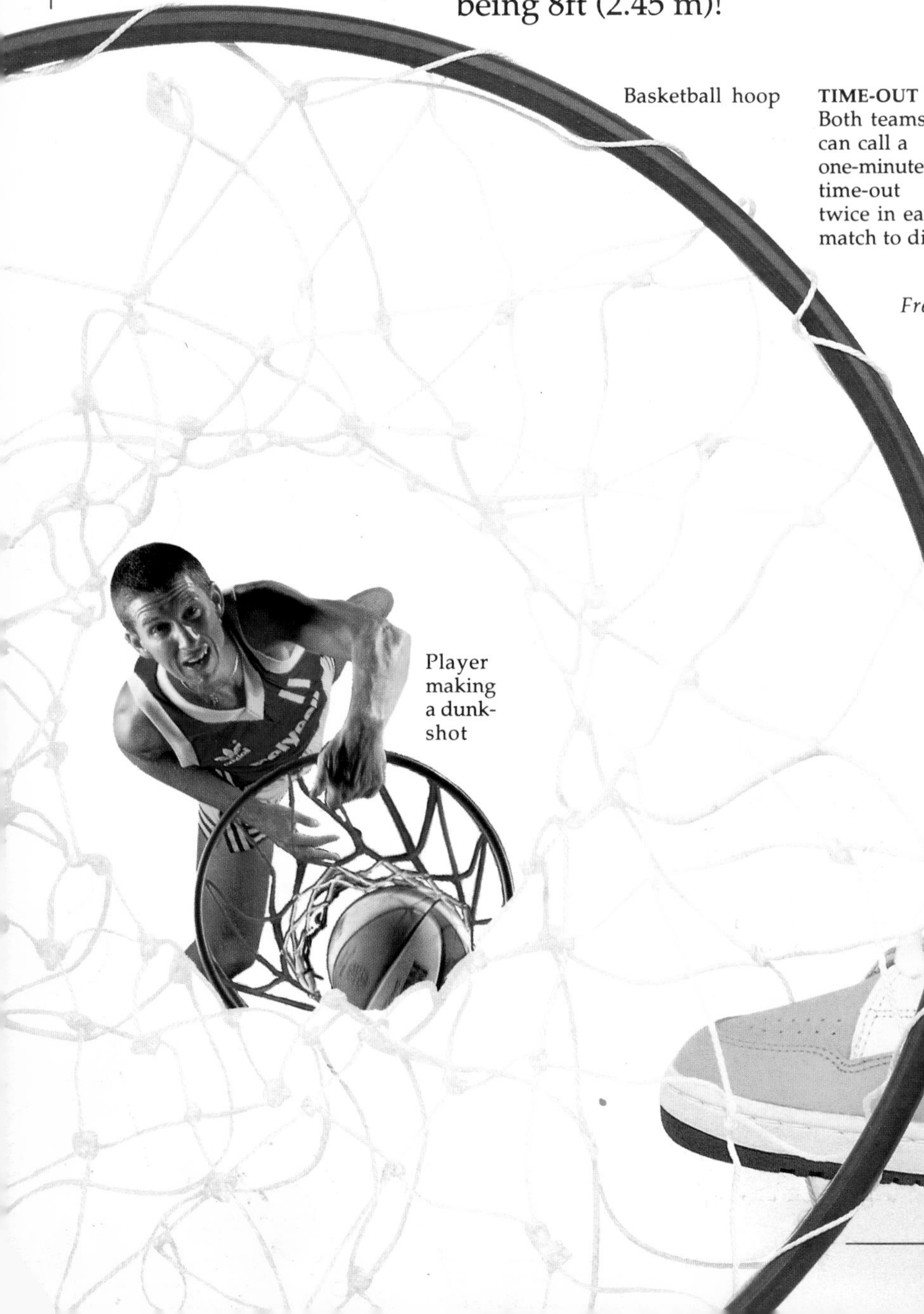

Basketball hoop

TIME-OUT
Both teams can call a one-minute time-out twice in each half of the match to discuss tactics.

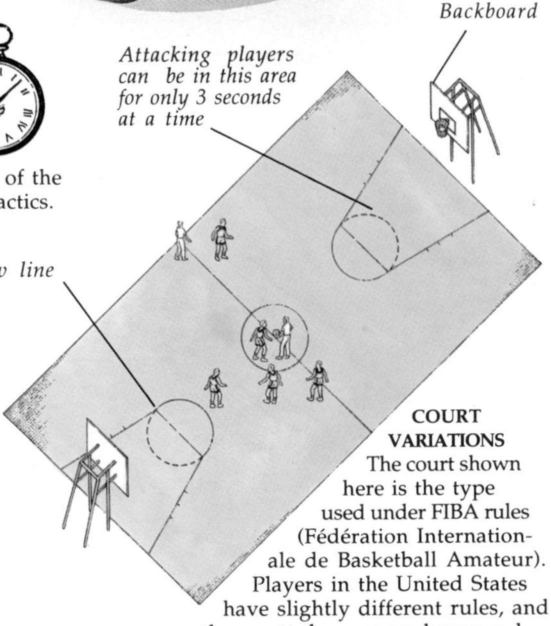

Attacking players can be in this area for only 3 seconds at a time

Backboard

Free-throw line

COURT VARIATIONS
The court shown here is the type used under FIBA rules (Fédération Internationale de Basketball Amateur). Players in the United States have slightly different rules, and the courts they use are larger and have different markings.

Player making a dunk-shot

Basketball shoes have high, padded ankles for added support.

CONVERSE®

Netball

Netball is played almost entirely by women. It is similar to basketball but played on a slightly larger court, with seven players on each side rather than five, and nets supported by poles instead of backboards. Like basketball, it originated in the United States in the second half of the last century.

MOVING WITH THE BALL
Netball players are not allowed to carry the ball. When holding it, the player can turn in any direction, but must keep one of her feet on the same spot.

Netball

PLAYING ZONES
Each player is only allowed in certain areas of the court. Players wear lettered vests to indicate their positions so the umpire knows if a player is in the wrong zone.

GD	WD
C	WA
GA	GS

Volleyball

This sport is like a cross between basketball and badminton (p. 35). Teams of six players hit a ball over a net using their hands and arms or any other part of their upper body. Each team may touch the ball up to three times before it crosses the net.

AT THE NET *left*
The height of the net means that attacking players have to jump high to smash the ball downward. No player is allowed to touch the net or reach over it into the opposing team's side of the court.

THE BALL *right*
The volleyball is lightweight and of a uniform color. It is smaller than a netball or a basketball.

Baseball

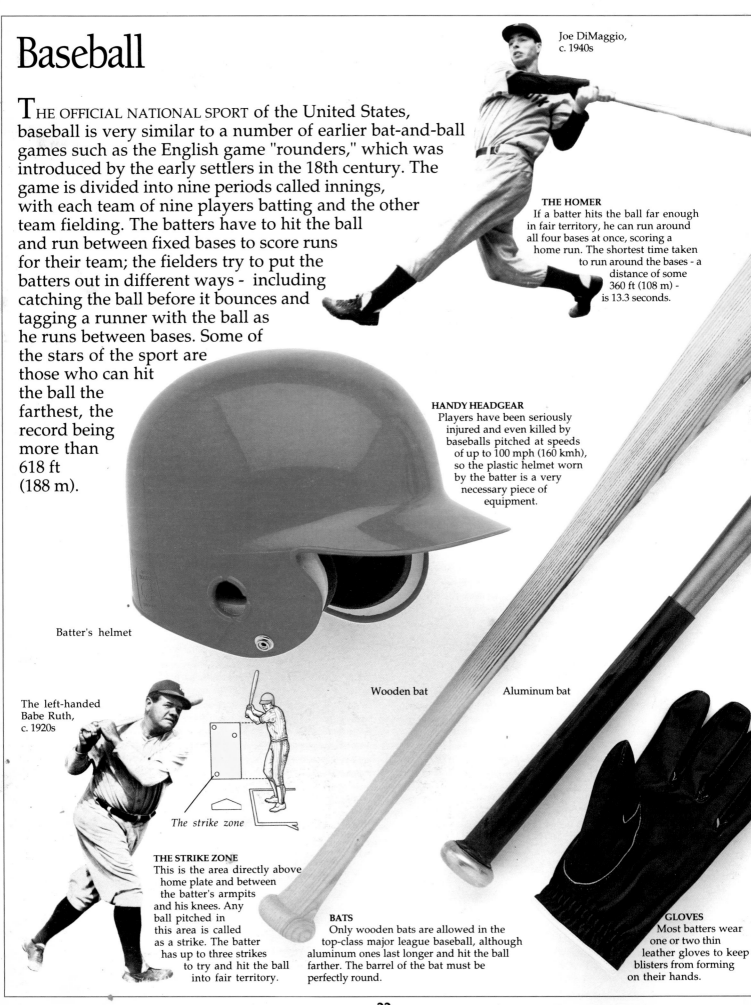

THE OFFICIAL NATIONAL SPORT of the United States, baseball is very similar to a number of earlier bat-and-ball games such as the English game "rounders," which was introduced by the early settlers in the 18th century. The game is divided into nine periods called innings, with each team of nine players batting and the other team fielding. The batters have to hit the ball and run between fixed bases to score runs for their team; the fielders try to put the batters out in different ways - including catching the ball before it bounces and tagging a runner with the ball as he runs between bases. Some of the stars of the sport are those who can hit the ball the farthest, the record being more than 618 ft (188 m).

Joe DiMaggio, c. 1940s

THE HOMER
If a batter hits the ball far enough in fair territory, he can run around all four bases at once, scoring a home run. The shortest time taken to run around the bases - a distance of some 360 ft (108 m) - is 13.3 seconds.

HANDY HEADGEAR
Players have been seriously injured and even killed by baseballs pitched at speeds of up to 100 mph (160 kmh), so the plastic helmet worn by the batter is a very necessary piece of equipment.

Batter's helmet

Wooden bat

Aluminum bat

The left-handed Babe Ruth, c. 1920s

The strike zone

THE STRIKE ZONE
This is the area directly above home plate and between the batter's armpits and his knees. Any ball pitched in this area is called as a strike. The batter has up to three strikes to try and hit the ball into fair territory.

BATS
Only wooden bats are allowed in the top-class major league baseball, although aluminum ones last longer and hit the ball farther. The barrel of the bat must be perfectly round.

GLOVES
Most batters wear one or two thin leather gloves to keep blisters from forming on their hands.

22

SHIRTS
Shirts cannot have any pattern or emblem that could be mistaken for a baseball, or any shiny glass or polished metal that could reflect the sun into another player's eyes. Each shirt must have a number at least 6 in (15 cm) high on the back. Some players also wear long-sleeved undershirts.

Baseball

INSIDE THE BALL
The baseball weighs between 5 and 5.5 oz (142-156 g), and has a very complex structure. Top-quality balls are covered in cowhide or horsehide treated with alum and are handstitched.

Grip for screwball

Red outer stitching

PITCHING
The pitcher must be able to throw fast and slow balls that curve in the air in various directions. The way the ball is gripped partly determines the type of pitch delivered.

Horsehide strips

Woolen strands

Cork center

Woolen yarn

Rubber inner casing

Cotton thread outer casing

A baseball pitcher

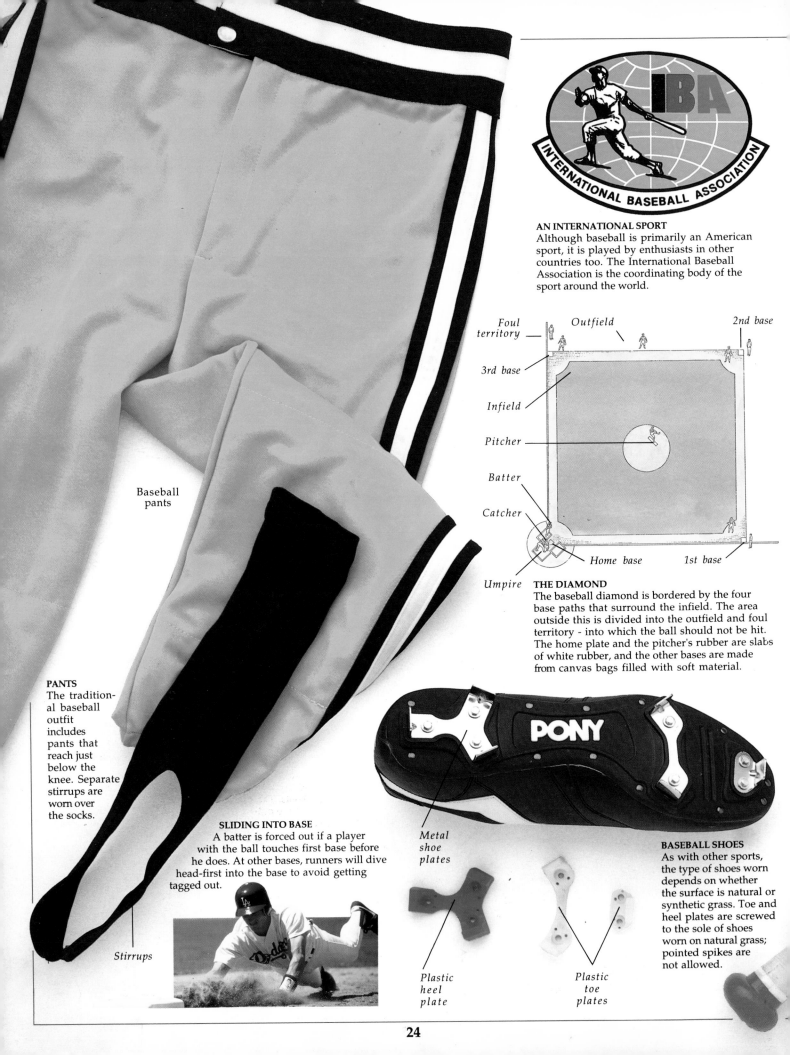

AN INTERNATIONAL SPORT
Although baseball is primarily an American sport, it is played by enthusiasts in other countries too. The International Baseball Association is the coordinating body of the sport around the world.

Foul territory

Outfield

2nd base

3rd base

Infield

Pitcher

Batter

Catcher

Umpire

Home base

1st base

THE DIAMOND
The baseball diamond is bordered by the four base paths that surround the infield. The area outside this is divided into the outfield and foul territory - into which the ball should not be hit. The home plate and the pitcher's rubber are slabs of white rubber, and the other bases are made from canvas bags filled with soft material.

Baseball pants

PANTS
The tradition-al baseball outfit includes pants that reach just below the knee. Separate stirrups are worn over the socks.

Stirrups

SLIDING INTO BASE
A batter is forced out if a player with the ball touches first base before he does. At other bases, runners will dive head-first into the base to avoid getting tagged out.

PONY

Metal shoe plates

Plastic heel plate

Plastic toe plates

BASEBALL SHOES
As with other sports, the type of shoes worn depends on whether the surface is natural or synthetic grass. Toe and heel plates are screwed to the sole of shoes worn on natural grass; pointed spikes are not allowed.

UMPIRE ON THE SPOT
Each game is controlled by up to four umpires. The plate umpire stands directly behind the batter and the catcher, so he can make all pitching and batting calls.

LOOKING THROUGH THE BARS
Because of the danger of being hit in the face with bat or ball, the catcher and the umpire need to wear more protective clothing than the other players. The face masks are made from thick wire coated in strong nylon.

Catcher's mask

Plastic-coated foam padding

Webbed pocket

Fingers laced together

Softball bat

SOFTBALL *below*
This sport, originally devised as an indoor version of baseball, is very popular in America. The main differences are that softball is played by both men and women, the ball is larger, the pitching is underarm, and the field is smaller.

Leather stitching

Fielding glove

Softball

CATCHING
The members of the fielding team wear large leather mitts to catch the ball in their non-throwing hand. The catcher wears a slightly different, more padded mitt.

Painted wooden shaft

Rounders ball

ROUNDERS
This is an English game, popular in schools. The principles are the same as those of baseball and softball, but the bat is much smaller and held in one hand, the diamond is smaller, and the bases are marked by vertical posts.

Tape grip

Bat must be no longer than 18.5 in (46 cm)

Rounders bat

Early bat-and-ball game

Cricket

CRICKET IS SIMILAR to baseball (p. 22), in the way teams take turns to bat and field. The two sports differ in that there are two cricket batsmen on the field at any one time and they must defend the "wicket" with their bat and score by running between the two wickets at opposite ends of the narrow "pitch". In addition, four runs are automatically scored if the ball is hit over the boundary of the field, and six if it crosses the boundary without touching the ground. Bat-and-ball games like cricket were probably played in England as long ago as the 13th century.

A gentleman cricketer

THE FIELD
The cricket "pitch" is a narrow strip of short grass in the center of the field, 66 ft (20 m) long, with a wicket at each end. "Overs" (sequences of six balls) are bowled (pitched) from alternate ends.

Wicketkeeper

Wicket

Batsman

Bowler

Umpire

Bowling "crease" (pitcher's boundary line)

Replica of an 18th-century bat

Screw-in spikes

SHOES
Many cricketers prefer to wear high-sided shoes with screw-in metal spikes. By tradition, most cricket clothing and footwear is white or off-white.

Wicketkeeper's gloves

Pimpled rubber

BOWLING
Cricketers bowl over-arm, and the ball bounces once before reaching the batsman. Slow bowlers spin the ball with their fingers so that it turns toward or away from the batsman, and faster bowlers bounce the ball off its raised seam to get a similar effect.

AN EARLY GAME
Cricket in the 18th century was played with five players on each team. There was only one wicket, and this had two stumps rather than three.

THE BALL
The cricket ball is made in a similar way to a baseball (p. 23) but is covered with red leather and has a straight-stitched seam.

Bails

Stumps

THE WICKETKEEPER
The wicketkeeper plays a similar role to the catcher in baseball (p. 21). Like the catcher, he wears leg guards because he is so close to the batsman. His well-padded gloves have pimpled-rubber palms to help grip the ball.

THE FIRST BATS
The word "cricket" may come from *cric*, the Old English term for a shepherd's crook, which the early cricket bats resembled. 18th-century bats were long and heavy with a curved blade. The modern style of straight bat was not used until the introduction of overarm bowling.

WICKETS
Modern wickets are made from ash, and are 28 in (71 cm) high. The wicket consists of three upright stumps and two bails which rest on the top. The batsmen is "bowled out" if the bowler (pitcher) knocks off one or both of the bails.

BATTING GLOVES
These protect the fingers from injury but allow enough freedom of movement to grip and wield the bat.

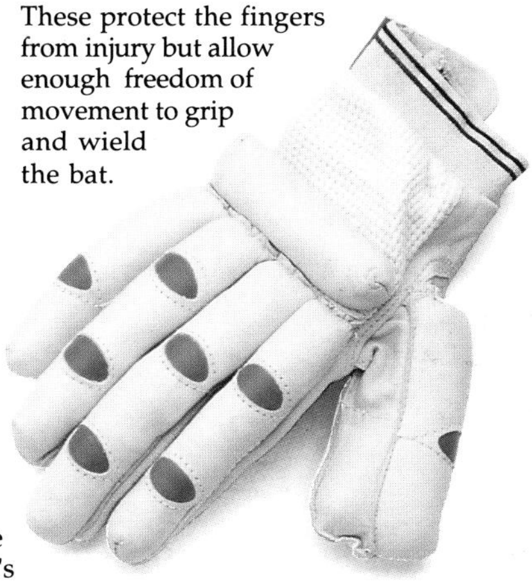

The weather vane depicting Old Father Time is a famous Lord's landmark

HAT TRICK *right*
Bowlers were once given hats if they "struck out" 3 batsmen in a row, hence the term "hat trick", used today if an ice hockey player scores 3 points in a game.

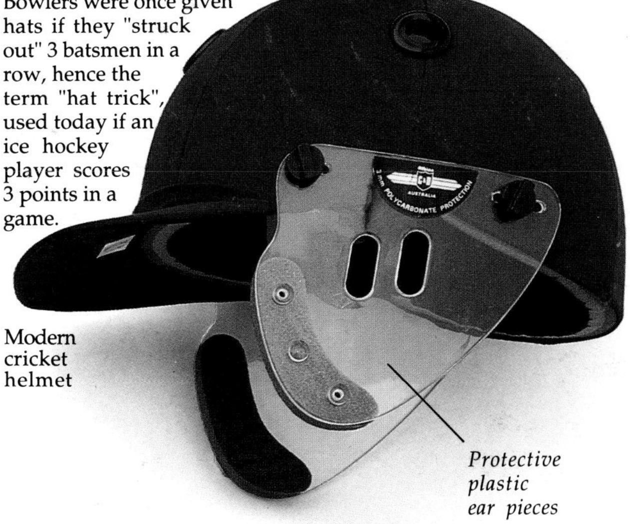

Modern cricket helmet

Protective plastic ear pieces

THE HOME OF CRICKET
Lord's cricket ground, known as the "home of cricket," was founded by Thomas Lord in 1787, and is the headquarters of the Marylebone Cricket Club (M.C.C.), which drew up the rules of the game. International matches are often played at Lord's; these last for five days and are known as "test" matches. The bat shown here has been signed by players taking part in a test match at Lord's.

COLORED CLOTHES
In floodlit cricket matches, each team wears a different-colored uniform. A white ball is used as it can be seen more easily.

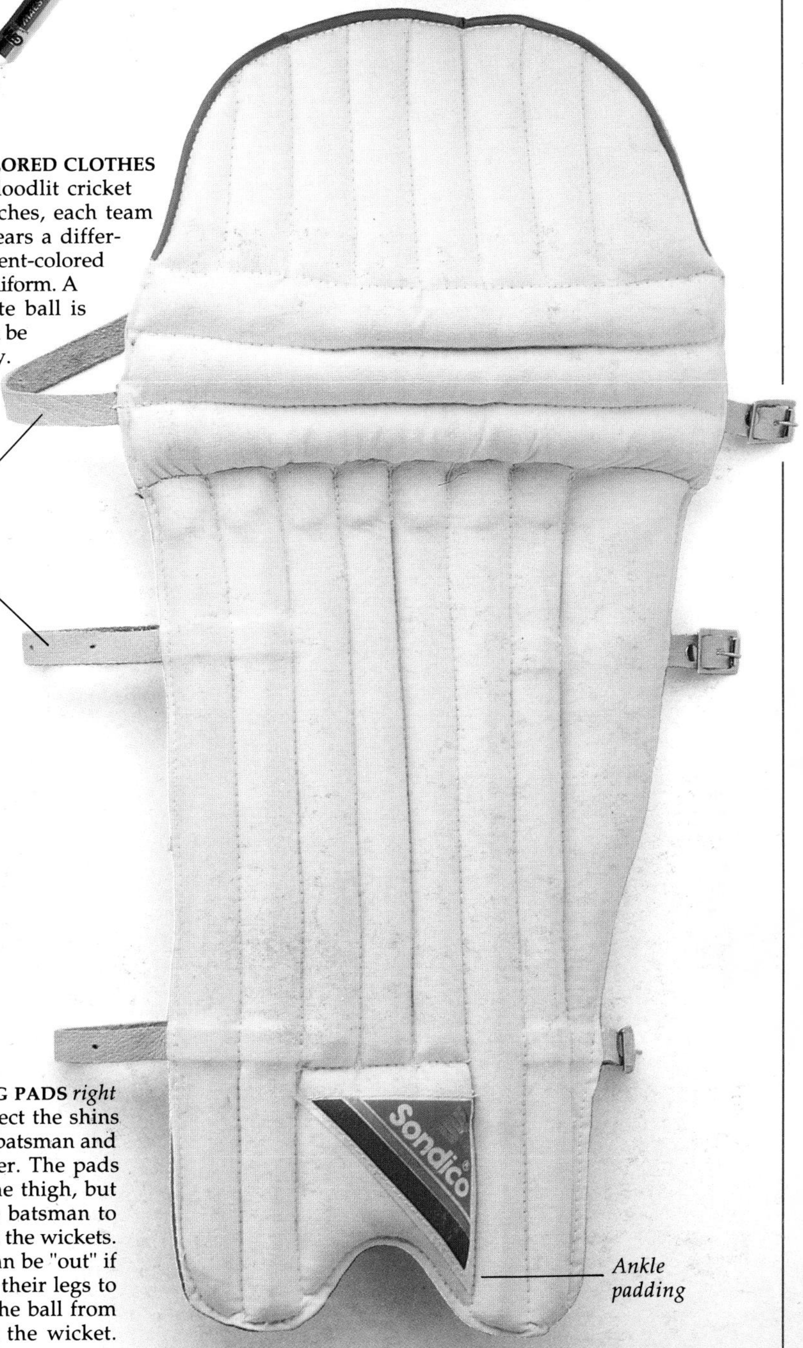

Fastening straps

METAL BAT
An aluminum bat was used by a few players during the 1970s, but the fashion did not last long, as aluminum bats proved no substitute for the traditional wooden variety.

Metal bats were hollow inside

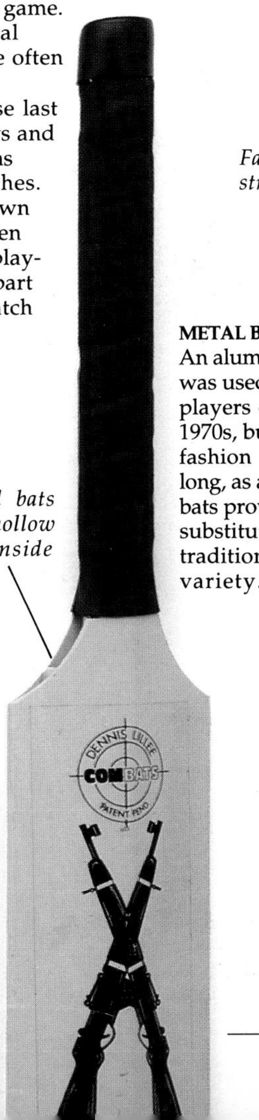

A MODERN BAT
Today's cricket bats are made from willow and have a cane handle, usually covered by a rubber grip. The average bat weighs about 2lb 5oz (1050 g) and is roughly half the weight of the old bat shown opposite.

LEG PADS *right*
These protect the shins of the batsman and wicketkeeper. The pads reach to the thigh, but still allow the batsman to run between the wickets. Batsmen can be "out" if they use their legs to keep the ball from hitting the wicket.

Ankle padding

How cricket bats are made

The introduction of fast overarm bowling in the early 19th century meant that batsmen needed lighter bats that could be swung more easily. The modern type of bat dates from that time, and despite various improvements in design, the style of the bat has changed little since then. The bat blade, which absorbs the impact of the ball, is made from willow, and the springy cane-and-rubber handle protects the hands from the shock of striking the ball.

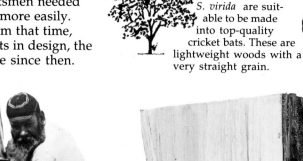

THE TREE
Of the 36 varieties of English willow, only *Salix coerulea* and *S. virida* are suitable to be made into top-quality cricket bats. These are lightweight woods with a very straight grain.

USING THE WOOD
Each section of trunk is used to make between six and eight bats, depending on its size and quality.

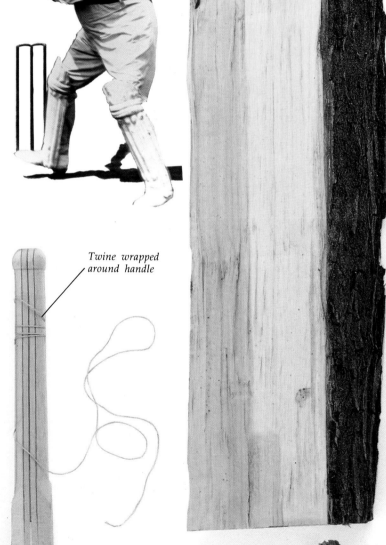

W.G. GRACE
Probably the most famous of all batsmen is Doctor William Gilbert ("W.G.") Grace, who dominated the sport throughout the second half of the 19th century. During his career, he scored over 54,000 runs.

Rubber   *Cane*

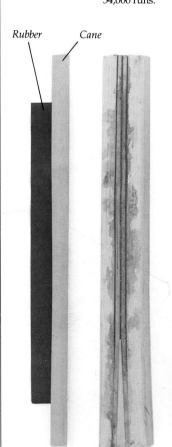

Twine wrapped around handle

1 SPLITTING THE TRUNK
Each 28 in (71 cm) length of willow trunk is cut into segments or "clefts"; then the bark is removed. The young outer "sapwood" is best for making bats; it is a lighter color than the inner "heartwood."

Sapwood

THE HANDLE
The handle is made from pieces of *Sarawak* cane formed into blocks with strips of rubber and bonded together tightly with strong glue.

2 THE SEASONING PROCESS
The clefts are sawed into "blades," stacked, and left to dry for 2-4 weeks. Then they are put into a kiln to dry for a further 4-6 weeks.

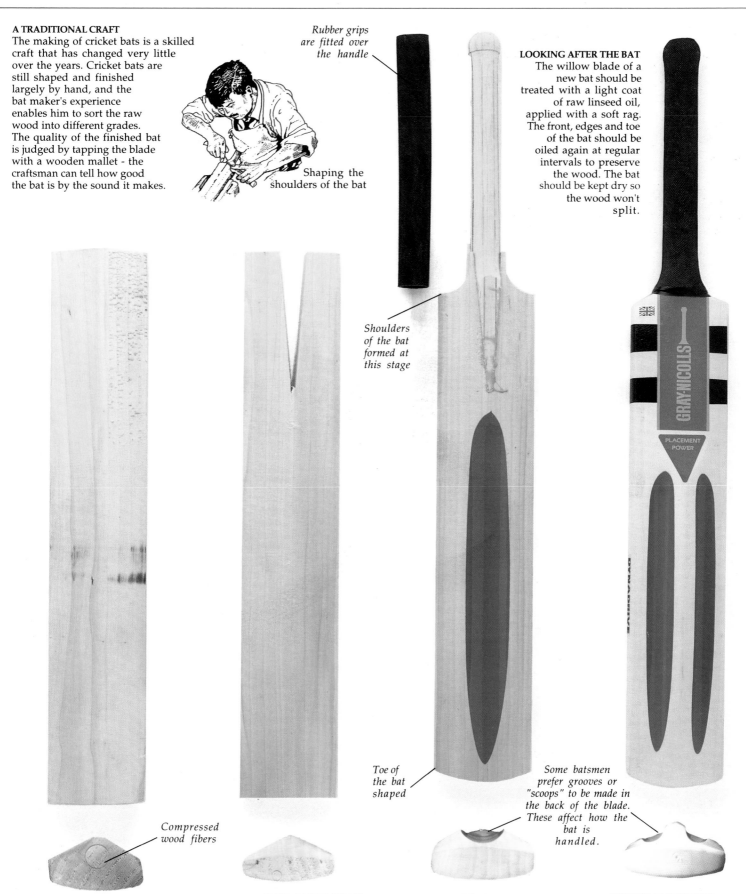

A TRADITIONAL CRAFT
The making of cricket bats is a skilled craft that has changed very little over the years. Cricket bats are still shaped and finished largely by hand, and the bat maker's experience enables him to sort the raw wood into different grades. The quality of the finished bat is judged by tapping the blade with a wooden mallet - the craftsman can tell how good the bat is by the sound it makes.

Shaping the shoulders of the bat

Rubber grips are fitted over the handle

Shoulders of the bat formed at this stage

LOOKING AFTER THE BAT
The willow blade of a new bat should be treated with a light coat of raw linseed oil, applied with a soft rag. The front, edges and toe of the bat should be oiled again at regular intervals to preserve the wood. The bat should be kept dry so the wood won't split.

Toe of the bat shaped

Some batsmen prefer grooves or "scoops" to be made in the back of the blade. These affect how the bat is handled.

Compressed wood fibers

3 SHAPING AND PRESSING
Now the dried blade is shaped and pressed by a special machine. The pressure of more than 2 tons hardens the bat and shows up any hidden weaknesses in the wood.

4 CUTTING THE SPLICE
The bat is planed and smoothed by hand, and the V-shaped slot or "splice" is cut into the top, ready for the handle to be inserted (*see opposite*).

5 FITTING THE HANDLE
The handle is turned on a lathe and shaped to fit the splice. Then it is fixed into place with strong glue. Twine is wrapped around the handle.

6 FINISHING TOUCHES
The completed bat is sanded and polished. If the wood is not a uniform color, it may be bleached or covered in linen before the maker's seal of approval is given.

Tennis

TENNIS IS PLAYED by two or four people on a court divided by a low net. Each player has a racket, and points are scored by hitting a ball over the net in such a way that it bounces inside the court and cannot be returned. "Real," or Royal, tennis originated in France during the Middle Ages and was very popular among the European noblemen of the 16th century, but it was not until the 19th century that "lawn tennis" was first played. The sport quickly became very popular with both men and women. Today tennis is played on clay, cement, wood, and plastic courts, as well as on grass.

Wooden frame

Angled racket head

Natural gut strings

REAL TENNIS
Real - or Royal - tennis used to be the sport of kings and was a favorite pastime of the French and English monarchy. Henry VIII of England built a court at his Hampton Court palace in the 16th century, that is still used by real tennis enthusiasts today.

An old-fashioned scoreboard

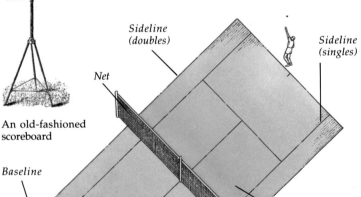

Sideline (doubles)

Sideline (singles)

Net

Baseline

The tennis court

Service court

Grip

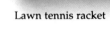

Lawn tennis racket

GAME, SET, AND MATCH
Opposing players serve alternate games. At least six games must be won to gain a set, and two - or sometimes three - sets are needed to win a match. Up to eleven officials, not including the umpire, are needed at top matches. They sit around the edge of the court and judge whether the ball is "in" or "out."

A STICKY START
Tennis first became popular in the 1870s, when it was known as *sphairistike* - the Greek word for "ball game." This was soon shortened to "sticky."

Hevea brasiliensis rubber tree

The tennis ball

The progression from real tennis, played on indoor courts, to lawn tennis, played in the gardens of "polite society," was not as obvious as it may seem. Indeed, before it was possible at all, somebody had to invent a ball that would bounce on grass!

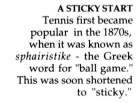

REAL FAILURES
The traditional real tennis balls were made from sheepskin and filled with sawdust, sand, or wool. They did not bounce on grass.

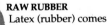

RAW RUBBER
Latex (rubber) comes from the stems of certain trees. It was not until the 19th century that rubber-tree seeds were brought to Europe and grown commercially.

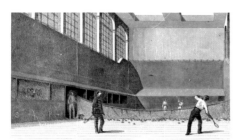

CLOISTER COURT
Real tennis courts have gallery "roofs" jutting out around three of the four sides, and points are won according to how the ball is hit into and through the galleries. The strange design of the court is like the monastery cloisters where the game was first played.

IN THE CHAIR
The tennis umpire sits in a high chair next to the net so he has the best possible view of the match. He announces the score after each point has been played.

Real tennis racket

WIMBLEDON
The oldest and most important tennis championships are held at the All England Tennis and Croquet Club, Wimbledon, London. The first championships were held in 1877.

Molded graphite frame

PUMA® HI-FLECK GRAPHITE

UNIVERSAL MIDSIZE

GRAPHITE · COMPOSITE

Throat

SPACE-AGE RACKET
The modern tennis racket is stronger and more powerful than ever before. Computers are used to help design the rackets, which are made from materials developed for the aerospace industry.

Synthetic strings

Head

HOW THE BALL IS MADE
The rubber is "vulcanized" (treated with sulfur at high temperatures) to make it stronger and more elastic. The hollow ball is formed from two halves bonded together.

COVERING
The plain rubber ball was rather slippery in wet conditions, so a flannel covering was invented. Modern balls are covered with a mixture of wool and man-made fibers.

Wilson 2

BALL CHANGES
The pressure inside the ball changes in different conditions and during play, so the balls used in major matches are kept refrigerated at 68°F (20°C), and replaced after every few games.

Wilson 2

Tennis rackets

The sport we know today as tennis can be traced back to the French game of *Jeu de Paume*, in which two players hit a ball to each other with the palm of their hand. Soon, pieces of wood and webbed gloves started to be used instead, and by the start of the 15th century, strung "rackets" had been invented. Today's rackets are the result of trial and error over the years; until very recently, there were no rules governing the design and proportions of the racket, and many different styles and materials have been used during the past 100 years. Different kinds of stringing have also been tried - even wire "strings" were used at one stage.

International Tennis Federation rules now state that the overall dimensions of any racket must not exceed 32 in (81.28 cm) in length and 12.5 in (31.75 cm) in width, and that there must only be one set of strings on each racket.

Woman player of 1890

Aluminum frame

Piano-wire strings

Solid ash frame

1900s *below*
By the early years of the 20th century, the familiar symmetrical (even) shape of the racket had been introduced. A popular feature of the period was the "fishtail" handle - considered to be the height of fashion. Grooves were often cut into the handle to improve the grip.

FIRST METAL RACKET *right*
During the 1920s, experimental rackets with aluminum frames were made. The fact that they were strung with piano wire did nothing for their appeal, as it meant that the wool-covered tennis balls quickly wore out.

1920s *above*
Leather grips were introduced around this time to make the racket much easier to hold. Most racket frames were still being made from a solid piece of ash, but the shafts were becoming narrower and the edges more rounded to reduce wind resistance.

Symmetrical head

Leather grip

Fishtail handle

Grooved grip

1880s *below*
The first lawn-tennis rackets were similar to those used in real tennis, with uneven pear-shaped heads. They weighed much the same as modern rackets but the natural gut was much coarser and strung more loosely than today.

Plain wooden handle

Uneven head

1930s *below*
The "Hazell's Streamline" racket has an unusual handle, designed to reduce wind resistance, and a laminated (layered) head. Using thin layers of different woods, rather than a solid piece, means the racket is lighter, stronger, and cheaper to make.

Forehand ground stroke

Backhand volley

Serve

USING THE RACKET
To achieve the maximum control over each stroke, the racket must travel exactly along the direction and height the player wishes the ball to go, but the racket is used in a different way for each type of shot. Ground strokes involve swinging the racket, whereas the volley needs a punching technique; the serving action is one of "throwing" the racket at the ball, and the lob is a scooping stroke.

Forehand lob

Laminated frame

Reinforced shoulders

Streamlined handle to reduce wind resistance

1950s *above*
This classic wooden racket was the most popular design for two decades. The frame has multiple laminations of ash and other woods that are used for decoration and to make the racket stronger. The "shoulders" are reinforced for added strength.

Narrow aluminum frame

Double stringing

1970s *above*
This decade saw the appearance of improved metal rackets. These could be made with a narrower frame than wooden rackets of the same strength, which meant they could travel faster through the air. Some rackets were double-strung to give extra spin to the ball (double stringing has since been banned).

Molded graphite frame

1980s *above*
Nowadays, top-class players don't use wooden rackets and very few use metal ones. Instead, racket frames are molded from a combination of materials such as carbon graphite, fiberglass, boron, and ceramic.

Table tennis and badminton

TABLE TENNIS AND BADMINTON are indoor sports in many ways similar to tennis. Badminton is played with a feather "shuttlecock" on a court with a high net, and table tennis is played with a light-weight ball on a rectangular table with a low net. Both sports date from the 1870s. The first "table tennis" match was between two British university students, using cigar boxes as bats and a champagne cork as a ball!

PING-PONG SET
The sport was also known as "Ping-Pong" because of the sound the ball made when it was hit with the paddle. It was a popular social activity around the turn of the century, when boxed Ping-Pong sets were sold in stores.

Paddle faces were made of parchment

Paddles had long wooden handles

PRICE FOURPENCE.
HOW TO PLAY
PING-PONG.
WITH DIAGRAMS AND LAWS.

Early net with brass posts

HOW PADDLES ARE MADE *below*
The blade of the paddle is made of plain wood, but this must be covered with pimpled rubber. The pimples may face inward or outward depending on the desired effect on the ball, but must be evenly spaced on the rubber.

Plywood blade of even thickness

Outward-facing pimples

White celluloid ball

Inward-facing pimples

THE GRIP
Some players prefer to hold the paddle as if it were a pen.

Cellular rubber

Rubber must be one color only

MODERN PADDLE
The sport became much more interesting in the 1920s, when the paddle was given a studded rubber face that enabled a player to put spin on the ball.

1901 MATCH *left*
Plain wooden paddles made for long, boring rallies, and the popularity of table tennis declined until rubber-faced paddles were introduced.

Badminton

Question: Which international sport is named after somebody's house? Answer: Badminton, called after the ancestral home of the Duke of Beaufort in Gloucestershire, England. The sport is thought to have been adapted from a children's game as an after-dinner entertainment for the duke's guests.

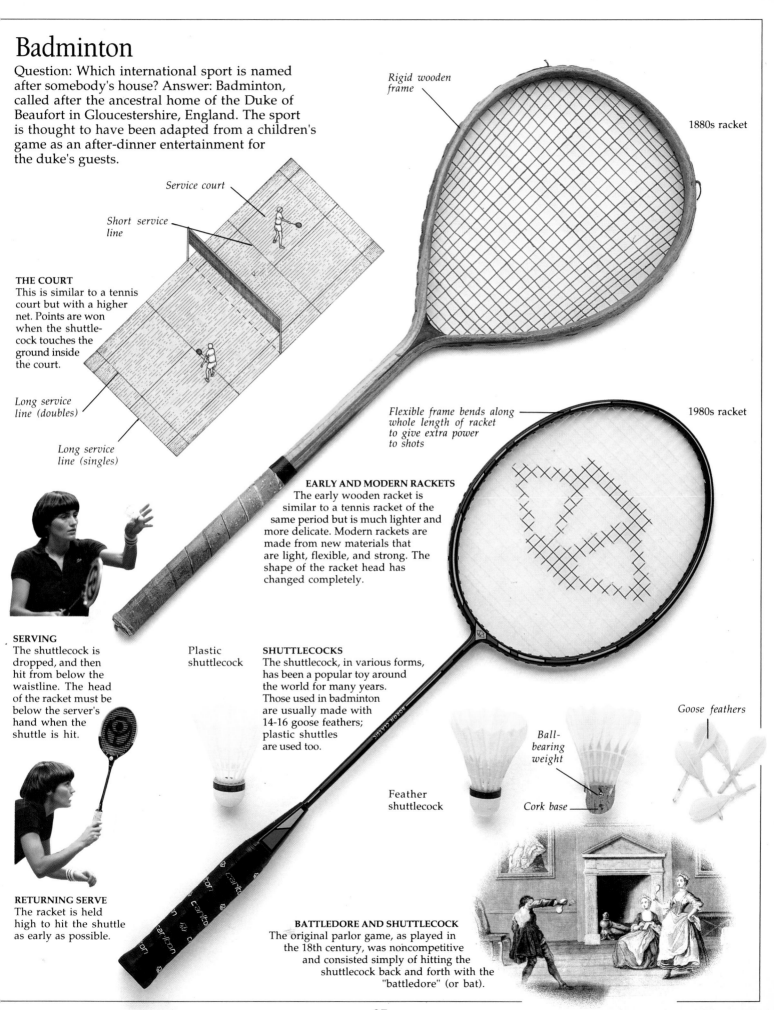

Rigid wooden frame

1880s racket

Service court

Short service line

THE COURT
This is similar to a tennis court but with a higher net. Points are won when the shuttlecock touches the ground inside the court.

Long service line (doubles)

Long service line (singles)

Flexible frame bends along whole length of racket to give extra power to shots

1980s racket

EARLY AND MODERN RACKETS
The early wooden racket is similar to a tennis racket of the same period but is much lighter and more delicate. Modern rackets are made from new materials that are light, flexible, and strong. The shape of the racket head has changed completely.

SERVING
The shuttlecock is dropped, and then hit from below the waistline. The head of the racket must be below the server's hand when the shuttle is hit.

Plastic shuttlecock

SHUTTLECOCKS
The shuttlecock, in various forms, has been a popular toy around the world for many years. Those used in badminton are usually made with 14-16 goose feathers; plastic shuttles are used too.

Goose feathers

Ball-bearing weight

Feather shuttlecock

Cork base

RETURNING SERVE
The racket is held high to hit the shuttle as early as possible.

BATTLEDORE AND SHUTTLECOCK
The original parlor game, as played in the 18th century, was noncompetitive and consisted simply of hitting the shuttlecock back and forth with the "battledore" (or bat).

Squash and racketball

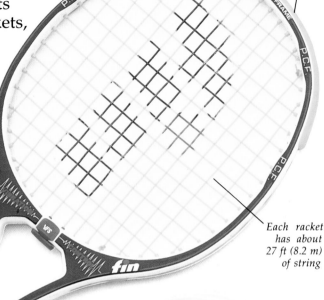

Protective strip prevents damage to the racket head

SQUASH, OR "SQUASH RACKETS," is one of several sports played on a court with four walls; others include rackets, fives, paddleball, racketball, and court handball. One player hits the ball against the front wall, and the other tries to return it before it has bounced more than once on the floor. The old game of rackets was first played in the 18th century in Fleet Prison, London; the inmates took to hitting a ball against the prison walls as a way of passing the time. A hundred years later, rackets players at Harrow School, England, invented squash as a practice game, its name coming from the soft or "squashy" ball that was used. Like the other racket sports, squash and racketball can be played by two (singles) or four players (doubles). In America, squash is played on a narrower court and with a much harder (almost solid) ball.

Each racket has about 27 ft (8.2 m) of string

| Yellow dot (very slow) | White dot (slow) | Red dot (fast) | Blue dot (very fast) |

COLOR-CODED BALLS
Temperature and other weather conditions affect the performance of the hollow rubber ball. Squash balls are made in four varieties - ranging from very slow for hot conditions to very fast for cold conditions. The different kinds of ball are coded with colored dots. Most top players use the very slow ball, which has a less pronounced bounce.

THE RACKET
Squash rackets have a smaller, rounder head than those used for badminton or tennis. Like other rackets, most modern squash rackets are now made from materials such as carbon graphite and fiberglass. Some rackets have a frame with a hollow core that reduces racket vibration when the ball is hit.

Synthetic strings

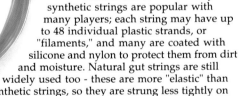

Natural gut strings

Squash racket

STRINGS
For all racket sports, the choice of strings is very important, as the string is the only part of the racket that actually touches the ball. Nowadays synthetic strings are popular with many players; each string may have up to 48 individual plastic strands, or "filaments," and many are coated with silicone and nylon to protect them from dirt and moisture. Natural gut strings are still widely used too - these are more "elastic" than synthetic strings, so they are strung less tightly on the racket.

EYE PROTECTORS
Some players wear special shatterproof goggles to protect their eyes in case they are struck by the fast-moving ball.

SPECTATOR SPORT
The development of glass and plexiglass walls meant that an audience could watch a match from all sides of the court. This made squash much more popular as a spectator sport.

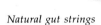

Squash court with plexiglass walls

Racketball
racket

Racketball

This very modern relative of squash was first played in the United States during the early 1950s. It evolved from court handball and, more directly, from paddleball - in which players used wooden bats, or paddles, rather than strung rackets. As with squash and badminton, points can only be won when a player is serving. When the server loses a rally, his opponent earns the right to serve. The winner is the first player to score 21 points.

THE BALL
The hollow rubber ball is larger than a squash ball. When dropped from a height of 100 in (2.5 m), it must bounce 68-72 in (1.7-1.8m) in a temperature of 76°F (24.5°C).

Racketball glove

THE RACKET
The racket has a slightly larger head than a squash racket, but the handle is much shorter. Some players use a wrist thong attached to the end of the handle.

FAST AND FURIOUS
Squash and racketball are two of the fastest and most energetic of all sports. Good players must be very fit and agile. Players must be ready to play within 10 seconds of the end of the previous rally, and are penalized if they try to delay the game longer in order to regain their strength.

Wrist thong

LEATHER GLOVE
Players may wear a glove on their racket hand to get a better grip on the handle. The sheepskin used for this glove has been treated to make it "tacky."

Squash/racketball shoe

Padded foam tongue for comfort

JAI ALAI
This sport, which comes from northern Spain, is played on a long, narrow court by players holding curved baskets, or *cestas*, made from woven reed and attached to a leather glove.

Basque jai alai player

INSIDE A SHOE
Modern sports shoes of all kinds are designed to be strong, light, and comfortable. Shoes worn by racket-sports players have to be well padded to avoid jarring the heels and ankles, and ventilated to allow the feet to "breathe."

Reinforced heel gives support

Rubber soles provide sure grip

Thick sole absorbs shock

Athletics

THE VARIOUS SPORTS that make up athletics are divided into two main groups: track events (running and walking) and field events (jumping and throwing). These are among the earliest and most basic forms of testing speed, strength, agility, and stamina, and can be traced back directly to the ancient Greek games, some 4,000 years ago. Most athletes only do one or two events, but a few choose to compete in a range of track and field events, the *heptathlon* for women (seven events held over two days) and the *decathlon* for men (ten events over two days).

Hollow relay batons

TEAM EVENT
The relay is the only athletics event in which teams compete directly against each other. A baton is passed between four team members, who each run either 100 m or 400 m.

Starting pistol

Blanks

FROM START TO FINISH
Races are started by firing a starting pistol. In top-class meetings, this triggers a highly accurate electronic timing device; ordinary stopwatches are used in lower levels of competition. The athlete is judged to have finished the race when his torso (not his arms, legs, head, or neck) crosses the line.

Stopwatch

Olympic torch-bearer

Track events

Races of up to one lap in length are run in eight lanes. Because the distance around the outside of the track is greater than the inside, the athletes start in a staggered line so that each one runs an equal distance.

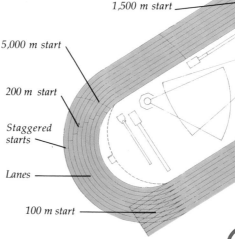

1,500 m start

5,000 m start

200 m start

Staggered starts

Lanes

100 m start

400 m start

Finishing line (all races)

The Olympic symbol

THE OLYMPIC GAMES
The Olympics are held every four years, and include athletics and a great variety of different sports. The Olympic symbol of five interlocking circles represents the five participating continents of the world.

ON THE BLOCKS *left*
Sprinters use starting blocks that are fixed to the track. They provide a firm base for the foot to push against at the start of the race. Blocks can be connected to a device that detects any false starts - when an athlete's foot leaves the blocks before the gun goes off.

CROSS-COUNTRY RUNNING
As well as track events, there are long-distance races run on roads and across country. Such courses may include obstacles like fences, ditches, and streams.

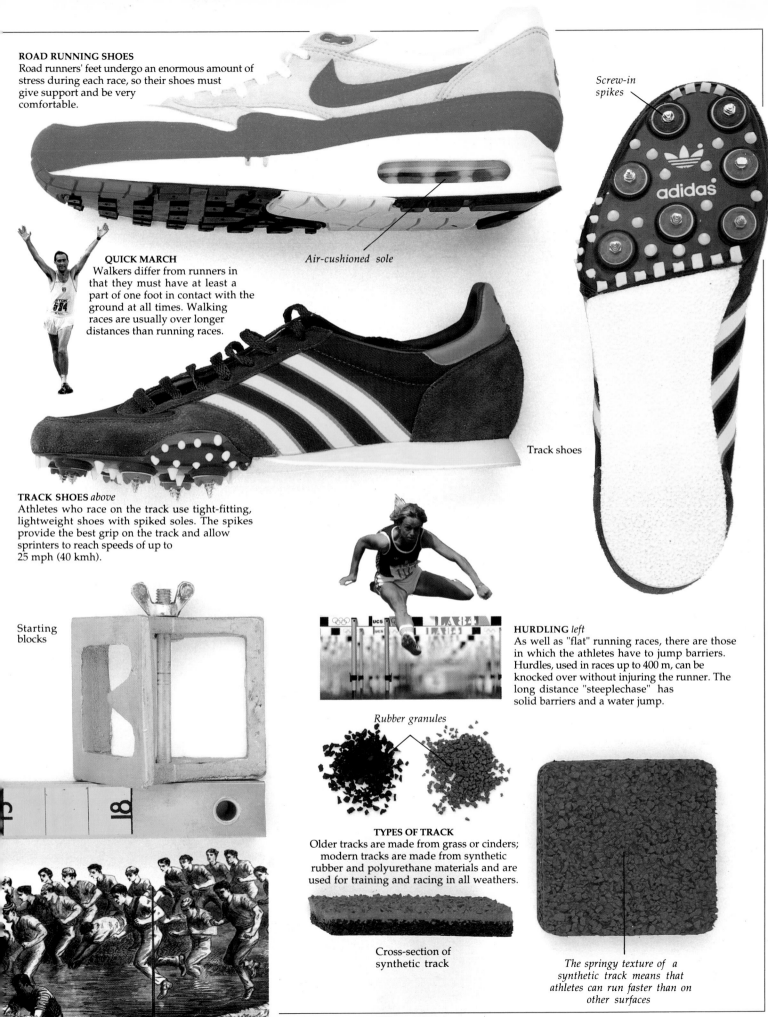

ROAD RUNNING SHOES
Road runners' feet undergo an enormous amount of stress during each race, so their shoes must give support and be very comfortable.

Screw-in spikes

Air-cushioned sole

QUICK MARCH
Walkers differ from runners in that they must have at least a part of one foot in contact with the ground at all times. Walking races are usually over longer distances than running races.

Track shoes

TRACK SHOES *above*
Athletes who race on the track use tight-fitting, lightweight shoes with spiked soles. The spikes provide the best grip on the track and allow sprinters to reach speeds of up to 25 mph (40 kmh).

Starting blocks

HURDLING *left*
As well as "flat" running races, there are those in which the athletes have to jump barriers. Hurdles, used in races up to 400 m, can be knocked over without injuring the runner. The long distance "steeplechase" has solid barriers and a water jump.

Rubber granules

TYPES OF TRACK
Older tracks are made from grass or cinders; modern tracks are made from synthetic rubber and polyurethane materials and are used for training and racing in all weathers.

Cross-section of synthetic track

The springy texture of a synthetic track means that athletes can run faster than on other surfaces

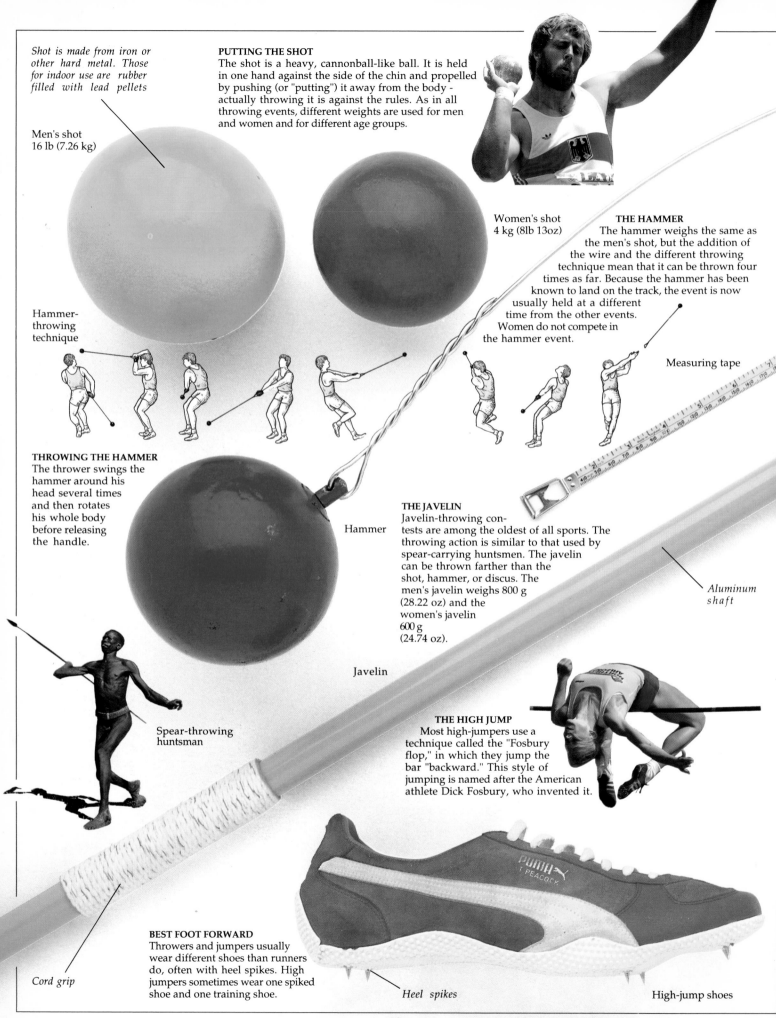

Shot is made from iron or other hard metal. Those for indoor use are rubber filled with lead pellets

PUTTING THE SHOT
The shot is a heavy, cannonball-like ball. It is held in one hand against the side of the chin and propelled by pushing (or "putting") it away from the body - actually throwing it is against the rules. As in all throwing events, different weights are used for men and women and for different age groups.

Men's shot
16 lb (7.26 kg)

Women's shot
4 kg (8lb 13oz)

THE HAMMER
The hammer weighs the same as the men's shot, but the addition of the wire and the different throwing technique mean that it can be thrown four times as far. Because the hammer has been known to land on the track, the event is now usually held at a different time from the other events. Women do not compete in the hammer event.

Hammer-throwing technique

Measuring tape

THROWING THE HAMMER
The thrower swings the hammer around his head several times and then rotates his whole body before releasing the handle.

Hammer

THE JAVELIN
Javelin-throwing contests are among the oldest of all sports. The throwing action is similar to that used by spear-carrying huntsmen. The javelin can be thrown farther than the shot, hammer, or discus. The men's javelin weighs 800 g (28.22 oz) and the women's javelin 600 g (24.74 oz).

Aluminum shaft

Javelin

Spear-throwing huntsman

THE HIGH JUMP
Most high-jumpers use a technique called the "Fosbury flop," in which they jump the bar "backward." This style of jumping is named after the American athlete Dick Fosbury, who invented it.

BEST FOOT FORWARD
Throwers and jumpers usually wear different shoes than runners do, often with heel spikes. High jumpers sometimes wear one spiked shoe and one training shoe.

Cord grip

Heel spikes

High-jump shoes

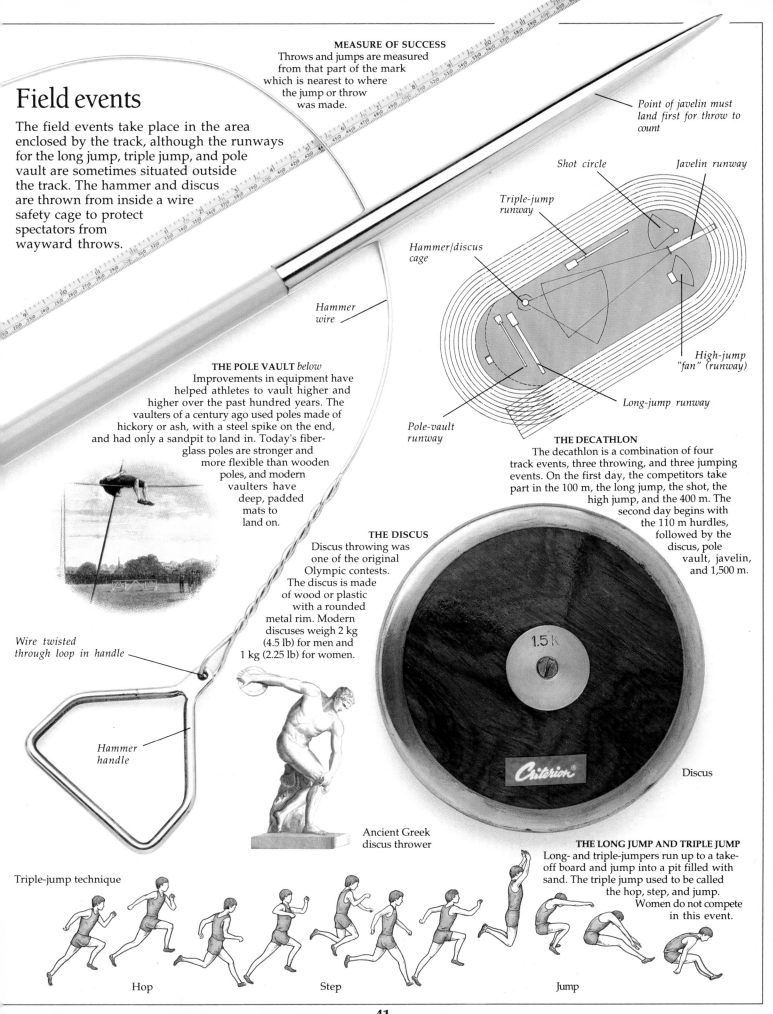

Field events

The field events take place in the area enclosed by the track, although the runways for the long jump, triple jump, and pole vault are sometimes situated outside the track. The hammer and discus are thrown from inside a wire safety cage to protect spectators from wayward throws.

MEASURE OF SUCCESS
Throws and jumps are measured from that part of the mark which is nearest to where the jump or throw was made.

Point of javelin must land first for throw to count

Shot circle

Javelin runway

Triple-jump runway

Hammer/discus cage

Hammer wire

High-jump "fan" (runway)

Long-jump runway

Pole-vault runway

THE POLE VAULT *below*
Improvements in equipment have helped athletes to vault higher and higher over the past hundred years. The vaulters of a century ago used poles made of hickory or ash, with a steel spike on the end, and had only a sandpit to land in. Today's fiberglass poles are stronger and more flexible than wooden poles, and modern vaulters have deep, padded mats to land on.

THE DECATHLON
The decathlon is a combination of four track events, three throwing, and three jumping events. On the first day, the competitors take part in the 100 m, the long jump, the shot, the high jump, and the 400 m. The second day begins with the 110 m hurdles, followed by the discus, pole vault, javelin, and 1,500 m.

THE DISCUS
Discus throwing was one of the original Olympic contests. The discus is made of wood or plastic with a rounded metal rim. Modern discuses weigh 2 kg (4.5 lb) for men and 1 kg (2.25 lb) for women.

Wire twisted through loop in handle

Hammer handle

1.5 K

Criterion®

Discus

Ancient Greek discus thrower

Triple-jump technique

THE LONG JUMP AND TRIPLE JUMP
Long- and triple-jumpers run up to a take-off board and jump into a pit filled with sand. The triple jump used to be called the hop, step, and jump. Women do not compete in this event.

Hop

Step

Jump

Gymnastics

GYMNASTICS IS A MIXTURE of different events, testing strength, agility, coordination, and balance. Gymnasts use standard apparatus (equipment) on which they perform a series of exercises that are marked by judges. Men compete in six events: the rings, pommel horse, parallel bars, high bar, vault, and floor exercises. Women also compete in the vault and floor exercises, as well as on the beam and uneven parallel bars. Many modern gymnasiums have other kinds of equipment that people can use to keep fit.

RIBBON RHYTHM
The floor exercises are performed on a marked-out area 40 ft (12 m) square. Gymnasts must make use of this whole area but are not allowed to step outside it. The exercises consist of tumbling, jumping, and balancing movements; women's floor exercises may be accompanied by music. A recent variation on the sport is "rhythmic" gymnastics, in which female gymnasts perform floor exercises with ribbons, balls, hoops, ropes, and Indian clubs.

PARALLEL BARS *below*
Movements performed on the parallel bars have names such as "peach basket" and "elephant lift." The record number of parallel bar "dips" (push-ups) is over 700 in a 30-minute period.

HANGING AROUND
The rings are suspended 8ft 2in (2.5 m) from the ground. All the movements must be performed without making the rings swing back and forth on their frame.

Wooden rings are 7 in (18 cm) in diameter

WALKING THE PLANK
Gymnasts do somersaults, cartwheels, and turns on the beam, which is 16.5 ft (5 m) long and 4 ft (120 cm) off the ground. Performing on the beam is a real balancing act, as it is only 4 in (10 cm) wide.

HIGH BAR
Exercises on the high bar must consist of nonstop swinging movements, with backward and forward swings and changes of grip. As with other events, the high bar is judged according to how difficult the exercises are and how well they are performed.

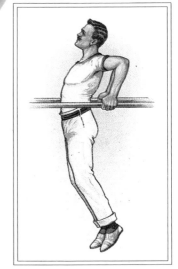

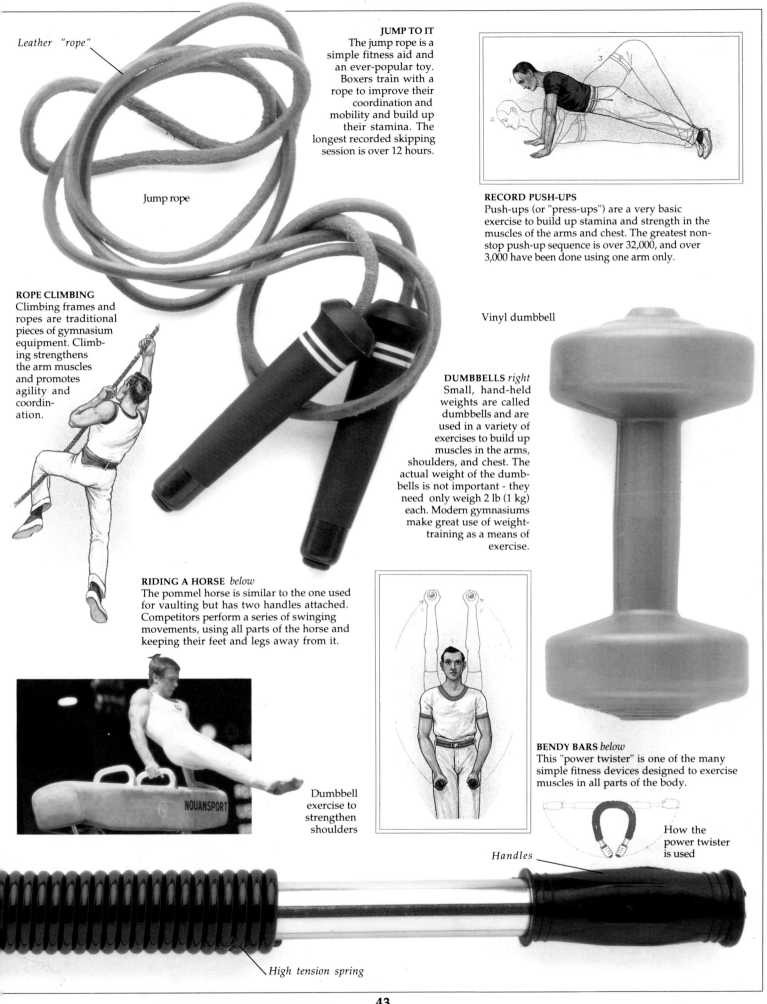

Leather "rope"

Jump rope

JUMP TO IT
The jump rope is a simple fitness aid and an ever-popular toy. Boxers train with a rope to improve their coordination and mobility and build up their stamina. The longest recorded skipping session is over 12 hours.

ROPE CLIMBING
Climbing frames and ropes are traditional pieces of gymnasium equipment. Climbing strengthens the arm muscles and promotes agility and coordination.

RIDING A HORSE *below*
The pommel horse is similar to the one used for vaulting but has two handles attached. Competitors perform a series of swinging movements, using all parts of the horse and keeping their feet and legs away from it.

NOUANSPORT

RECORD PUSH-UPS
Push-ups (or "press-ups") are a very basic exercise to build up stamina and strength in the muscles of the arms and chest. The greatest non-stop push-up sequence is over 32,000, and over 3,000 have been done using one arm only.

Vinyl dumbbell

DUMBBELLS *right*
Small, hand-held weights are called dumbbells and are used in a variety of exercises to build up muscles in the arms, shoulders, and chest. The actual weight of the dumbbells is not important - they need only weigh 2 lb (1 kg) each. Modern gymnasiums make great use of weight-training as a means of exercise.

Dumbbell exercise to strengthen shoulders

BENDY BARS *below*
This "power twister" is one of the many simple fitness devices designed to exercise muscles in all parts of the body.

How the power twister is used

Handles

High tension spring

Weightlifting

THE LIFTING OF WEIGHTS is one of the oldest and most simple forms of testing strength. Modern weightlifters compete against each other according to their body weight, as heavier men can usually lift the larger weights. In recent years, a great many people have discovered how training with weights helps build up the strength and stamina needed in other sports. Others use weights to develop muscles "for their own sake" and compete in special bodybuilding contests.

DISK WEIGHTS *below*
These cast-iron disks range from 0.25 kg (0.5 lb) up to 25 kg (56 lb), so that any weight can be added to the bar by a combination of disks. The greatest weight ever raised by a human is 6,270 lb (2,844 kg), equal to the combined weight of three dozen fully grown men.

1.25 kg
(2.75 lb)

2.5 kg
(5.5 lb)

CIRCUS STRONGMAN *left*
The modern form of weightlifting, using a bar and weighted disks, only dates from the end of the last century. Before then, strongmen performed great lifting feats as part of circus and fairground shows.

Weight-training gloves

BACK SUPPORT *above*
Lifters use wide belts to protect their backs from injury.

MUSCLE POWER
Male and female bodybuilders train with weights in order to make their muscles as big as possible. Then they oil their bodies to make the muscles stand out even more, and parade in front of judges in special bodybuilding contests.

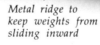

Metal ridge to keep weights from sliding inward

Hand grips

Female bodybuilder

Rough-textured metal where bar is gripped by lifter

LOADING THE BAR
The disk weights are attached to a bar that is 7ft 4in (220 cm) long and weighs 20 kg (44 lb). The weight of the bar forms part of the total weight lifted. The largest weights are always on the inside and the smallest on the outside. This is so gradual increases in the weight can be made quickly after each successful lift.

"Clean"...

CLEAN AND JERK
One of the standard weightlifting techniques is the two-part "clean and jerk," where the bar is first lifted onto the chest and then, when the lifter has steadied himself, pushed up over the head in a separate action. The lifter must "lock" his elbows and knees to complete the lift.

...and "jerk"

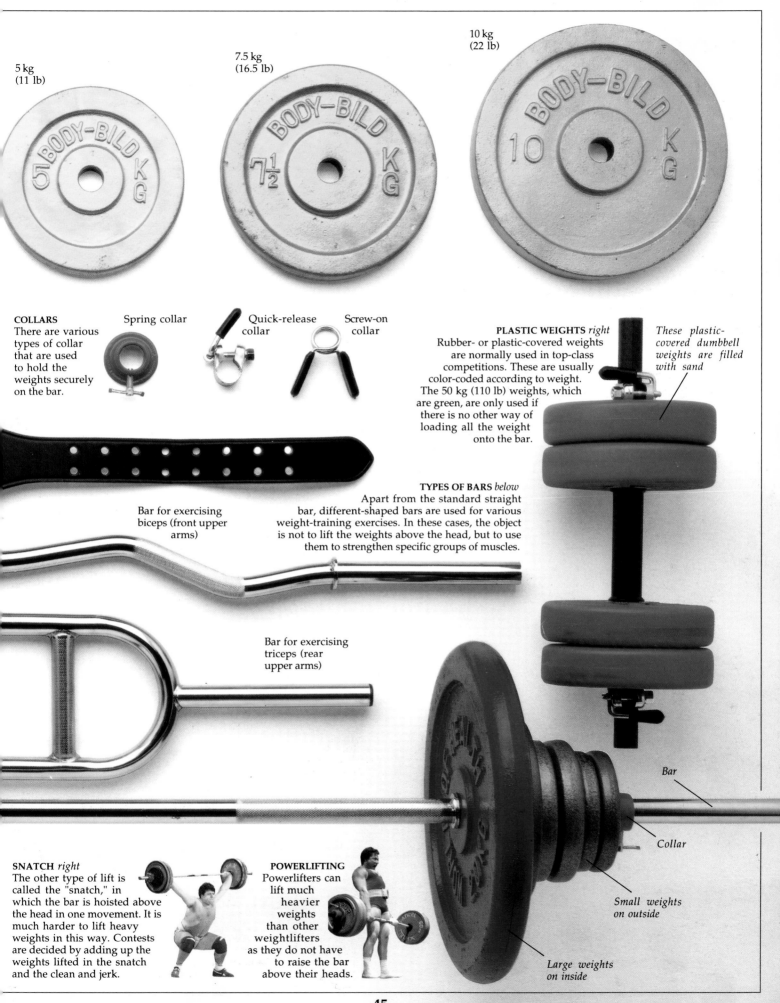

5 kg
(11 lb)

7.5 kg
(16.5 lb)

10 kg
(22 lb)

COLLARS
There are various types of collar that are used to hold the weights securely on the bar.

Spring collar

Quick-release collar

Screw-on collar

PLASTIC WEIGHTS *right*
Rubber- or plastic-covered weights are normally used in top-class competitions. These are usually color-coded according to weight. The 50 kg (110 lb) weights, which are green, are only used if there is no other way of loading all the weight onto the bar.

These plastic-covered dumbbell weights are filled with sand

Bar for exercising biceps (front upper arms)

TYPES OF BARS *below*
Apart from the standard straight bar, different-shaped bars are used for various weight-training exercises. In these cases, the object is not to lift the weights above the head, but to use them to strengthen specific groups of muscles.

Bar for exercising triceps (rear upper arms)

Bar

Collar

Small weights on outside

SNATCH *right*
The other type of lift is called the "snatch," in which the bar is hoisted above the head in one movement. It is much harder to lift heavy weights in this way. Contests are decided by adding up the weights lifted in the snatch and the clean and jerk.

POWERLIFTING
Powerlifters can lift much heavier weights than other weightlifters as they do not have to raise the bar above their heads.

Large weights on inside

45

Boxing

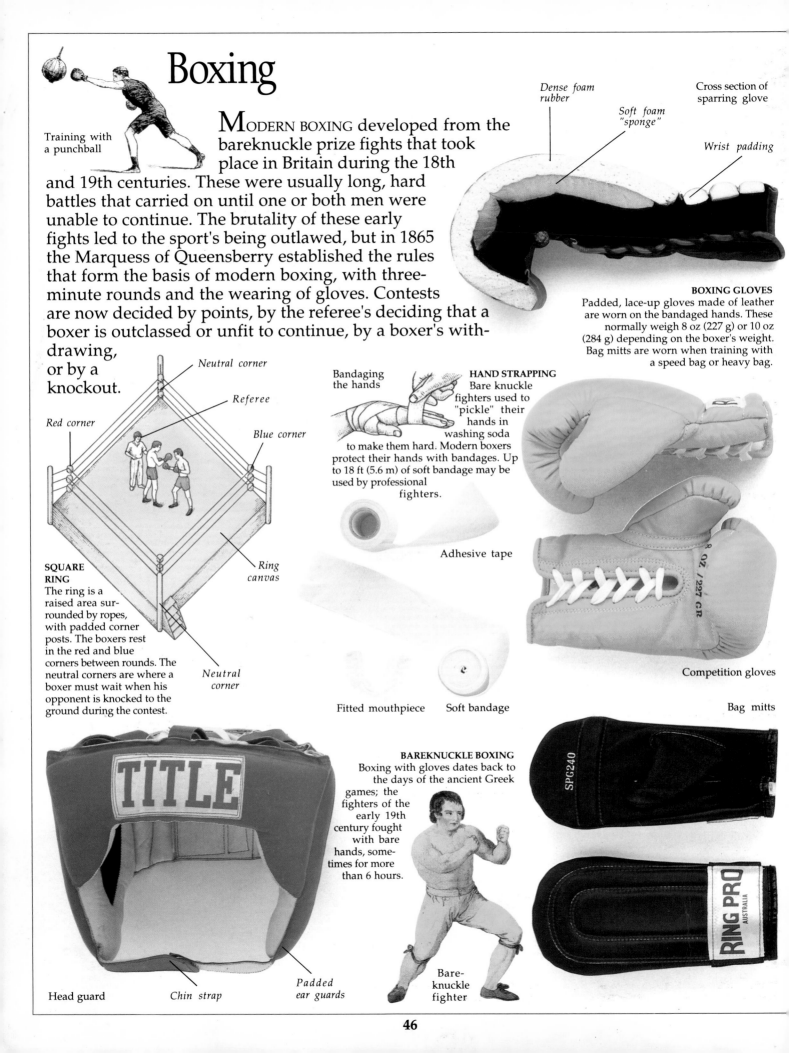

Training with a punchball

MODERN BOXING developed from the bareknuckle prize fights that took place in Britain during the 18th and 19th centuries. These were usually long, hard battles that carried on until one or both men were unable to continue. The brutality of these early fights led to the sport's being outlawed, but in 1865 the Marquess of Queensberry established the rules that form the basis of modern boxing, with three-minute rounds and the wearing of gloves. Contests are now decided by points, by the referee's deciding that a boxer is outclassed or unfit to continue, by a boxer's withdrawing, or by a knockout.

Dense foam rubber

Soft foam "sponge"

Cross section of sparring glove

Wrist padding

BOXING GLOVES
Padded, lace-up gloves made of leather are worn on the bandaged hands. These normally weigh 8 oz (227 g) or 10 oz (284 g) depending on the boxer's weight. Bag mitts are worn when training with a speed bag or heavy bag.

Neutral corner

Referee

Red corner

Blue corner

SQUARE RING
The ring is a raised area surrounded by ropes, with padded corner posts. The boxers rest in the red and blue corners between rounds. The neutral corners are where a boxer must wait when his opponent is knocked to the ground during the contest.

Ring canvas

Neutral corner

Bandaging the hands

HAND STRAPPING
Bare knuckle fighters used to "pickle" their hands in washing soda to make them hard. Modern boxers protect their hands with bandages. Up to 18 ft (5.6 m) of soft bandage may be used by professional fighters.

Adhesive tape

Fitted mouthpiece

Soft bandage

Competition gloves

Bag mitts

BAREKNUCKLE BOXING
Boxing with gloves dates back to the days of the ancient Greek games; the fighters of the early 19th century fought with bare hands, sometimes for more than 6 hours.

Head guard

Chin strap

Padded ear guards

Bareknuckle fighter

AMATEUR OR PROFESSIONAL? *above*
Amateur fights are fought over three rounds of three minutes each, compared to up to 15 rounds for professional championship bouts. Amateurs always wear singlets and the protective headguard that professionals use only when sparring (practicing). Every boxer wears a mouthpiece, molded to the shape of his mouth, to protect his teeth. A lace-up protector is worn under the trunks to guard against any stray punches.

Elasticized belt

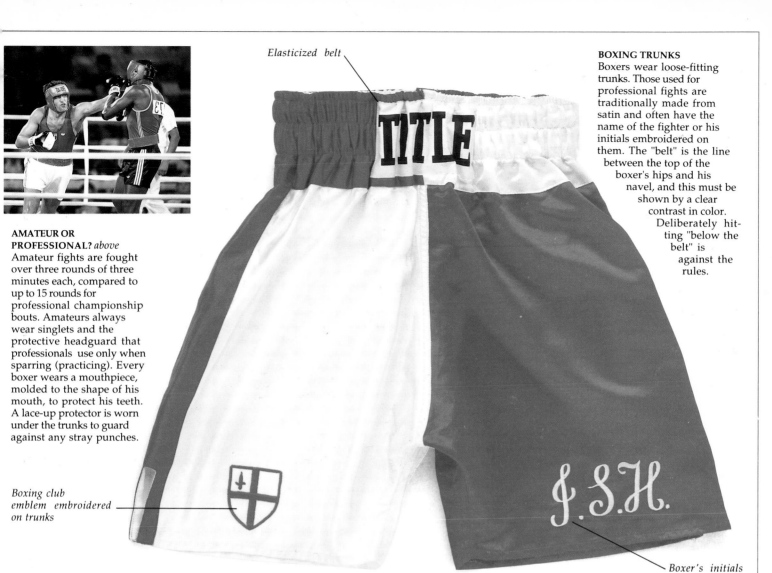

BOXING TRUNKS
Boxers wear loose-fitting trunks. Those used for professional fights are traditionally made from satin and often have the name of the fighter or his initials embroidered on them. The "belt" is the line between the top of the boxer's hips and his navel, and this must be shown by a clear contrast in color. Deliberately hitting "below the belt" is against the rules.

Boxing club emblem embroidered on trunks

Boxer's initials

The points system

The judges award points to each boxer at the end of every round. The maximum number of points per round (20) is given to the boxer who has been most skillful in landing his punches during that round; after an equal round, both boxers might get 20 points. To score points, a punch must be made with the knuckle part of the glove on the front or sides of the opponent's head or upper body. At the end of the last round, the man with the highest total of points is declared the winner.

Direct left-hand blow to the body

FANCY FOOTWORK
The ability to move quickly and smoothly around the ring is an important aspect of boxing. Fighters practice their "dancing" with a jump rope as part of their training. The tall boxing shoes are lightweight and have a thin sole with no heel.

High sides provide support for boxer's ankles

Ducking to avoid left-hand punch and countering with right-hand blow to jaw

Ducking to the right avoids left-hand blow to the head

Thin, flat sole

Lightweight leather uppers

Martial arts

MARTIAL ARTS are those skills that are used in battle and therefore include fencing, shooting and archery, as well as the sports described here. However, the term is usually used to describe the various combat sports that come from the Far East, of which judo and karate are the most widely practiced. *Judo* means "the soft way" and involves throwing and holding movements. *Karate*, on the other hand, means "empty hand" and is a mixture of punching and kicking techniques. The martial arts were first practiced by the ancient Japanese samurai warriors, who were armed with bows and swords. The unarmed combat techniques, from which modern judo and karate evolved, enabled the warriors to continue fighting if they were suddenly disarmed by their opponent.

Film fighter Bruce Lee helped make the martial arts popular in the 1970s

KUNG FU WEAPONS
As well as the various forms of unarmed combat, martial artists learn to master weapons such as the *nunchaku*, two wooden handles joined by a metal chain. This weapon developed from a tool used in the Chinese rice fields. Nunchakus with safe rubber handles are used in sporting competitions

Nunchaku

KENDO *below*
The traditional Japanese art of *kendo* is a form of fencing with wooden swords. The competitors, or *kendoka*, wear traditional padded clothing. Each bout lasts for just 3-5 minutes.

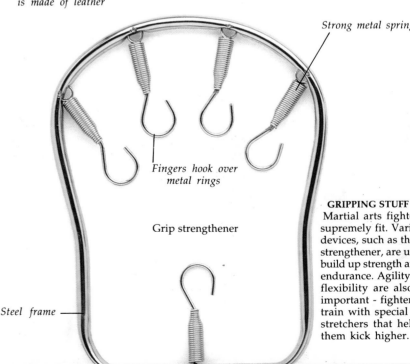

Leather hilt

Round "tsuba," or shield, is made of leather

Shinai

Strong metal springs

SUMO WRESTLING
The origins of Japanese *sumo* wrestling, in which contestants try to push each other out of the ring, date back to the 1st century B.C. The wrestlers put on weight by eating a high-protein stew - the heaviest wrestler on record was 496 lb (225 kg). Ritual is an important part of the sport.

Fingers hook over metal rings

Grip strengthener

GRIPPING STUFF
Martial arts fighters are supremely fit. Various devices, such as this grip strengthener, are used to build up strength and endurance. Agility and flexibility are also important - fighters train with special leg-stretchers that help them kick higher.

Steel frame

KENDO EQUIPMENT

The *kendoka* wear protective masks, gloves, breastplates, and aprons. The kendo sword is called a *shinai* and is made from four strips of bamboo lashed together with string and leather. It must be less than 47 in (118 cm) long.

Leather tip

Bamboo strips

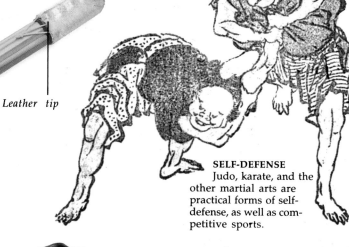

SELF-DEFENSE
Judo, karate, and the other martial arts are practical forms of self-defense, as well as competitive sports.

Red belt
9th-11th *dan*

Black belt
1st-5th *dan*

Judo

Judo students are trained to make use of an opponent's strength to overcome him, while saving their own energy. Sporting bouts are strictly controlled, and the object is to display superior technique rather than to injure the opponent. Different levels of points are awarded according to the standard of throwing and holding movements.

Brown belt
1st *kyu*

Blue belt
2nd *kyu*

SMASHING TECHNIQUE
The special physical and mental training of karate fighters enables them to break slabs of concrete and blocks of wood with their hands, feet, or head.

Green belt
3rd *kyu*

"Semicontact" gloves

KARATE GLOVES
The many different forms of karate have different rules about the amount of physical contact allowed and the protective clothing worn by the contestants. Various gloves are sometimes used in practice and in competitions.

Karate

Karate contests usually last two minutes and are controlled by a referee and four judges. Actual physical contact is not required to score points - as with judo, it is superior technique that counts.

Orange belt
4th *kyu*

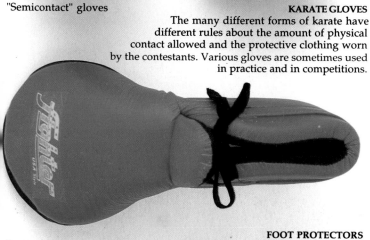

Foot protectors

FOOT PROTECTORS
These padded shoes slip over the bare feet of the fighter to protect them when he kicks at an opponent.

JUDO BELTS *right*
Fighters are awarded colored belts to show the grade they have reached. The highest level reached by most people is the black belt, but there are three levels above this - red-and-white striped, red, and white belts.

Yellow belt
5th *kyu*

Fencing

FENCING IS A COMBAT SPORT using swords and takes place on a narrow *piste* (strip) 14 m (46 ft) long. The winner is the fencer who scores the greater number of "hits" on his opponent. The three types of modern sword - the *foil*, *épée*, and *saber* - are descendants of the *rapier*, which was a popular court weapon in the 16th century. The rapier and dagger replaced the heavier sword and "buckler" (shield) that had been carried before. Fencing swords do not have cutting blades, and the tip is formed into a blunt button to prevent injuries.

16th-century duelist

METAL JACKET
In some contests electronic equipment is used to show when a hit has been scored. Fencers have to wear special jackets covering the target area; these are made from woven metal threads that conduct the electricity, so the scoreboard lights up when they are touched by the tip of the sword.

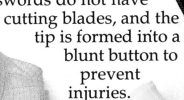

MESH MASK
The traditional mask protects the face and head, and a padded bib protects the throat. The fine mesh is made from stainless steel or molded plastic. It allows the fencer to see out but prevents any accidental injuries to the eyes.

CLOTHING
The fencer's clothes must allow him freedom of movement and give maximum protection. They must be white and made from stong material, and there must be no fastenings in which a sword may become caught.

GAUNTLET
A long white glove, or gauntlet, is worn only on the sword hand. It is slightly padded and extends halfway up the fencer's forearm.

Guard

Leather pad

"Tang"

Blade

Steel foil pommel

Insert brass screw

Alternative "pistol-grip" handle

THE SWORD
Swords are subject to strict rules governing their design and safety. The total length of any type of sword must not be more than 44 in (110 cm) - 42 in (105 cm) for the saber.

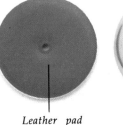

Gripping the handle

THE BLADE
The blade is square in cross section and has a groove running along its whole length. In electric-sword contests, the wire runs down this groove and is taped into place.

THE SABER

The saber may have a straight or curved blade; any curve must be continuous and less than 1.5 in (4 cm). The sword must weigh less than 1 lb (500 g) and the guard must measure no more than 6 in x 5.5 in (15 cm x 14 cm). Unlike the other swords, the edges of the saber - as well as its tip - can be used to register hits.

THE FOIL

This light sword was developed specially for fencing practice in the 18th century. It weighs the same as the saber, but its guard must have a diameter of no more than 4.5 in (12 cm). In electric foil contests, a hit registers only when pressure on the point is at least 1 lb (500 g).

THE EPEE

This is the traditional dueling sword, heavier than the foil and saber, with a maximum weight of 1.5 lb (750 g) and a guard no larger than 5.5 in (13.5 cm) in diameter. A pressure of 1.5 lb (750 g) is needed to score a hit in electric épée bouts. Foils and épées usually have a strap, called a martingale, attaching the sword to the fencer's hand.

DUELISTS

The sport of fencing developed directly from the use of the sword in warfare and dueling. Gentlemen used to fight duels regularly as a way of settling "matters of honor," but these resulted in so many deaths that they were banned in many countries. Duelists often carried a sword in one hand and a dagger in the other.

The target area in saber competitions is the trunk and arms

The target area for foil is the trunk, not including the arms

The target area for épée is the whole of the opponent's body

SWORD HILTS

The hilt (handle) of the modern sporting saber most closely resembles those of dueling swords, which were designed to protect the sword hand.

Modern saber hilt

16th-century rapier hilt

CAVALRY CHARGE

The saber used in modern fencing competition is a light version of the sword used by cavalry troops in the 18th and 19th centuries. The weapon was specially designed for use by troops on horseback and had a flat, curved blade.

Martingale

USING ELECTRICITY

Official foil and épée competitions now use an electric scoring system in which the sword tips are connected to lights by a long wire that passes underneath each fencer's jacket.

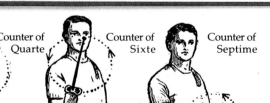

Counter of Quarte

Counter of Sixte

Counter of Septime

Counter of Seconde

Button

FENCING TECHNIQUE

These circular movements - which are made by moving the fingers and wrist only - are used to deflect the opponent's blade. Many of the fencing terms date from the 16th or 17th century, when the light court sword was introduced in France.

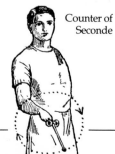

Archery

VARIOUS FORMS of bow and arrow have been used to fight battles and as hunting tools for thousands of years. Modern sporting bows are designed and made according to the same principles, although the sights, stabilizers, and other attachments make them look very different. Competitors in target archery shoot a certain number of arrows at targets fixed at different distances - 30 m, 50 m, 70 m, and 90 m for men, and 30 m, 50 m, 60 m, and 70 m for women. The points scored are added up to give a total, and the archer with the highest total is the winner. Crossbows are sometimes used in separate competitions.

Cupid's arrows cause people to fall in love

THE BAYEAUX TAPESTRY
Archers and slingers used to be less effective in battle than an army's main forces of cavalry and infantry (foot soldiers), until the introduction of the longbow in the Middle Ages.

The Dacron string is taken off the bow after each shooting session

Hardwood laminate (layered) limbs

"Riser"

VICTORIAN ARCHERS
The bows used by 19th-century British archers were usually made from two pieces of wood spliced (joined) together in the center. Those made from a single piece are called "self bows".

PROTECTION
A "bracer" is worn on the arm that holds the bow, to protect it against the bowstring. A glove or finger tab is worn on the drawing hand.

THE MODERN BOW
Until recently, bows were always made from wood, the best being yew. Modern bows are usually made from laminates and other materials, such as fiberglass and carbon. These are much stronger and therefore more reliable.

Sight ring attachment

BOWSIGHT *left*
A sight can be fixed to the side of the bow to help the archer concentrate his or her aim.

Finger tab

Magnesium handle

Archer's glove

STABILIZERS *below*
These are screwed into the "risers" to make the bow more stable while shooting so each shot is consistent.

The "nock" rests on the string

There are three feather "fletches" on each arrow

Bracer

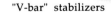

"V-bar" stabilizers

HUNTING WEAPON *left*
Like many other weapons, the bow and arrow was first used to help man catch his food. In the case of the Indians, it was used to kill buffalo, which also provided hides to make clothing and shelter.

MINI ARROWS
Crossbows fire "bolts," which are much shorter than arrows but must be at least 12 in (30 cm) long.

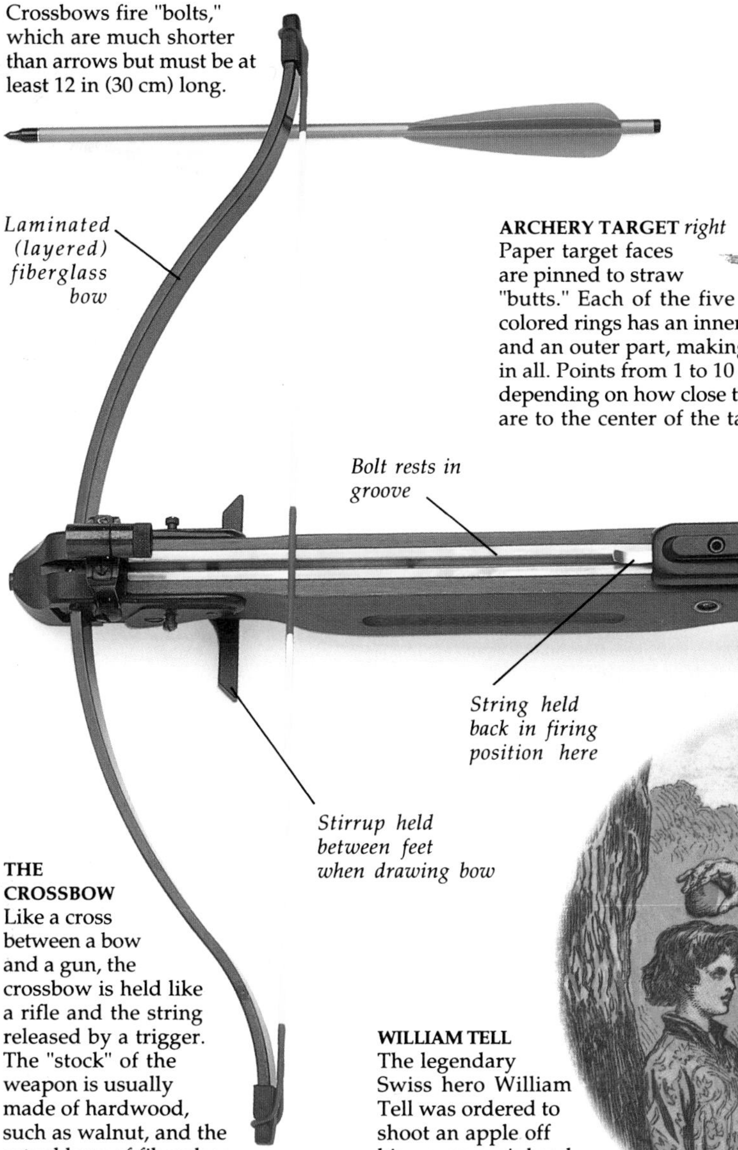

Laminated (layered) fiberglass bow

ARCHERY TARGET *right*
Paper target faces are pinned to straw "butts." Each of the five colored rings has an inner and an outer part, making ten areas in all. Points from 1 to 10 are scored depending on how close the arrows are to the center of the target - the bull's-eye.

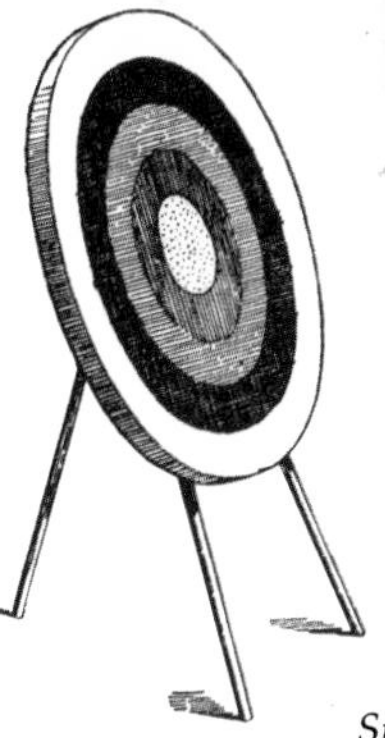

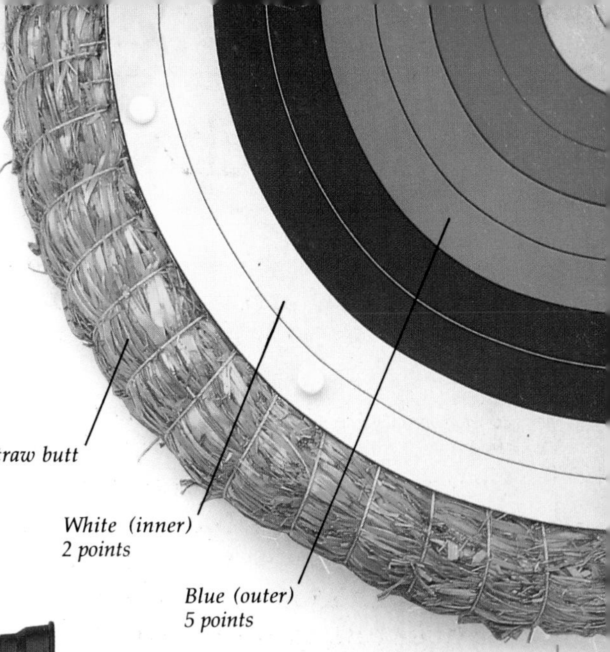

Straw butt

White (inner) 2 points

Blue (outer) 5 points

Bolt rests in groove

Aiming sight

String held back in firing position here

Stirrup held between feet when drawing bow

THE CROSSBOW
Like a cross between a bow and a gun, the crossbow is held like a rifle and the string released by a trigger. The "stock" of the weapon is usually made of hardwood, such as walnut, and the actual bow of fiberglass or some similar material.

WILLIAM TELL
The legendary Swiss hero William Tell was ordered to shoot an apple off his young son's head as a punishment. The legend usually says that he used a crossbow, but this picture shows him with a longbow.

Metal tip

THE PARTS OF AN ARROW *above*
The craft of making arrows is known as "fletching." Cedar and pine are the woods traditionally used to make the best arrows.

Wooden shaft

THE QUIVER *right*
This is the "holster" that holds the arrows. It is usually worn on a belt around the archer's waist. The arrows in this quiver have aluminum shafts and plastic fletches.

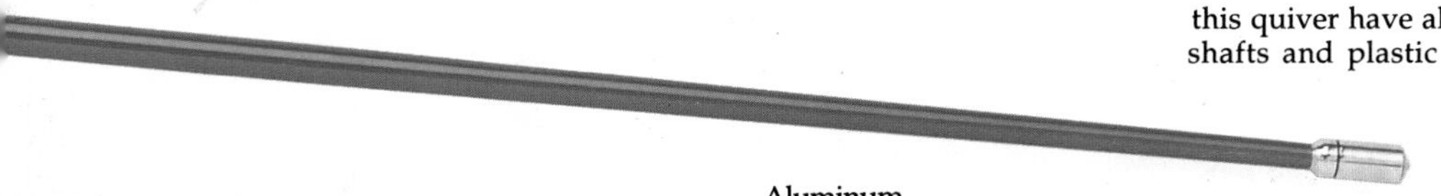

Aluminum long-rod stabilizer

LONGSHOT *left*
Modern bows are very powerful. A "footbow," in which the arrow is drawn back with both hands, can shoot an arrow well over a mile. The record for a handbow is over 3,600 ft (1,100 m).

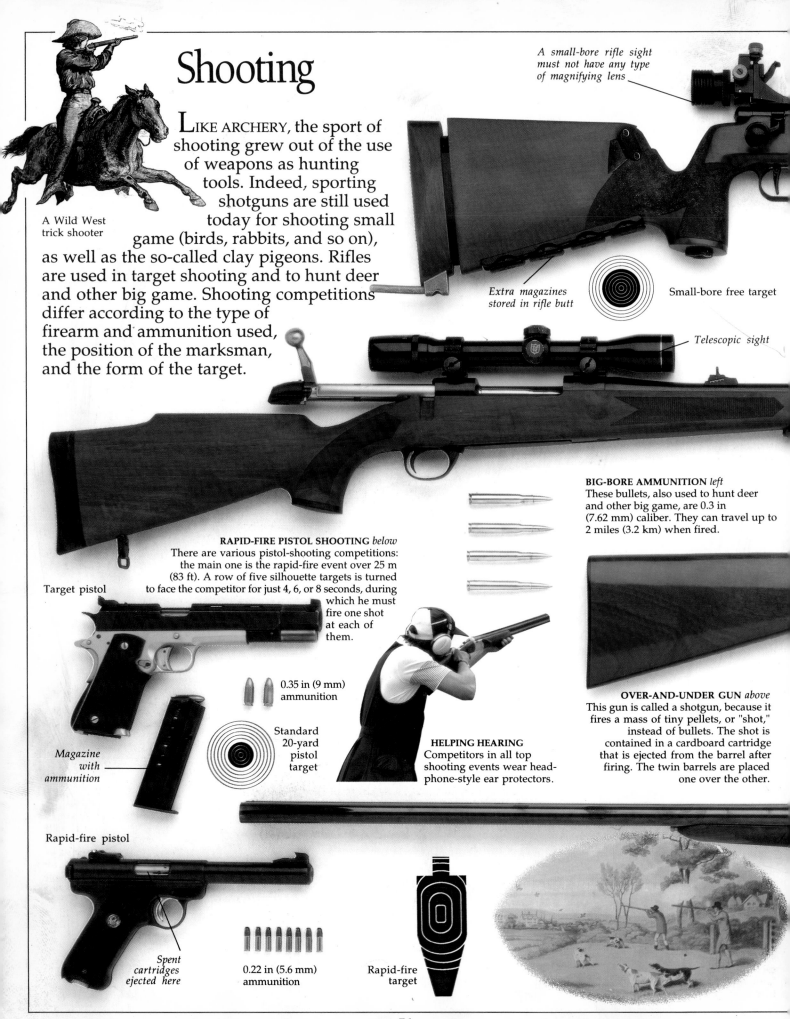

Shooting

LIKE ARCHERY, the sport of shooting grew out of the use of weapons as hunting tools. Indeed, sporting shotguns are still used today for shooting small game (birds, rabbits, and so on), as well as the so-called clay pigeons. Rifles are used in target shooting and to hunt deer and other big game. Shooting competitions differ according to the type of firearm and ammunition used, the position of the marksman, and the form of the target.

A Wild West trick shooter

A small-bore rifle sight must not have any type of magnifying lens

Extra magazines stored in rifle butt

Small-bore free target

Telescopic sight

BIG-BORE AMMUNITION *left*
These bullets, also used to hunt deer and other big game, are 0.3 in (7.62 mm) caliber. They can travel up to 2 miles (3.2 km) when fired.

RAPID-FIRE PISTOL SHOOTING *below*
There are various pistol-shooting competitions: the main one is the rapid-fire event over 25 m (83 ft). A row of five silhouette targets is turned to face the competitor for just 4, 6, or 8 seconds, during which he must fire one shot at each of them.

Target pistol

0.35 in (9 mm) ammunition

Standard 20-yard pistol target

Magazine with ammunition

HELPING HEARING
Competitors in all top shooting events wear head-phone-style ear protectors.

OVER-AND-UNDER GUN *above*
This gun is called a shotgun, because it fires a mass of tiny pellets, or "shot," instead of bullets. The shot is contained in a cardboard cartridge that is ejected from the barrel after firing. The twin barrels are placed one over the other.

Rapid-fire pistol

Spent cartridges ejected here

0.22 in (5.6 mm) ammunition

Rapid-fire target

SMALL-BORE FREE RIFLE *below*
This weapon is fired from a distance of 50 m (165 ft) at a round target 6.5 in (16.24 cm) across. The diameter, or "caliber," of the bullets used is 0.22 in (5.6 mm).

Barrel sight

Ammunition for small-bore free rifle

THE BIATHLON
This is a modern sport combining cross-country skiing and rifle shooting. Competitors ski a course of up to 20 km (12.5 miles) and stop for three or four sessions of shooting at targets from a range of 150 m (495 ft).

ANNIE GET YOUR GUN
The remarkable Annie Oakley was a famous trick shooter: as part of her act, she would shoot a cigarette from between the lips of her husband and split a playing card from a distance of 30 paces.

BIG - BORE RIFLE *above*
This hunting rifle is fired over a distance of 1,000 ft (305 m) at a target 39 in (1 m) across. The term "rifle" refers to the spiral groove inside the barrel of the guns that causes the bullets to spin through the air as they are fired.

Air-pistol pellets

Over-and-under barrels

AIR WEAPONS
Air pistols and rifles use compressed air or carbon dioxide to fire tiny pellets from a range of 10 m (33 ft) at targets just 1.8 in (4.6 cm) across. These pellets have to be loaded one at a time.

The wooden grip is specially shaped to fit the hand exactly

Cartridge

Pellets

"BB" 4.3 mm
(0.172 in)
shot

"No. 9" 2.0 mm
(0.08 in)
shot

TYPES OF SHOT
Different sizes of shot are used for different purposes. Large pellets travel farther and are used to shoot birds; smaller pellets scatter over a wide area more quickly and are used in clay-pigeon shooting.

CLAY PIGEONS
These small, saucer-shaped clay disks are launched two at a time from special traps on the ground, and their flight resembles that of game birds.

A traditional hunting scene *left*

SIDE-BY-SIDE GUN *above*
This traditional sporting gun is used to shoot small game birds. Its barrels are alongside each other rather than "over and under." Special "gun dogs" are trained to retrieve birds that have been shot by their masters.

Bowling sports

THERE ARE TWO main kinds of bowling sports: those in which the object is to knock down pins or skittles, and those in which the players try to get their bowls (balls) nearer to the target ball, or "jack," than their opponent. Modern tenpin bowling was "invented" when the game of skittles - which had nine pins arranged in a diamond formation - was banned in some states in the 1840s; the players merely added another pin and put them all in a triangle.

Crown-green bowls jack

Crown-green bowls foot mat ("footer")

CROWN-GREEN BOWLS *above*
This game is played on a square grass lawn that is raised slightly to form a "crown" in the center. The jack is larger than the one used in the more popular flat-green version.

Crown-green bowl, or "wood"

Boule

BOULES *above*
The sport of boules, or pétanque, is played mainly by the French. The heavy metal spheres are rolled or thrown at a small wooden jack. The field usually has a sandy surface.

Boules technique

Bowls technique

BOWLING TECHNIQUES *above*
The object of bowls and boules is the same, but boules can be thrown, and bowls must always be rolled along the ground. Each bowl is weighted or "biased" on one side so that it curves gently when it is rolled.

BOWLING SHOES
These have flat soles to avoid damaging the green.

Flat-green wood

Flat-green jack

FLAT-GREEN BOWLS
Traditionally, each set of four bowls, or "woods," was made from a single log of the heavy wood *lignum vitae*. The black or brown bowls are now often made from rubber or composition materials instead.

SIR FRANCIS DRAKE
The English admiral Sir Francis Drake is believed to have been playing a form of bowls at Plymouth when the Spanish invasion fleet, or Armada, was sighted in 1588.

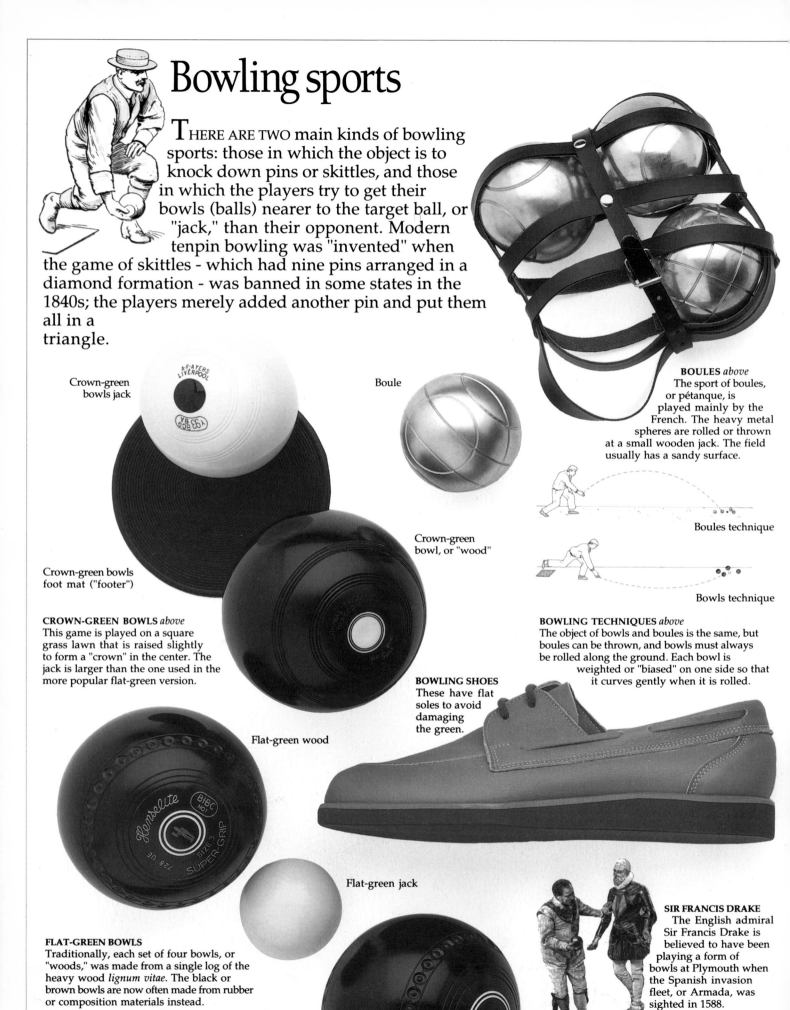

A MEDIEVAL BOWLING GAME
Games in which balls are thrown or rolled along the ground toward a target are among the oldest and most popular of all, dating back to the days of the ancient Egyptians.

MARBLES *below*
Roman children used to play a game like marbles, flicking nuts into an area marked on the floor. There are many different forms of the sport, using balls made from glass or baked clay.

Marbles

SKITTLES
The object of this game is to knock over as many of the skittles as possible with a single throw.

Most bowlers use a three-finger grip

Brunswick

GRM2688

Black Beauty

Bowling ball

TENPIN BOWLING
Bowlers roll the heavy ball down a narrow lane, trying to knock down the pins at the other end. Points are scored for each pin knocked down. The ball is made from hard rubber composition or plastic, and may weigh up to 16 lb (7.26 kg). Finger holes are drilled into the ball to make gripping easier.

THE LANE
The pins are set out in a triangular pattern at the far end of the lane, which may be made from plastic or thin strips of pine or maple wood.

Pins

CURLING *above*
This is a bowling sport on ice; players slide round "stones" toward a target area called a "house." Brushes are used to sweep away frost and moisture from in front of the running stone. This helps to keep it straight and makes it go farther.

Curling stone

THE PINS
The ten pins are made from maple wood and covered in plastic to protect them against the impact of the ball. Each pin stands on a numbered spot within the formation.

Golf

THE ORIGINS OF GOLF are not clear, but it almost certainly belongs to the same family of sports as bowling and croquet. The modern form of the game was first played in Scotland some 400 years ago. Golfers hit a small ball with clubs from a starting point ("tee") into a hole located some distance away. Modern golf courses have eighteen holes, and the object is to hit the ball into each hole, and so complete the round, using as few strokes as possible.

GOLF CLUBS
A player may use no more than 14 different clubs in any round of golf. Most players use three or four wooden clubs ("woods"), nine or ten metal clubs ("irons"), and a "putter." The ball must be hit with only the head of the club.

WOODS
These clubs have large heads made from wood, or sometimes plastic or metal, and have longer shafts than other clubs. They are capable of hitting the ball a long way and are used for the first tee shot - the "drive" - and for other long shots. The most commonly-used woods are numbered 1 to 5. The number 1 wood, known as the "driver," is the largest.

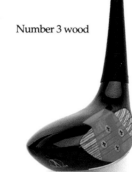

Number 1 wood   Number 3 wood   Number 5 wood

CLUB HEADS
Wooden clubs are made from persimmon or laminates (layers) of other woods. Face inserts and metal sole plates keep the club from being damaged.

A TYPICAL HOLE *below*
The length of a hole may be between 300-2000 ft (100-600 m). This length determines its "par" - the number of strokes normally needed to get the ball into the hole. If a player completes a hole in a shot less than par, he scores a "birdie." Two shots less scores an "eagle"; three shots less, a "double eagle". The length and features of each course vary a great deal.

THE SWING *left*
The ball is placed on a small wooden or plastic tee, which raises it off the ground. The golfer takes a great swing at the ball, following through with his club. Hitting the ball straight into the hole from the tee is a "hole in one."

Practice ball

Golf ball

Tee

The "tee" is a smooth, level area from which the first shot is taken

Club head ———

METAL WOODS
Some woods are not wooden at all, but made from metal or plastic.

GOLF BALLS
These are covered with over 400 "dimples," which help the ball fly long and straight when hit. Players use lightweight "air balls" to practice their technique.

Shaft

THE ORIGINS OF GOLF
A stick-and-ball game called "bandy-ball" - a cross between golf and hockey - was played in the 14th century.

HEAD COVERS
Special sleeves protect the heads of clubs from the weather when they are not being used.

IRONS

The heads of the metal clubs are narrower than the woods; they are made from chromium-plated steel and used for shorter shots. The irons are numbered 1 to 10. The head of each is angled differently for different kinds of shots - a number 1 iron hits the ball farther and lower than a number 2, and so on.

Number 2 iron
(18-degree angle)

Number 3 iron
(21-degree angle)

Number 4 iron
(24-degree angle)

Number 5 iron
(27-degree angle)

Number 6 iron
(31-degree angle)

Number 7 iron
(35-degree angle)

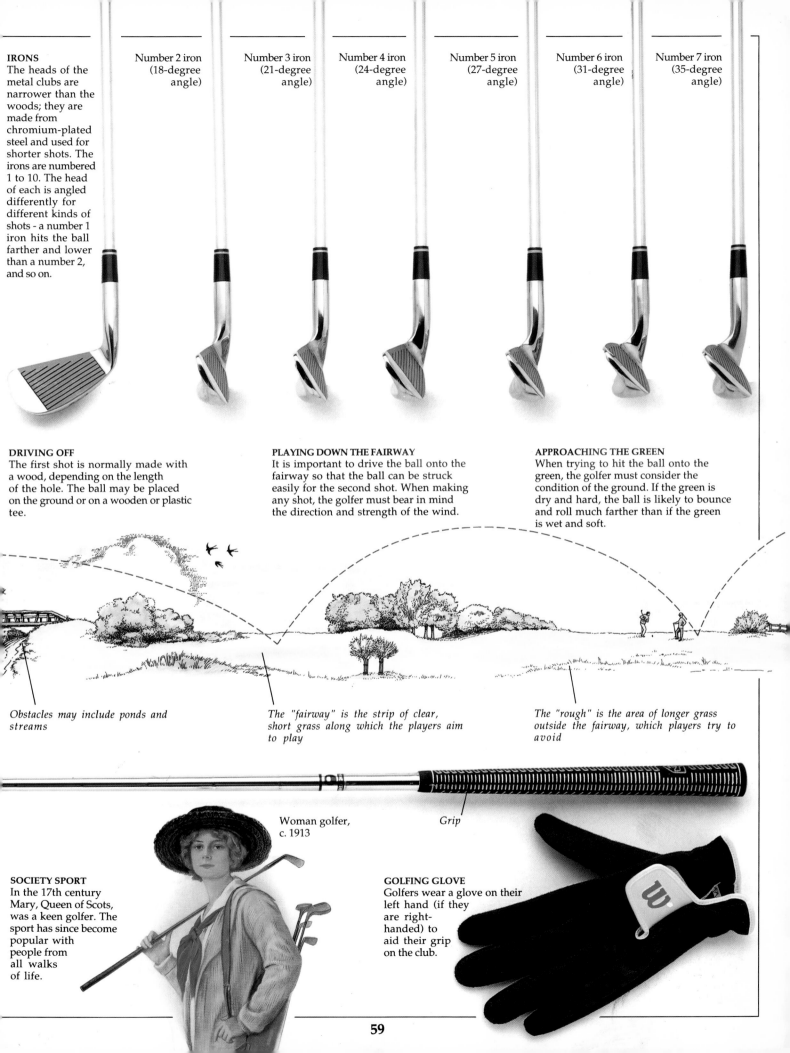

DRIVING OFF

The first shot is normally made with a wood, depending on the length of the hole. The ball may be placed on the ground or on a wooden or plastic tee.

PLAYING DOWN THE FAIRWAY

It is important to drive the ball onto the fairway so that the ball can be struck easily for the second shot. When making any shot, the golfer must bear in mind the direction and strength of the wind.

APPROACHING THE GREEN

When trying to hit the ball onto the green, the golfer must consider the condition of the ground. If the green is dry and hard, the ball is likely to bounce and roll much farther than if the green is wet and soft.

Obstacles may include ponds and streams

The "fairway" is the strip of clear, short grass along which the players aim to play

The "rough" is the area of longer grass outside the fairway, which players try to avoid

Woman golfer,
c. 1913

Grip

SOCIETY SPORT

In the 17th century Mary, Queen of Scots, was a keen golfer. The sport has since become popular with people from all walks of life.

GOLFING GLOVE

Golfers wear a glove on their left hand (if they are right-handed) to aid their grip on the club.

Pitching wedge, used to "chip" the ball onto the green (48-degree angle)

Sand wedge, used to get the ball out of a bunker (55-degree angle)

PUTTERS
Putters are light clubs, usually made of metal, and are used only on the putting green. They have flat faces but come in many different designs to suit each player's taste.

Standard center-shaft putter

Large-head putter with angled neck

Small-head center-shaft putter

GETTING OUT OF TROUBLE
If the ball is accidentally hit into a bunker, it can be very difficult to get out. A sand wedge may be used to lift the ball onto the green.

PUTTING
Once the ball is on the green, a putter is used to hit it along the ground and into the hole.

THE PUTTING TECHNIQUE
The ball must be struck with the head of the club - not pushed or "scraped" along the ground. The golfer must take into account the direction of any slope when making his stroke.

Sand traps, or "bunkers," are often placed close to the green

The "green" is the area of very short grass where the hole is located

The hole is marked with a flag known as, the "pin"

BALL MARKERS
On the green, players may pick up their ball and mark its position with a small disk while an opponent takes his putt.

GOLF SHOES
Golfers wear shoes with spiked soles to help them stand firm when they are swinging their clubs. The most expensive pair of shoes in the world are mink-lined golf shoes with gold trim and ruby-tipped spikes.

THE CADDIE
The caddie is an assistant who carries the bag of clubs around the course. This is an 18th-century caddie.

Croquet

Croquet has much in common with lawn bowls (p. 56), but like golf, the sport involves hitting a ball at a target with a club - or, in this case, a "mallet." A game consists of scoring points by hitting colored balls through a series of arches, or "wickets," in a certain order. The secret of the sport is to keep the balls of your own side close together, and those of the opposing side as far apart as possible. The winner is the player or team that gets all its balls to the end of the course first.

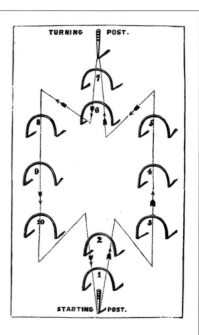

PEGGING OUT
The balls must be hit through each of the six wickets twice, and a point is scored for each wicket. At the end of the course, the player hits the ball against the wooden peg to score an extra point, making a total of 13 for each ball.

THE TEN-WICKET GAME
Modern croquet matches use just six wickets, but the old-fashioned form of the game used ten. The broad, round-topped wickets used at that time were thought to be much too easy to get the ball through, so they were replaced with the modern narrower kind.

A BYGONE AGE
Croquet, like golf, was a fashionable social pastime during the 19th century. The popularity of the sport declined as lawn tennis (p. 30) became all the rage in the late 19th century, but it is now enjoying a revival.

The handle of the mallet is usually made of ash

THE CROQUET SHOT
If a player hits his ball into another ball, he is allowed to make a "croquet" shot. He places his ball against the other ball and hits it so that both balls are sent in different directions.

WICKETS
The iron wickets are just wide enough for the balls to pass through. They are painted white, and the crown of the last wicket, or "rover," is red.

THE BALLS
Each player or team plays with two of the four balls, which are traditionally made from boxwood or composite material.

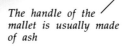

MALLETS
Players must hit the ball, rather than push it, with the head of the mallet, which is about 32 in (80 cm) long from the tip of the handle to the base of the head.

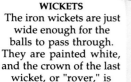

SINGLES AND DOUBLES
Two players may compete with two balls each, or four players can compete as two teams, with one ball per player. Each player must use the same colored ball throughout the game. Blue and black always play against red and yellow.

The boxwood mallet head may be square or cylindrical

HOCKEY ON HORSEBACK
The sport of polo is like a cross between field hockey (p. 16) and croquet played by teams of four riders on horseback. Long-handled mallets made from sycamore or ash are used to hit a ball toward goals set 900 ft (275 m) apart.

Pool and snooker

THESE INDOOR SPORTS are played on a rectangular table that has "pockets" at the corners and in the middle of the longest sides. Players use long wooden cues to hit balls into the pockets and score points. In the "8-ball" version, each player tries to sink his or her set of balls before the other player sinks his or her set. Both sports evolved from the game of billiards, which dates back to around the 15th century, when it was probably played outdoors on grass. King Louis XI of France is thought to have been the first to play the game indoors.

THE ROYAL MACE
Billiards was popular at the French court at Versailles. Players in Louis XIV's day had to hit the ball with a "mace" - a stick some 3 ft (1 m) long, flattened at one end into a spoon shape.

Over 35 miles (56 km) of woolen yarn are needed to cover a 12ft 6in x 6ft 7in (4 m x 2 m) table

Plain colors

THE TABLE
The first tables were made from oak and marble; the modern slate-bed tables were not introduced until the 1830s. The use of the rigid slate ensures that the playing surface is completely flat. The table is covered with a fine-quality woolen cloth.

8-ball

Slate bed screwed to wooden underframe

Striped colors

POCKETS
Balls that fall into the holes are collected in string pockets.

POOL BALLS
The pool balls are divided into two groups - numbers 1-7 are called "solids," and numbers 9-15 are called "stripes." In "8-ball" pool each player must pocket all the balls in one of these groups and then sink the black 8-ball to win.

Cue ball

Two-piece cues have a screw attachment

62

Snooker

The game of snooker was invented by a British Army officer in India in 1875. The term "snooker" was a nickname for military cadets in England at the time. Players score points by sinking the red balls, after which they may attempt a colored ball, which is worth more points. Sunk colored balls are replaced on their spots until no reds are left. The players then try to sink the colored balls in a certain order, finishing with the black ball.

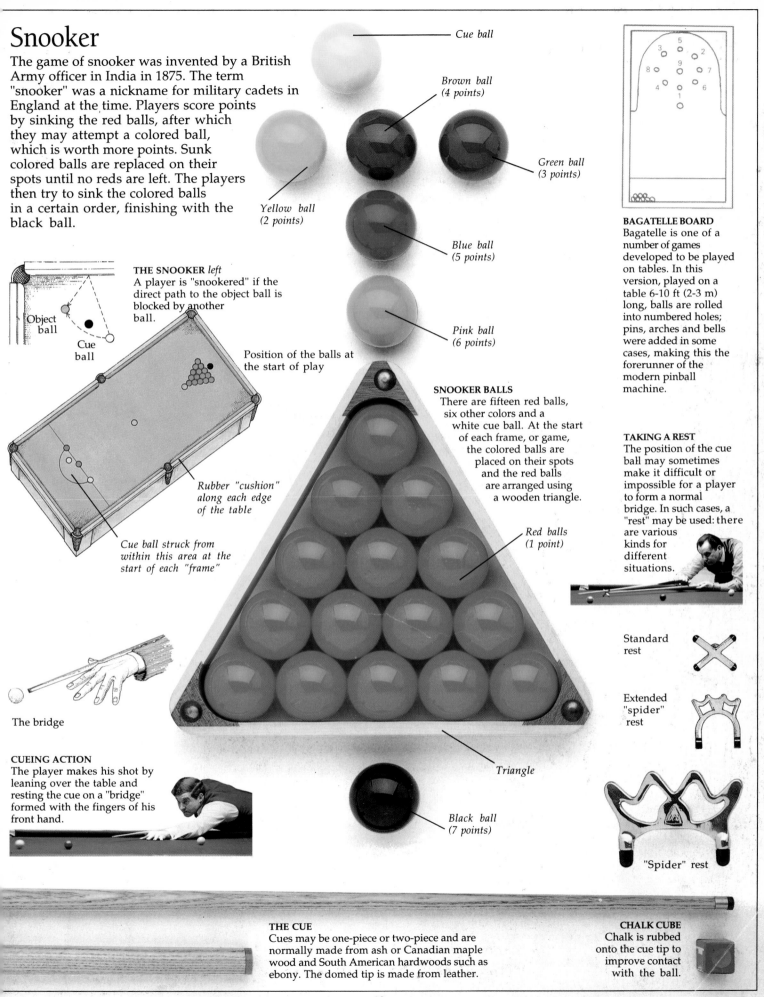

Cue ball

Brown ball
(4 points)

Green ball
(3 points)

Yellow ball
(2 points)

Blue ball
(5 points)

Pink ball
(6 points)

THE SNOOKER *left*
A player is "snookered" if the direct path to the object ball is blocked by another ball.

Object ball

Cue ball

Position of the balls at the start of play

Rubber "cushion" along each edge of the table

Cue ball struck from within this area at the start of each "frame"

The bridge

CUEING ACTION
The player makes his shot by leaning over the table and resting the cue on a "bridge" formed with the fingers of his front hand.

SNOOKER BALLS
There are fifteen red balls, six other colors and a white cue ball. At the start of each frame, or game, the colored balls are placed on their spots and the red balls are arranged using a wooden triangle.

Red balls
(1 point)

Triangle

Black ball
(7 points)

BAGATELLE BOARD
Bagatelle is one of a number of games developed to be played on tables. In this version, played on a table 6-10 ft (2-3 m) long, balls are rolled into numbered holes; pins, arches and bells were added in some cases, making this the forerunner of the modern pinball machine.

TAKING A REST
The position of the cue ball may sometimes make it difficult or impossible for a player to form a normal bridge. In such cases, a "rest" may be used: there are various kinds for different situations.

Standard rest

Extended "spider" rest

"Spider" rest

THE CUE
Cues may be one-piece or two-piece and are normally made from ash or Canadian maple wood and South American hardwoods such as ebony. The domed tip is made from leather.

CHALK CUBE
Chalk is rubbed onto the cue tip to improve contact with the ball.

Index

Acknowledgments

Dorling Kindersley would like to thank:
Grandstand Sports and Leisure
Geron Way
Edgware Road
London NW2

A & D Billiards & Pool Services Ltd, Amateur Athletics Association, Amateur Boxing Association, Amateur Fencing Association, Badminton Association of England Ltd, Bapty and Co. Ltd, Billiards and Snooker Control Council, British Amateur Baseball and Softball Federation, British Amateur Gymnastics Association, British Amateur Weight Lifters' Association, British American Football Association, British Ice Hockey Federation, British Racketball Association, British Tenpin Bowling Association,

Jonathan Buckley, Continental Sports Products Co., The Croquet Association, Dragon Martial Arts, English Basketball Association, English Bowling Association, English Table Tennis Association, The Football Association, The Football League Ltd, C.L. Gaul & Co. Ltd, James Gilbert Ltd, Grand National Archery Society, Grays of Cambridge (International) Ltd, Gridiron Sports, International Hockey Federation, Quicks the Archery Specialist, Leon Paul Equipment Co. Ltd, Charlie Magri Sports, Martial Arts Commission, Marylebone Cricket Club, Minerva Football Co. Ltd, Diana Morgan, Newitt & Co. Ltd, Professional Golfers Association, The Rugby Football Union, Len Smiths (School & Sports) Ltd, Squash Rackets Association, Wilson Sporting Goods

Co. Ltd, Wimbledon Lawn Tennis Museum.

Ray Owen for artwork

Polyflex running-track materials (pp. 3 and 39) used by courtesy of Recreational Surfaces Ltd

Picture credits
t=top b=bottom m=middle l=left r=right

All-sport (UK): 6tr, bm; 7m; 9b; 10t, mr; 11tr; 13tm, ml; 14br; 16ml; 18tr; 19tm, br; 20tl, bl; 21bl; 23bm; 26mr; 27m; 35ml, bl, 36bl; 37ml; 38tl, bl; 39tl, m; 40tr; 47tl; 48bl, mr; 50bl; 52br; 55tl; 61b; 63mr, bl.
BBC Hulton Picture Library: 10br; 13br; 18tl; 22tr, bl; 25bl; 28ml; 38ml; 40bl; 44tm; 50tl; 51tr, m; 52bl; 53m; 54tl; 55tr; 57tl, tr; 62tr.
The British Library: 54br.
The British Museum: 49tm.
Colorsport/SIPA: 7tm, tr; 9m; 14tr; 15tl;

24bl; 27tl; 31tr, ml; 34m; 42tr, bl; 43bl; 44ml, bm, br; 45bl, bm; 49m; 54m; 58ml.
The Mansell Collection: 34bm; 35br; 56br; 58br.
Mary Evans Picture Library: 8t; 14tl, ml; 15mr; 16tr, bl; 17mr; 25tl, br; 26tl, m; 30br; 31tl; 32tl; 34tl; 37br; 39bl; 41ml, bm; 46bm; 52tl, tr, mr; 57bl; 59bl; 60bl; 61ml.

Cigarette card illustrations on pp. 42-3 reproduced courtesy of W.D & H.O. Wills

Illustrations by Will Giles: 10m, bl; 30ml; 35tl; 38mr; 40tr; 57m; 62bl; 63ml.

Illustrations by Sandra Pond: 6m; 13tr, m; 16mr; 19tl; 20mr; 21tl; 22bl; 24mr; 26tr; 39m; 40b; 46ml, m; 51m.

Illustration by Coral Mula: 58-60m.

Picture research by:
Joanne King

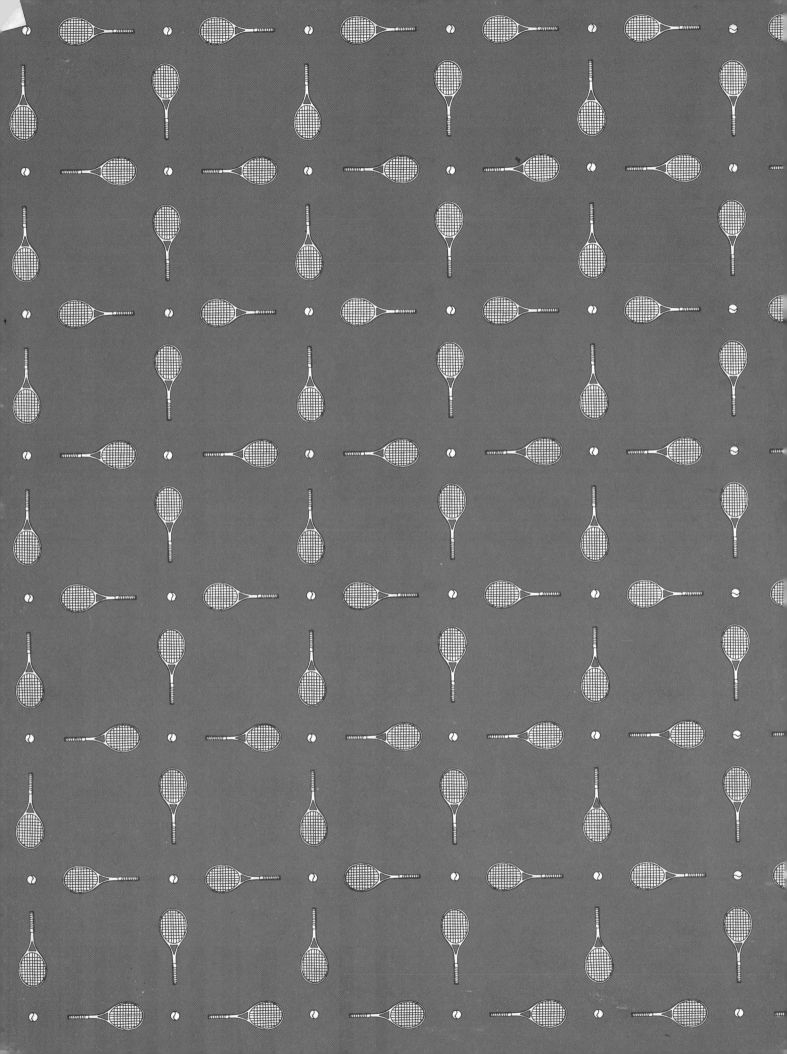